Adventures of
Huckleberry Finn

*A Bold American Classic of Freedom,
Friendship & the Spirit of Rebellion on the
Mississippi River*

A Modern Translation
Adapted for the Contemporary Reader

Mark Twain

Translated by Tim Zengerink

Table of Contents

Preface
Message to the Reader

Rebuilding the Greatest Library in Human History

Thousands of years ago, the Library of Alexandria was the heart of global knowledge — a sanctuary where the wisdom of every known civilization was gathered and shared freely.

And then, it was lost.

Now, we're rebuilding it — and you are invited to join us.

At the Library of Alexandria, we've set out to make every book available to every person on Earth — not just in print, but in every language, every format, and for every reader.

Here's how we do it:

- **Deluxe Print Editions at True Printing Cost** - Order any book as a high-quality paperback, elegant hardcover, or stunning boxset — and only pay what it costs to print. No markups. No middlemen.
- **Unlimited Access to the Greatest Works** - Enjoy thousands of timeless classics — from Plato to Shakespeare to Tolstoy — in beautiful, modern eBook and audiobook editions. Read and listen without limits — for every reader, everywhere.
- **Modern Translations for Every Language & Dialect** - We're reimagining the classics in clear, accessible language — and translating them into every dialect imaginable. Everyone deserves to understand humanity's greatest ideas.

When you visit **LibraryofAlexandria.com**, you're not just accessing books — you're joining a global movement to restore, preserve, and share the wisdom of civilization.

Join us today at LibraryofAlexandria.com

Together, we'll ensure the light of human wisdom never fades again.

With gratitude,

The Modern Library of Alexandria Team

Visit:
www.libraryofalexandria.com
Or scan the code below:

Introduction:
Adventures of Huckleberry Finn

You are about to embark on one of the most significant and transformative journeys in all of literature. Do not be deceived by its opening pages, which may feel like a simple continuation of a boy's adventure story. The book you hold is something far more profound, more dangerous, and more true. It is a journey that begins on the land, in the stifling, well-meaning world of "sivilization," but finds its soul on the water, aboard a primitive raft drifting down the vast, muddy, and majestic Mississippi River. This is a book that peels back the skin of a nation to expose the fierce, often ugly, contradictions of its heart. It is at once a thrilling escape story, a brilliant and biting satire of a society choking on its own hypocrisy, and one of the most moving portraits of a friendship ever written.

At the center of this journey is one of literature's most unforgettable creations: Huckleberry Finn, a boy who is an outcast by nature and a hero by instinct. Uneducated, superstitious, and born into the lowest rung of white society, Huck is a child of the frontier, more comfortable in the woods and on the water than in a starched collar. It is through his eyes—clear, unsentimental, and unburdened by the prejudices of formal education—that we will witness the world. His voice, colloquial, ungrammatical, and breathtakingly authentic, was a revolution in itself, and it is this voice that will guide us through a moral wilderness. The journey down the river is more than a physical escape; it is a flight toward freedom in its deepest sense, and a profound, often unconscious, search for a moral compass in a world where society's rules are revealed to be profoundly and tragically wrong. Ernest Hemingway famously declared that "All modern American literature comes from one book by Mark Twain called

Huckleberry Finn." He was right. Open the first page, push the raft into the current, and prepare to understand why.

The Author and His River: The World of Mark Twain

It is impossible to separate the river that flows through these pages from the man who created it. The Mississippi was Mark Twain's lifeblood, his university, and the central, defining metaphor of his imagination. To understand the depth, authenticity, and profound moral vision of this novel, one must first understand the world of Samuel Langhorne Clemens, the man who became Mark Twain. He was born in Missouri in 1835, on the edge of the American frontier, in a slave-holding state. His childhood town of Hannibal, on the west bank of the Mississippi, would become the fictional St. Petersburg of his books, a place he would remember with a complex mixture of idyllic nostalgia and clear-eyed revulsion. This was his world: a sleepy, rough-hewn town where the rhythms of life were dictated by the seasons and the ceaseless, powerful current of the great river. It was the main artery of the nation, a bustling highway of steamboats, keelboats, and makeshift rafts, carrying a constant traffic of commerce, ideas, and humanity in all its forms—from genteel ladies and prosperous merchants to rough-decked raftsmen, desperate fugitives, and itinerant preachers.

Young Sam Clemens absorbed it all. He absorbed the dialects of the rivermen, the folklore of the slaves, the rigid social codes of the townspeople, and the ever-present, casual brutality of the institution of slavery. This last point is crucial. Clemens grew up in a world where the ownership of human beings was an accepted, legal, and religiously sanctioned fact of life. His own family owned slaves. This intimate, firsthand knowledge of slavery's reality—not as an abstract political issue, but as a lived, human experience—

would become the great, troubling, and ultimately defining moral subject of his greatest work.

The most formative experience of his young adulthood was his time as a steamboat pilot on the Mississippi. For four years, he trained and worked on the river, mastering its every bend, snag, and sandbar. This was, as he would later say, the education that mattered. It taught him not just the geography of the river, but the character of the people who lived on and by it. He learned to "read" the water, to see the hidden dangers beneath the placid surface—a skill that would become a perfect metaphor for his literary project of revealing the hidden hypocrisies beneath the placid surface of society. His very pen name, "Mark Twain," is a riverman's term, a leadsman's cry meaning "two fathoms deep," a measure of safe water. It is a name that speaks of deep knowledge and a mastery of the treacherous currents. When he wrote this novel, years after the Civil War had ended and the era of the steamboat was fading, he was drawing on a deep well of memory. He was summoning a lost world, not to romanticize it, but to put it on trial. He was using the landscape of his own youth to conduct a searching moral autopsy on the soul of the nation that had produced him.

Twain's genius was that he was both an insider and an outsider. He was a Southerner who had, for a brief and confused period, even served with a Confederate militia. But he was also a man who had left the South behind, who had traveled the world, and who had become a celebrated satirist and lecturer, one of the most famous Americans of his day. This dual perspective allowed him to write about the pre-Civil War South with an authority and a critical distance that no other writer could match. He knew its charms and its horrors, its codes of honor and its savage cruelties. This novel is his definitive statement on that world, a powerful act of looking back, an attempt to grapple with the great, unresolved questions of his country's past through the eyes of a boy who never knew he was asking them.

A Revolution in Voice:
The Language of the People

Perhaps the most revolutionary aspect of this novel, and the key to its enduring power, is the voice of Huckleberry Finn himself. Before you read a single chapter, you will be met by a "NOTICE" from the author, in which he states, with a straight-faced, satirical seriousness, that several dialects have been used in the book and have been rendered with "painstaking" care. This is not a joke; it is a declaration of artistic independence and a clue to one of the most significant achievements in the history of the novel. Up to this point, serious American literature was largely written in a formal, "literary" English, a language that bore little resemblance to the way most Americans actually spoke. With this book, Mark Twain tore down that wall. He chose to tell his epic story not in the polished prose of a New England scholar, but in the ungrammatical, slang-filled, and gloriously authentic vernacular of a poor, uneducated boy from the Missouri frontier.

This choice was an act of profound literary and cultural significance. By placing Huck's voice at the center of the narrative, Twain was asserting that the story of this boy, and the language of the common people, were worthy of the highest art. Huck's voice is the ultimate tool of realism. It is immediate, intimate, and utterly convincing. We do not feel like we are reading a story about Huck; we feel like we are listening to him, sitting beside him on the raft as he tells us his tale. This intimacy is what makes his moral journey so powerful. We are not watching him from a distance; we are inside his head, experiencing his confusion, his fear, and his dawning realizations right alongside him.

Huck's language is also a source of brilliant dramatic irony. As an uneducated child, he often describes the events and people he encounters without fully understanding their social or moral significance. He will report on a scene of incredible hypocrisy or cruelty with a simple, literal-minded directness, and it is in the gap between his naive description and our own more sophisticated understanding that the full force of Twain's satire is unleashed. He doesn't need to tell us that a character is a fool or a scoundrel; he simply lets Huck describe what the person says and does, and we are left to draw our own, devastating conclusions. Huck's plain, honest language acts as a kind of moral acid, dissolving the pretentious and self-serving rhetoric of the "sivilized" world he is fleeing.

It is impossible to discuss the novel's language without addressing its most controversial element: its repeated use of a racial slur. For a modern reader, encountering this word can be a jarring and painful experience. It is essential to understand that Twain's purpose in using it was not to endorse the racism it represents, but to expose it. He was writing a realistic novel set in a deeply racist society, and this was the word that white people, from the kindest to the cruelest, used to refer to Black people. To have avoided it would have been a profound act of historical dishonesty. Twain puts the word in the mouths of his characters to force the reader to confront the casual, ingrained, and dehumanizing nature of the prejudice that permeated every corner of that society. The novel is a blistering attack on that prejudice, and the ugliness of the language is a crucial part of that attack. The story's central moral drama revolves around Huck's struggle to see the man, Jim, beyond the hateful label that society has assigned to him. The language is not the novel's flaw; it is an inseparable part of its unflinching and courageous confrontation with the nation's original sin.

The Journey Within:
Society, Conscience, and the Mighty Mississippi

The physical journey down the river is the frame for a much deeper and more important journey: Huck's journey into his own conscience. The novel is structured around a powerful central contrast between the world of the River and the world of the Shore. The raft, floating on the vast, untamed current, becomes a kind of floating sanctuary, a primitive Eden. It is a space of freedom, of natural beauty, and of profound, instinctual morality. It is on the raft, under the stars, that Huck and his companion, the runaway slave Jim, forge one of the most powerful and moving friendships in literature. Stripped of all social conventions, they form a makeshift family, a bond of mutual dependence, trust, and genuine affection that stands in stark opposition to every social law of their time.

The Shore, by contrast, is the domain of "sivilization," and nearly every time Huck and Jim set foot on it, they encounter a world that is corrupt, violent, foolish, and grotesquely hypocritical. Twain uses these episodes on the shore to create a panoramic satire of Southern society. We meet feuding, "aristocratic" families who attend church with their rifles, listening to sermons on brotherly love before going back to murdering each other over a long-forgotten grudge. We meet a pair of comically inept and vicious con men, the "Duke" and the "King," who swindle and cheat their way through the riverside towns, preying on the ignorance and sentimentality of the populace. We see lynch mobs, drunken sadists, and pious slave-owners, a whole gallery of characters who represent the moral bankruptcy of a society built on a foundation of lies. Huck's journey is a process of education, but not the kind Miss Watson intended. It is a systematic disillusionment, a process of learning that the values and rules of the civilized world he has been taught to respect are, in fact, monstrous.

The moral climax of the book, and the source of its enduring power, is the terrible choice that Huck is ultimately forced to make. All his life, he has been taught by his church, his community, and his own conscience (or what he thinks is his conscience) that helping a slave to escape is a sin, a crime against property and a betrayal of his race that will condemn his soul to "everlasting fire." As he and Jim travel farther south, deeper into slave territory, this internal conflict becomes unbearable. He must choose between the laws of society, which he believes to be the laws of God, and the loyalty and love he feels for his friend. This is the heart of the novel: the struggle between a received, socially-constructed morality and a deeply felt, personal, and humane one. The decision Huck makes in this moment is a thunderous declaration of independence, not just for himself, but for the American conscience.

You are about to read a book that is often funny, frequently thrilling, and, in the end, profoundly moving. It is a story that will take you into the very heart of a nation at war with itself, a nation of breathtaking beauty and unspeakable cruelty. It is a journey that will test the limits of friendship and the courage of a boy's soul. The raft is waiting.

Huckleberry Finn

Scene: The Mississippi Valley

Time: Forty to fifty years ago

Chapter I.

You don't know about me unless you have read a book called The Adventures of Tom Sawyer, but that doesn't matter. That book was written by Mr. Mark Twain, and he told the truth, mostly. There were things that he exaggerated, but mostly he told the truth. That's nothing unusual. I've never seen anybody who hasn't lied at one time or another, except maybe Aunt Polly, or the widow, or perhaps Mary. Aunt Polly—who is Tom's Aunt Polly—and Mary, and the Widow Douglas are all described in that book, which is mostly a true book, with some exaggerations, as I mentioned before.

Here's how the book ends: Tom and I discovered the money that the robbers had hidden in the cave, and it made us wealthy. We each received six thousand dollars—all in gold. It was an incredible amount of money when it was stacked up. Judge Thatcher took our money and invested it, earning us a dollar each day throughout the entire year—more than anyone could figure out how to spend. The Widow Douglas took me in as her son and said she would civilize me; but living in the house all the time was difficult, considering how strictly proper and respectable the widow was in everything she did; so when I couldn't tolerate it any longer, I ran away. I put on my old torn clothes and returned to my sugar barrel, and felt free and content. But Tom Sawyer tracked me down and told me he was planning to form a gang of robbers, and I could join if I returned to the widow's house and became respectable. So I went back.

The widow cried over me and called me a poor lost lamb, along with many other names, but she never meant any harm by it. She put me back in those new clothes, and all I could do was sweat and sweat, feeling completely cramped up. Well, then the same old routine started up again. The widow rang a bell for supper, and you had to be there on time. When you reached the table, you couldn't start eating right away, but had to wait for the widow to bow her head and mumble a little over the food, even though there wasn't really anything wrong with it—except that everything was cooked separately. In a barrel of leftovers it's different; things get mixed together, and the juices blend around, making everything taste better.

After dinner she brought out her book and taught me about Moses and the Bulrushes, and I was eager to learn everything about him; but eventually she mentioned that Moses had been dead for a very long time; so then I didn't care about him anymore, because I don't have any interest in dead people.

Before long I wanted to smoke, and I asked the widow if I could. But she refused. She said it was a bad habit and wasn't clean, and I had to try not to do it anymore. That's just how some people are. They criticize something when they don't know anything about it. There she was worrying about Moses, who wasn't related to her and was no good to anyone since he was dead, you see, yet she found plenty of fault with me for doing something that had some benefit. And she used snuff too; naturally that was perfectly fine because she did it herself.

Her sister, Miss Watson, a reasonably thin old unmarried woman wearing glasses, had recently moved in with her and immediately started working on me with a spelling book. She pushed me fairly hard for about an hour, and then the widow told her to let up. I couldn't have endured it much longer. Then for an hour everything was extremely boring, and I felt restless. Miss Watson would say, "Don't put your feet up there, Huckleberry," and "Don't slouch like that, Huckleberry—sit up straight," and before long she would say, "Don't yawn and stretch like that, Huckleberry—why don't you try to behave?" Then she told me all about hell, and I said I wished I was there. She became angry then, but I didn't mean any harm. All I wanted was to go somewhere; all I wanted was a change, I wasn't picky. She said it was sinful to say what I said; said she wouldn't say it for anything in the world; she was going to live in such a way as to go to heaven. Well, I couldn't see any benefit in going where she was going, so I decided I wouldn't try for it. But I never said so, because it would only cause trouble, and wouldn't do any good.

Now she had gotten started, and she continued telling me everything about heaven. She explained that all anyone would need to do there was walk around all day with a harp and sing, for all eternity. So I wasn't very impressed by it. But I didn't say that out loud. I asked her if she thought Tom Sawyer would end up there, and she said definitely not. I was happy to hear that, because I wanted him and me to stay together.

Miss Watson kept nagging at me, and it became tiresome and lonely. Eventually they brought the enslaved people in for prayers, and then everyone went off to bed. I went up to my room with a piece of candle and placed it on the table. Then I sat down in a chair by the window and tried to think of something cheerful, but it was no use. I felt so lonely I almost wished I was dead. The stars were shining, and the leaves rustled in the woods so mournfully; and I heard an owl, far off, hooting about somebody who was dead, and a whippoorwill and a dog crying about somebody who was going to die; and the wind was trying to whisper something to me, and I couldn't figure out what it was, and so it made cold shivers run over me. Then far out in the woods I heard that kind of sound that a ghost makes when it wants to tell about something that's on its mind and can't make itself understood, and so can't rest easy in its grave, and has to go about that way every night grieving. I got so downhearted and scared I really wished I had some company. Pretty soon a spider went crawling up my shoulder, and I flicked it off and it landed in the candle; and before I could move it was all shriveled up. I didn't need anybody to tell me that was a terribly bad sign and would bring me some bad luck, so I was scared and nearly shook the clothes off of me. I got up and turned around in my tracks three times and crossed my chest every time; and then I tied up a little lock of my hair with a thread to keep witches away. But I had no confidence. You do that when you've lost a horseshoe that you've found, instead of nailing it up over the door, but I had never heard anybody say it was any way to keep off bad luck when you'd killed a spider.

I sat down again, trembling all over, and pulled out my pipe for a smoke since the house was completely silent as death now, and the widow wouldn't find out. Well, after a long while I heard the clock far off in the town strike boom—boom—boom—twelve times; and everything was quiet again—quieter than before. Soon I heard a twig break down in the darkness among the trees—something was moving. I sat still and listened carefully. Then I could just barely make out a "meow! meow!" down there. That was perfect! I whispered, "meow! meow!" as quietly as I could, and then I blew out the light and climbed out of the window onto the shed. Then I slid down to the ground and crept among the trees, and sure enough, there was Tom Sawyer waiting for me.

Chapter II.

We walked carefully along a path through the trees toward the back of the widow's garden, crouching low so the branches wouldn't hit our heads. As we passed by the kitchen, I tripped over a root and made a noise. We crouched down and stayed perfectly still. Miss Watson's enslaved man, named Jim, was sitting in the kitchen doorway; we could see him quite clearly because there was light behind him. He stood up and craned his neck for about a minute, listening. Then he said:

"Who's there?"

He listened for a while longer; then he came tiptoeing down and stood right between us; we could have touched him, almost. Well, it was probably minutes and minutes that there wasn't a sound, and we were all there so close together. There was a spot on my ankle that started itching, but I didn't dare scratch it; and then my ear began to itch; and next my back, right between my shoulders. It seemed like I would die if I couldn't scratch. Well, I've noticed that thing plenty of times since. If you are with important people, or at a funeral, or trying to go to sleep when you aren't sleepy—if you are anywhere where it wouldn't be appropriate for you to scratch, then you will itch all over in more than a thousand places. Pretty soon Jim says:

"Tell me, who are you? Where are you? I'll be darned if I didn't hear something. Well, I know what I'm going to do: I'm going to sit down here and listen until I hear it again."

So he sat down on the ground between Tom and me. He leaned his back against a tree and stretched his legs out until one of them almost touched one of mine. My nose started to itch. It itched until tears came to my eyes. But I didn't dare scratch it. Then it started to itch on the inside. Next I began itching underneath. I didn't know how I was going to sit still. This misery went on for about six or seven minutes, but it seemed much longer than that. I was itching in eleven different places now. I figured I couldn't stand it for more than a minute longer, but I clenched my teeth hard and got ready to try. Just then Jim started to breathe heavily; next he began to snore—and then I was comfortable again pretty soon.

Tom gave me a signal—a quiet sound with his mouth—and we crept away on our hands and knees. When we were ten feet away, Tom whispered to me that he wanted to tie Jim to the tree for fun. But I said no; Jim might wake up and cause a commotion, and then they'd discover I wasn't in bed. Then Tom said he didn't have enough candles, and he would sneak into the kitchen to get some more. I didn't want him to try it. I said Jim might wake up and come after us. But Tom wanted to risk it; so we slipped in there and grabbed three candles, and Tom left five cents on the table as payment. Then we got out, and I was eager to get away; but nothing would satisfy Tom except that he had to crawl over to where Jim was, on his hands and knees, and play some trick on him. I waited, and it felt like a long time, everything was so quiet and lonely.

As soon as Tom returned, we hurried along the path, around the garden fence, and eventually reached the steep hilltop on the other side of the house. Tom said he had slipped Jim's hat off his head and hung it on a branch right above him, and Jim stirred a little, but he didn't wake up. Later, Jim claimed the witches had cast a spell on him and put him in a trance, and rode him all over the state, and then placed him back under the trees again, and hung his hat on a branch to show who had done it. And the next time Jim told the story, he said they rode him down to New Orleans; and after that, every time he told it he embellished it more and more, until eventually he said they rode him all over the world, and exhausted him nearly to death, and his back was covered with saddle sores. Jim was extremely proud of this experience, and he became so conceited that he would hardly acknowledge the other enslaved people. Enslaved people would travel miles to hear Jim tell about it, and he was more respected than any enslaved person in that region. Unfamiliar enslaved people would stand with their mouths open and stare at him all over, as if he were a marvel.

Enslaved people are always talking about witches in the dark by the kitchen fire; but whenever someone was talking and pretending to know all about such things, Jim would appear and say, "Hm! What do you know about witches?" and that person was silenced and had to take a back seat. Jim always kept that five-cent piece around his neck with a string, and said it was a charm the devil had given to him with his own hands, and told him he could cure anybody with it and summon witches whenever he wanted to just by saying something to it; but he never revealed what it was he said to it. Enslaved people would come from all around there and give Jim anything they had, just for a glimpse of that five-cent piece; but they wouldn't touch it, because the devil had handled it. Jim was nearly ruined as a servant, because he became arrogant on account of having seen the devil and been ridden by witches.

When Tom and I reached the edge of the hilltop, we looked down into the village and could see three or four lights twinkling, where there might be sick people; and the stars above us were sparkling beautifully; and down by the village was the river, a whole mile wide, and incredibly still and magnificent. We went down the hill and found Jo Harper and Ben Rogers, and two or three more of the boys, hiding in the old tannery. So we untied a small boat and rowed down the river two and a half miles, to the big scar on the hillside, and went ashore.

We walked over to a cluster of bushes, and Tom made everyone promise to keep the secret, then revealed a hole in the hillside, hidden deep within the thickest part of the bushes. We lit our candles and crawled inside on our hands and knees. After traveling roughly two hundred yards, the cave opened up into a larger space. Tom explored among the different passages, and soon crouched down under a wall where you wouldn't have noticed there was an opening. We moved through a narrow corridor and entered what looked like a room, damp and humid and cold, and there we came to a stop. Tom said:

"Now, we'll start this band of robbers and call it Tom Sawyer's Gang. Everybody that wants to join has got to take an oath, and write his name in blood."

Everyone was willing. So Tom pulled out a sheet of paper on which he had written the oath, and read it aloud. It required every boy to swear loyalty to the band and never reveal any of the secrets; and if anyone harmed any boy in the band, whichever boy was assigned to kill that person and his family had to do it, and he couldn't eat and he couldn't sleep until he had killed them and carved a cross into their chests, which was the symbol of the band. And nobody who didn't belong to the band could use that mark, and if he did he had to be prosecuted; and if he did it again he had to be killed. And if anybody who belonged to the band revealed the secrets, he had to have his throat slit, and then have his body burned up and the ashes scattered everywhere, and his name crossed off the list with blood and never spoken again by the gang, but have a curse placed on it and be forgotten forever.

Everyone said it was a truly beautiful oath, and they asked Tom if he had come up with it himself. He said he had created some of it, but the rest came from pirate books and robber books, and every gang that had class used one like it.

Some thought it would be a good idea to kill the families of boys who revealed the secrets. Tom said it was a smart plan, so he picked up a pencil and wrote it down. Then Ben Rogers said:

"Here's Huck Finn, he doesn't have any family; what are you going to do about him?"

"Well, doesn't he have a father?" says Tom Sawyer.

"Yes, he has a father, but you can never find him these days. He used to lie drunk with the hogs in the tannery, but he hasn't been seen in these parts for a year or more."

They discussed it among themselves, and they were planning to exclude me because they said every boy had to have a family member or someone to kill, or else it wouldn't be fair to the others. Well, nobody could come up with a solution—everyone was stuck and sat quietly. I was almost ready to cry; but suddenly I thought of an idea, and so I suggested Miss Watson—they could kill her. Everyone said:

"Oh, she'll be fine. That's perfectly all right. Huck can come in."

Then they all pricked their fingers with a pin to draw blood for signing, and I made my mark on the paper.

"Now," says Ben Rogers, "what kind of business does this Gang do?"

"Nothing but robbery and murder," Tom said.

"But who are we going to rob?—houses, or cattle, or—"

"Nonsense! Stealing cattle and things like that isn't robbery; it's burglary," says Tom Sawyer. "We aren't burglars. That's not our style at all. We are highwaymen. We stop stagecoaches and carriages on the road, wearing masks, and kill the people and take their watches and money."

"Must we always kill the people?"

"Oh, absolutely. That's the best approach. Some experts disagree, but most believe it's best to kill them—except for certain ones that you bring back to the cave here and keep until they're ransomed."

"Ransomed? What does that mean?"

"I don't know. But that's what they do. I've seen it in books; and so of course that's what we've got to do."

"But how can we do it if we don't know what it is?"

"Look, we absolutely have to do this. Haven't I told you it's written in the books? Do you really want to do something different from what the books say and mess everything up?"

"Oh, that sounds great to say, Tom Sawyer, but how on earth are we going to ransom these guys if we don't know how to do it to them? That's what I'm trying to figure out. So what do you think it means?"

"Well, I don't know. But maybe if we keep them until they're ransomed, it means that we keep them until they're dead."

"Now, that's more like it. That'll work. Why couldn't you have said that before? We'll keep them until they're ransomed to death; and they'll be a troublesome bunch too—eating up everything and always trying to escape."

"What are you talking about, Ben Rogers? How could they possibly escape when there's a guard watching them, ready to shoot them if they make even the slightest move?"

"A guard! Well, that sounds good. So someone has to stay up all night and never get any sleep, just to watch them. I think that's foolish. Why can't someone just take a club and ransom them as soon as they arrive?"

"Because it's not in the books that way—that's why. Now, Ben Rogers, do you want to do things properly, or don't you?—that's the point. Don't you think that the people who wrote the books know what's the right thing to do? Do you think you can teach them anything? Not by a long shot. No, sir, we'll just go ahead and ransom them in the proper way."

"All right. I don't mind, but I think it's a foolish way, anyway. Say, do we kill the women, too?"

"Well, Ben Rogers, if I were as clueless as you, I wouldn't show it. Kill the women? No way; nobody has ever read anything like that in the books. You bring them to the cave, and you treat them with perfect politeness; and eventually they fall in love with you and never want to go home again."

"Well, if that's how it is, I agree, but I don't believe in it. Pretty soon we'll have the cave so cluttered up with women and men waiting to be ransomed that there won't be any room for the robbers. But go ahead, I don't have anything to say."

Little Tommy Barnes had fallen asleep, and when they woke him up, he was frightened and started crying, saying he wanted to go home to his mother and didn't want to be a robber anymore.

So they all made fun of him and called him a crybaby, which made him angry, and he said he would go straight and tell everyone all the secrets. But Tom gave him five cents to keep quiet and said we would all go home and meet next week to rob somebody and kill some people.

Ben Rogers mentioned that he could only get away on Sundays since he was usually busy the rest of the week, so he suggested they start the following Sunday. However, all the other boys argued that it would be wrong to begin on a Sunday, and that ended the discussion. They decided to meet up again soon to choose a proper day, and then we voted Tom Sawyer as our first captain and Jo Harper as second captain of the Gang before heading home.

I climbed up the shed and crept into my window just before dawn was breaking. My new clothes were all greased up and covered with clay, and I was completely exhausted.

Chapter III.

Well, I received a thorough scolding in the morning from old Miss Watson because of my clothes, but the widow didn't scold me. Instead, she simply cleaned off the grease and clay, and looked so sorry that I thought I would try to behave for a while if I could. Then Miss Watson took me into the closet and prayed, but nothing came of it. She told me to pray every day, and that whatever I asked for I would receive. But that wasn't true. I tried it. Once I got a fishing line, but no hooks. It was no good to me without hooks. I tried for the hooks three or four times, but somehow I couldn't make it work. Eventually, one day, I asked Miss Watson to try for me, but she said I was a fool. She never told me why, and I couldn't figure it out in any way.

I sat down one time back in the woods and had a long think

about it. I said to myself, if a person can get anything they pray for, why doesn't Deacon Winn get back the money he lost on pork? Why can't the widow get back her silver snuffbox that was stolen? Why can't Miss Watson gain weight? No, I said to myself, there's nothing to it. I went and told the widow about it, and she said the thing a person could get by praying for it was "spiritual gifts." This was too much for me, but she told me what she meant—I must help other people, and do everything I could for other people, and look out for them all the time, and never think about myself. This included Miss Watson, as I understood it. I went out in the woods and turned it over in my mind a long time, but I couldn't see any advantage in it—except for the other people; so at last I figured I wouldn't worry about it anymore, but just let it go. Sometimes the widow would take me aside and talk about Providence in a way to make a person's mouth water; but maybe the next day Miss Watson would take over and knock it all down again. I decided I could see that there were two Providences, and a poor fellow would stand a considerable chance with the widow's Providence, but if Miss Watson's got him there wasn't any help for him anymore. I thought it all out, and figured I would belong to the widow's if he wanted me, though I couldn't figure out how he was going to be any better off then than what he was before, seeing I was so ignorant, and so kind of low-down and worthless.

Dad hadn't been seen for more than a year, and that was comfortable for me; I didn't want to see him anymore. He used to always beat me when he was sober and could get his hands on me; though I used to head to the woods most of the time when he was around. Well, around this time he was found in the river drowned, about twelve miles above town, so people said. They figured it was him, anyway; said this drowned man was just his size, and was ragged, and had unusually long hair, which was all like Dad; but they couldn't make anything out of the face, because it had been in the water so long it wasn't much like a face at all. They said he was floating on his back in the water. They took him and buried him on the bank. But I wasn't comfortable long, because I happened to think of something. I knew very well that a drowned man doesn't float on his back, but on his face. So I knew, then, that this wasn't Dad, but a woman dressed up in a man's clothes. So I was uncomfortable again. I figured the old man would turn up again eventually, though I wished he wouldn't.

We played robber for about a month, and then I quit. All the boys did. We hadn't robbed anyone or killed any people, but only pretended. We used to jump out of the woods and charge down on pig-drivers and women in carts taking garden produce to market, but we never bothered any of them. Tom Sawyer called the pigs "ingots," and he called the turnips and other vegetables "jewelry," and we would go to the cave and discuss what we had done, and how many people we had killed and wounded. But I couldn't see any profit in it. One time Tom sent a boy to run around town with a blazing stick, which he called a signal (which was the sign for the gang to get together), and then he said he had received secret news from his spies that the next day a whole group of Spanish merchants and rich Arabs was going to camp in Cave Hollow with two hundred elephants, and six hundred camels, and over a thousand pack mules, all loaded down with diamonds, and they only had a guard of four hundred soldiers, so we would lie in ambush, as he called it, and kill them all and take their things. He said we must polish up our swords and guns, and get ready. He never could go after even a turnip cart without having to polish up all the swords and guns for it, though they were only wooden strips and broomsticks, and you could polish them until you died, and then they weren't worth a handful of ashes more than what they were before. I didn't believe we could beat such a crowd of Spaniards and Arabs, but I wanted to see the camels and elephants, so I was there the next day, Saturday, in the ambush; and when we got the signal we rushed out of the woods and down the hill. But there weren't any Spaniards and Arabs, and there weren't any camels or elephants. It was nothing but a Sunday school picnic, and only a beginner's class at that. We broke it up, and chased the children up the hollow; but we never got anything except some doughnuts and jam, though Ben Rogers got a rag doll, and Jo Harper got a hymn book and a religious pamphlet; and then the teacher charged in, and made us drop everything and run.

I didn't see any diamonds, and I told Tom Sawyer so. He said there were loads of them there, anyway; and he said there were Arabs there, too, and elephants and things. I said, why couldn't we see them, then? He said if I wasn't so ignorant, but had read a book called Don Quixote, I would know without asking. He said it was all done by enchantment. He said there were hundreds of soldiers there, and elephants and treasure, and so on, but we had enemies which he called magicians; and they had turned the whole thing into a children's Sunday school, just out of spite. I said, all right; then the thing for us to do was to go for the magicians. Tom Sawyer said I was a fool.

"Why," he said, "a magician could summon a bunch of genies, and they would destroy you in an instant before you could blink. They're as tall as a tree and as wide as a church."

"Well," I said, "suppose we got some genies to help us—can't we beat the other group then?"

"How are you going to get them?"

"I don't know. How do they get them?"

"Why, they rub an old tin lamp or an iron ring, and then the genies come rushing in, with thunder and lightning crackling all around and smoke billowing everywhere, and whatever they're commanded to do, they immediately go and do it. They don't think twice about uprooting an entire shot tower and smacking a Sunday school superintendent over the head with it—or any other person for that matter."

"What makes them run around like that?"

"Why, whoever rubs the lamp or the ring. They belong to whoever rubs the lamp or the ring, and they have to do whatever he says. If he tells them to build a palace forty miles long out of diamonds, and fill it full of chewing gum, or whatever you want, and bring an emperor's daughter from China for you to marry, they have to do it—and they have to do it before sunrise the next morning, too. And more: they have to move that palace around over the country wherever you want it, you understand."

"Well," I said, "I think they're a bunch of idiots for not keeping the palace for themselves instead of throwing it away like that. And what's more—if I were one of them, I'd tell a man to go to hell before I'd drop everything I was doing and come running just because he rubbed some old tin lamp."

"That's ridiculous, Huck Finn. You'd be forced to appear whenever he rubbed it, whether you felt like it or not."

"What! and I as tall as a tree and as big as a church? All right, then; I would come; but I bet I'd make that man climb the highest tree there was in the country."

"Darn, there's no point in talking to you, Huck Finn. You don't seem to know anything at all—complete fool."

I thought about all this for two or three days, and then I decided I would see if there was anything to it. I got an old tin lamp and an iron ring, and went out into the woods and rubbed and rubbed until I was sweating like crazy, planning to build a palace and sell it; but it was no use, none of the genies appeared. So then I figured that all that stuff was just one of Tom Sawyer's lies. I thought he believed in the Arabs and the elephants, but I saw things differently. It had all the characteristics of a Sunday school story.

———————

Chapter IV.

Well, three or four months passed by, and winter had really set in by now. I had attended school almost every day and could spell and read and write a little bit, and I could recite the multiplication table up to six times seven equals thirty-five, and I don't think I could ever advance beyond that even if I lived forever. I don't put any faith in mathematics, anyway.

At first I hated the school, but gradually I got to the point where I could tolerate it. Whenever I became extremely tired I skipped school, and the punishment I received the next day did me good and lifted my spirits. So the longer I attended school the easier it became. I was getting somewhat accustomed to the widow's ways as well, and they weren't so harsh on me. Living in a house and sleeping in a bed felt quite restrictive most of the time, but before the cold weather arrived I would sometimes sneak out and sleep in the woods, and that provided me with relief. I preferred the old ways best, but I was beginning to appreciate the new ones a little bit too. The widow said I was progressing slowly but steadily, and performing very satisfactorily. She said she wasn't ashamed of me.

One morning I accidentally knocked over the salt shaker at breakfast. I quickly reached for some of the spilled salt to throw over my left shoulder and ward off the bad luck, but Miss Watson got there before me and stopped me. She said, "Take your hands away, Huckleberry; you're always making such a mess!" The widow spoke up for me, but that wasn't going to prevent the bad luck, I knew that well enough. I left after breakfast, feeling anxious and nervous, and wondering where the misfortune would strike me, and what form it would take. There are ways to prevent some types of bad luck, but this wasn't one of those situations; so I didn't try to do anything, but just wandered around feeling dejected and staying alert.

I walked down to the front garden and climbed over the wooden steps that led through the tall board fence. About an inch of fresh snow covered the ground, and I noticed someone's footprints. The tracks had come up from the quarry and lingered around the fence crossing for some time, then continued along the garden fence. It seemed strange that whoever it was hadn't come inside after standing there for so long. I couldn't figure it out. Something about it felt odd and puzzling. I was about to follow the trail around the fence, but I bent down to examine the footprints more closely first. At first glance, I didn't see anything unusual, but then I did. There was a cross carved into the left boot heel, made with large nails, meant to ward off the devil.

I jumped up immediately and raced down the hill. I glanced back over my shoulder from time to time, but I didn't see anyone. I reached Judge Thatcher's place as quickly as I could. He said:

"Why, my boy, you are completely out of breath. Did you come for your interest?"

"No, sir," I said; "is there some for me?"

"Oh, yes, the half-yearly payment came in last night—over a hundred and fifty dollars. That's quite a fortune for you. You should let me invest it together with your six thousand, because if you take it, you'll just spend it."

"No, sir," I said, "I don't want to spend it. I don't want it at all—not the six thousand either. I want you to take it; I want to give it to you—the six thousand and everything."

He looked surprised. He couldn't seem to figure it out. He says:

"What do you mean by that, my boy?"

"Don't ask me any questions about it, please," I said. "You'll take it, won't you?"

He says:

"Well, I'm confused. Is something wrong?"

"Please take it," I said, "and don't ask me anything—then I won't have to tell any lies."

He thought about it for a moment, and then he said:

"Oh, I see! I think I understand now. You want to sell me all your property—not give it to me. That's the right way to think about it."

Then he wrote something on a piece of paper, read it over, and said:

"There; you see it says 'for a consideration.' That means I have bought it from you and paid you for it. Here's a dollar for you. Now you sign it."

So I signed it and left.

Miss Watson's slave, Jim, had a hair-ball as big as your fist, which had been taken out of the fourth stomach of an ox, and he used to do magic with it. He said there was a spirit inside of it, and it knew everything. So I went to him that night and told him my father was here again, for I found his tracks in the snow. What I wanted to know was, what he was going to do, and was he going to stay? Jim got out his hair-ball and said something over it, and then he held it up and dropped it on the floor. It fell pretty solid, and only rolled about an inch. Jim tried it again, and then another time, and it acted just the same. Jim got down on his knees, and put his ear against it and listened. But it wasn't any use; he said it wouldn't talk. He said sometimes it wouldn't talk without money. I told him I had an old smooth counterfeit quarter that wasn't any good because the brass showed through the silver a little, and it wouldn't pass anywhere, even if the brass didn't show, because it was so smooth it felt greasy, and so that would give it away every time. (I figured I wouldn't say anything about the dollar I got from the judge.) I said it was pretty bad money, but maybe the hair-ball would take it, because maybe it wouldn't know the difference. Jim smelled it and bit it and rubbed it, and said he would manage so the hair-ball would think it was good. He said he would split open a raw Irish potato and stick the quarter in between and keep it there all night, and next morning you couldn't see any brass, and it wouldn't feel greasy anymore, and so anybody in town would take it in a minute, let alone a hair-ball. Well, I knew a potato would do that before, but I had forgotten it.

Jim placed the quarter beneath the hair-ball and crouched down to listen once more. This time he said the hair-ball was working properly. He explained that it would reveal my entire fortune if I desired it to. I told him to proceed. So the hair-ball spoke to Jim, and Jim relayed its message to me. He said:

"Your old father doesn't know yet what he's going to do. Sometimes he thinks he'll go away, and then again he thinks he'll stay. The best way is to rest easy and let the old man take his own way. There are two angels hovering around about him. One of them is white and shiny, and the other one is black. The white one gets him to go right a little while, then the black one sails in and busts it all up. A person can't tell yet which one is going to fetch him at the last. But you are all right. You're going to have considerable trouble in your life, and considerable joy. Sometimes you're going to get hurt, and sometimes you're going to get sick; but every time you're going to get well again. There are two girls flying about you in your life. One of them's light and the other one is dark. One is rich and the other is poor. You're going to marry the poor one first and the rich one by and by. You want to keep away from the water as much as you can, and don't run no risk, because it's down in the bills that you're going to get hanged."

When I lit my candle and went up to my room that night, there sat my father himself!

Chapter V.

I had closed the door behind me. When I turned around, there he was. I used to be afraid of him constantly because he beat me so often. I thought I was scared now too, but after a moment I realized I was wrong—that is, after the initial shock, you could say, when my breathing caught because his appearance was so unexpected; but immediately afterward I saw that I wasn't really afraid of him anymore.

He was nearly fifty years old, and he certainly looked it. His hair was long, tangled, and greasy, hanging down so that you could see his eyes gleaming through it as if he were peering from behind vines. The hair was completely black without any gray, just like his long, disheveled whiskers. There was no natural color in his face where it was visible; it was white, but not the kind of white you'd see on another person—this was a sickening white that made your skin crawl, the pale white of a tree frog or a fish's belly. His clothes were nothing more than rags. He sat with one ankle resting on his other knee, and the boot on that foot was torn open with two of his toes poking through, which he wiggled from time to time. His hat lay on the floor—an old black slouch hat with the top collapsed inward like a broken lid.

I stood there looking at him; he sat there looking at me, with his chair tilted back a little. I set the candle down. I noticed the window was open; so he had climbed in by the shed. He kept looking me all over. After a while he says:

"Stiff, formal clothes—extremely so. You think you're quite important, don't you?"

"Maybe I am, maybe I'm not," I said.

"Don't give me any of your attitude," he says. "You've gotten pretty fancy since I've been gone. I'll bring you down a notch before I'm finished with you. You're educated too, they say—can read and write. You think you're better than your father now, don't you, because he can't? I'll make you pay for that. Who told you that you could mess around with such high-and-mighty nonsense, huh?—who told you that you could?"

"The widow. She told me."

"The widow, huh? And who told the widow she could stick her nose into something that's none of her business?"

"No one ever told her."

"Well, I'll teach her not to interfere. And listen here—you quit that school, you understand? I'll teach people not to raise a boy who puts on airs around his own father and pretends to be better than he really is. Don't let me catch you messing around with that school again, you hear? Your mother couldn't read, and she couldn't write either, before she died. None of the family could before they died. I can't; and here you are puffing yourself up like this. I'm not the kind of man to tolerate it—you understand? Now, let me hear you read."

I picked up a book and started reading something about General Washington and the wars. After I'd been reading for about half a minute, he struck the book with his hand and sent it flying across the room. He said:

"That's right. You can do it. I had my doubts when you told me. Now listen here; you stop putting on airs. I won't stand for it. I'll be watching you, you little show-off; and if I catch you around that school I'll give you a good beating. Before you know it, you'll get religion too. I've never seen such a son."

He picked up a small blue and yellow picture showing some cows and a boy, and said:

"What's this?"

"It's something they give me for learning my lessons well."

He ripped it apart and said:

"I'll give you something better—I'll give you a beating with a leather strap."

He sat there mumbling and growling for a minute, and then he said:

"Aren't you quite the fancy gentleman? A bed and bedding and a mirror and a piece of carpet on the floor—while your own father has to sleep with the hogs in the tannery. I've never seen such a son. I guarantee I'll knock some of these fancy airs out of you before I'm finished with you. Why, there's no limit to your pretensions—they say you're wealthy. Really?—how is that possible?"

"They lie—that's how."

"Listen here—watch how you talk to me; I'm at the end of my rope right now—so don't give me any attitude. I've been in town for two days, and all I've heard is talk about you being rich. I heard about it way down the river, too. That's why I came. You get me that money tomorrow—I want it."

"I don't have any money."

"It's a lie. Judge Thatcher's got it. You get it. I want it."

"I don't have any money, I'm telling you. You can ask Judge Thatcher; he'll tell you the same thing."

"All right. I'll ask him; and I'll make him pay up, too, or I'll find out why not. Say, how much money do you have in your pocket? I want it."

"I only have a dollar, and I want that to—"

"It doesn't matter what you want it for—you just pay up."

He took it and bit it to check if it was real, and then he said he was heading downtown to buy some whiskey; he mentioned he hadn't had a drink all day. After he stepped out onto the shed, he stuck his head back inside and cursed at me for acting fancy and trying to be superior to him; and just when I thought he had left, he returned and poked his head in once more, warning me about that school because he planned to wait for me and beat me if I didn't quit going.

The next day he was drunk, and he went to Judge Thatcher's house and harassed him, trying to force him to hand over the money; but he couldn't succeed, and then he swore he'd use the law to make him give it up.

The judge and the widow took legal action to convince the court to remove me from his custody and allow one of them to become my guardian; however, it was a new judge who had recently arrived, and he wasn't familiar with the old man; therefore he declared that courts shouldn't interfere and break up families if it could be avoided; he stated he would prefer not to take a child away from its father. Consequently, Judge Thatcher and the widow had to abandon their efforts.

That delighted the old man so much he couldn't sit still. He said he'd beat me with a cowhide whip until I was black and blue if I didn't get some money for him. I borrowed three dollars from Judge Thatcher, and my father took it and got drunk, and went around town making noise and swearing and shouting and acting wild; and he kept this up all over town, banging a tin pan, until almost midnight; then they put him in jail, and the next day they brought him before the court, and jailed him again for a week. But he said he was satisfied; said he was the boss of his son, and he'd make things difficult for him.

When he was released, the new judge said he was going to make a man of him. So he brought him to his own house, dressed him up clean and neat, and invited him to eat breakfast, dinner, and supper with the family, treating him wonderfully well. After supper, he spoke with him about temperance and similar matters until the old man cried, saying he had been a fool and wasted his life; but now he was going to turn over a new leaf and become a man that nobody would be ashamed of, and he hoped the judge would help him and not look down on him. The judge said he could hug him for those words; so he cried, and his wife cried as well; father said he had always been a man who was misunderstood before, and the judge said he believed it. The old man said that what a man who was down needed was sympathy, and the judge agreed; so they cried again. And when it was bedtime, the old man stood up and held out his hand, and said:

"Look at it, gentlemen and ladies; take hold of it; shake it. Here's a hand that once belonged to a pig, but that's not what it is anymore; it's the hand of a man who has begun a new life, and who would rather die than go back to his old ways. Remember these words—don't forget that I said them. It's a clean hand now; shake it—don't be afraid."

So they shook it, one after the other, all around, and cried. The judge's wife kissed it. Then the old man signed a pledge—made his mark. The judge said it was the most sacred moment on record, or something like that. Then they put the old man in a beautiful room, which was the guest room, and sometime during the night he got extremely thirsty and climbed out onto the porch roof and slid down a support post and traded his new coat for a jug of cheap whiskey, and climbed back up again and had a great time; and toward daylight he crawled out again, drunk as could be, and rolled off the porch and broke his left arm in two places, and was nearly frozen to death when somebody found him after sunrise. And when they came to look at that guest room they had to measure the mess before they could get through it.

The judge felt somewhat irritated. He said he figured someone might be able to reform the old man with a shotgun, perhaps, but he didn't know any other way.

Chapter VI.

Well, pretty soon the old man was up and around again, and then he went after Judge Thatcher in the courts to make him give up that money, and he went after me, too, for not quitting school. He caught me a couple of times and beat me, but I went to school just the same, and avoided him or outran him most of the time. I didn't want to go to school much before, but I figured I'd go now to spite pap. That lawsuit was a slow business—it seemed like they were never going to get started on it; so every now and then I'd borrow two or three dollars from the judge for him, to keep from getting a beating. Every time he got money he got drunk; and every time he got drunk he caused trouble around town; and every time he caused trouble he got jailed. He was perfectly content—this kind of thing was right up his alley.

He started spending too much time around the widow's house, so she finally told him that if he didn't stop loitering there, she would cause problems for him. Well, wasn't he angry? He said he would show who was Huck Finn's boss. So he waited for me one day in the spring, and caught me, and took me up the river about three miles in a small boat, and crossed over to the Illinois shore where it was wooded and there weren't any houses except an old log cabin in a place where the trees were so thick you couldn't find it unless you knew where it was.

He kept me with him constantly, and I never had an opportunity to escape. We lived in that old cabin, and he always locked the door and placed the key under his head at night. He had a gun that he had stolen, I believe, and we fished and hunted, and that's what we survived on. Every so often he would lock me inside and go down to the store, three miles away, to the ferry, and traded fish and game for whiskey, and brought it home and got drunk and had a good time, and beat me. The widow eventually discovered where I was, and she sent a man over to try to get me; but my father drove him away with the gun, and it wasn't long after that until I had grown accustomed to being where I was, and enjoyed it—except for the beating part.

It was relaxing and enjoyable, lounging around comfortably all day, smoking and fishing, with no books or studying required. Two months or more passed by, and my clothes became completely torn and dirty, and I couldn't understand how I had ever come to enjoy it so much at the widow's house, where you had to wash yourself, eat from a plate, comb your hair, go to bed and wake up at regular times, constantly struggle with books, and deal with old Miss Watson constantly nagging you. I no longer wanted to return there. I had stopped swearing because the widow disapproved of it, but now I started doing it again since my father had no problem with it. Those were pretty good times up in the woods, all things considered.

But gradually my father became too quick with his hickory switch, and I couldn't tolerate it anymore. I was covered in welts all over. He also started going away frequently and locking me inside. One time he locked me in and disappeared for three days. It was terribly lonely. I figured he had drowned, and I would never get out again. I was frightened. I decided I would figure out some way to escape from there. I had attempted to get out of that cabin many times before, but I couldn't discover any way out. There wasn't a window large enough for even a dog to squeeze through. I couldn't climb up the chimney; it was too narrow. The door was made of thick, solid oak planks. My father was quite careful not to leave a knife or any tool in the cabin when he went away; I think I had searched the place more than a hundred times; well, I spent almost all my time doing it, since it was practically the only way to pass the time. But this time I finally discovered something; I found an old rusty wood saw without a handle; it was tucked between a rafter and the roof's clapboards. I oiled it up and started working. There was an old horse blanket nailed against the logs at the cabin's far end behind the table, to prevent the wind from blowing through the gaps and extinguishing the candle. I crawled under the table and lifted the blanket, then began sawing out a section of the large bottom log—big enough for me to crawl through. Well, it was quite a lengthy task, but I was nearing completion when I heard my father's gun firing in the woods. I eliminated all traces of my work, dropped the blanket and concealed my saw, and soon after my father came inside.

Dad wasn't in a good mood—so he was acting like his usual self. He said he had been downtown, and everything was going badly. His lawyer told him he thought he would probably win his lawsuit and get the money if they ever actually started the trial; but there were ways to delay it for a long time, and Judge Thatcher knew how to do that. And he said people believed there would be another trial to take me away from him and give me to the widow as my guardian, and they thought it would succeed this time. This upset me quite a bit, because I didn't want to go back to the widow's house anymore and be so restricted and civilized, as they called it. Then the old man started swearing, and he cursed everything and everybody he could think of, and then cursed them all over again to make sure he hadn't missed anyone, and after that he finished up with a kind of general curse all around, including a good number of people whose names he didn't know, so he called them what's-his-name when he got to them, and kept right on with his cursing.

He said he wanted to see the widow take me in. He told me he would keep watch, and if they tried to pull any tricks like that on him, he knew of a place six or seven miles away where he could hide me, and they could search until they collapsed without ever finding me. That made me quite worried again, but only for a moment; I figured I wouldn't stick around long enough to give him that opportunity.

The old man made me go to the boat and get the supplies he had bought. There was a fifty-pound bag of cornmeal, a slab of bacon, ammunition, and a four-gallon jug of whiskey, along with an old book and two newspapers for packing, plus some rope. I carried up a load and went back to sit on the front of the boat to rest. I thought everything through, and I figured I would take the gun and some fishing lines and head into the woods when I escaped. I figured I wouldn't stay in one spot, but would just walk straight across the country, mostly at night, and hunt and fish to survive, and get so far away that the old man and the widow could never find me again. I decided I would cut my way out and leave that night if my father got drunk enough, and I expected he would.

35

I got so caught up in planning that I didn't realize how long I had been sitting there until the old man yelled and asked me if I was asleep or had drowned.

I carried everything up to the cabin, and by then it was getting dark. While I was making dinner, the old man had a drink or two and started getting worked up, beginning his ranting again. He had been drunk in town and had spent the night lying in the gutter, and he looked terrible. Anyone would have thought he was Adam—he was completely covered in mud. Whenever the alcohol started affecting him, he almost always went after the government, and this time he said:

"Call this a government! Why, just look at it and see what it's like. Here's the law standing ready to take a man's son away from him—a man's own son, which he has had all the trouble and all the anxiety and all the expense of raising. Yes, just as that man has got that son raised at last, and ready to go to work and begin to do something for him and give him a rest, the law up and goes for him. And they call that government! That isn't all, either. The law backs that old Judge Thatcher up and helps him to keep me out of my property. Here's what the law does: The law takes a man worth six thousand dollars and upwards, and jams him into an old trap of a cabin like this, and lets him go around in clothes that aren't fit for a hog. They call that government! A man can't get his rights in a government like this. Sometimes I've a mighty notion to just leave the country for good and all. Yes, and I told them so; I told old Thatcher so to his face. Lots of them heard me, and can tell what I said. Says I, for two cents I'd leave the blamed country and never come near it again. Those are the very words. I says look at my hat—if you call it a hat—but the lid raises up and the rest of it goes down till it's below my chin, and then it isn't rightly a hat at all, but more like my head was shoved up through a joint of stove-pipe. Look at it, says I—such a hat for me to wear—one of the wealthiest men in this town if I could get my rights."

"Oh, yes, this is a wonderful government, wonderful. Why, look here. There was a free Black man there from Ohio—mixed race, almost as white as a white man. He had the whitest shirt on you ever saw, too, and the shiniest hat; and there isn't a man in that town that's got as fine clothes as what he had; and he had a gold watch and chain, and a silver-headed cane—the most distinguished old gray-headed gentleman in the State. And what do you think? They said he was a professor in a college, and could speak all kinds of languages, and knew everything. And that isn't the worst. They said he could vote when he was at home. Well, that did it for me. I thought, what is the country coming to? It was election day, and I was just about to go and vote myself if I wasn't too drunk to get there; but when they told me there was a State in this country where they'd let that Black man vote, I backed out. I said I'll never vote again. Those are the very words I said; they all heard me; and the country may rot for all I care—I'll never vote again as long as I live. And to see the calm way of that Black man— why, he wouldn't have given me the road if I hadn't shoved him out of the way. I said to the people, why isn't this Black man put up at auction and sold?—that's what I want to know. And what do you think they said? Why, they said he couldn't be sold until he'd been in the State six months, and he hadn't been there that long yet. There, now—that's an example. They call that a government that can't sell a free Black man until he's been in the State six months. Here's a government that calls itself a government, and pretends to be a government, and thinks it is a government, and yet has got to sit stock-still for six whole months before it can take hold of a prowling, thieving, infernal, white-shirted free Black man, and—"

Dad was going on so much he never noticed where his unsteady legs were taking him, so he tumbled head over heels over the barrel of salt pork and scraped both his shins, and the rest of his speech was filled with the angriest kind of language—mostly directed at the Black man and the government, though he cursed at the barrel some too, off and on. He hopped around the cabin quite a bit, first on one leg and then on the other, holding first one shin and then the other one, and finally he suddenly lashed out with his left foot and gave the barrel a thundering kick. But that wasn't smart thinking, because that was the boot that had a couple of his toes sticking out of the front end of it; so now he let out a scream that practically made a person's hair stand on end, and down he went in the dirt, and rolled there, and clutched his toes; and the swearing he did then surpassed anything he had ever done before. He said so himself afterwards. He had heard old Sowberry Hagan in his prime, and he said it beat him too; but I figure that was probably exaggerating it a bit, maybe.

After dinner, my father grabbed the jug and said he had enough whiskey there for two drinking binges and one case of delirium tremens. That was always his expression. I figured he would be completely drunk within an hour, and then I would steal the key or saw my way out, one way or another. He drank and drank, and eventually collapsed on his blankets; but luck wasn't on my side. He didn't fall into a deep sleep, but remained restless. He groaned and moaned and tossed around in every direction for a long time. Finally I became so sleepy I couldn't keep my eyes open no matter what I tried, and so before I realized what was happening I was fast asleep, with the candle still burning.

I don't know how long I was asleep, but suddenly there was a terrible scream and I woke up. There was my father looking wild, jumping around in every direction and yelling about snakes. He said they were crawling up his legs; then he would leap and scream, saying one had bitten him on the cheek—but I couldn't see any snakes. He started running around and around the cabin, shouting "Get him off! get him off! he's biting me on the neck!" I had never seen a man look so wild in the eyes. Soon he was completely exhausted, and fell down gasping; then he rolled over and over incredibly fast, kicking things in every direction, and swinging and grasping at the air with his hands, and screaming and saying there were devils holding onto him. He tired himself out eventually, and lay still for a while, moaning. Then he lay even stiller, and didn't make a sound. I could hear the owls and the wolves far off in the woods, and it seemed terribly quiet. He was lying over by the corner. After a while he raised up partway and listened, with his head tilted to one side. He said, very quietly:

"Stomp—stomp—stomp; that's the dead; stomp—stomp—stomp; they're coming after me; but I won't go. Oh, they're here! don't touch me—don't! hands off—they're cold; let go. Oh, leave a poor soul alone!"

Then he dropped down on his hands and knees and crawled away, pleading with them to leave him alone, and he wrapped himself up in his blanket and squirmed underneath the old pine table, still begging; and then he started crying. I could hear him through the blanket.

After a while he rolled out and jumped to his feet looking wild, and when he saw me he came after me. He chased me around and around the place with a clasp-knife, calling me the Angel of Death, and saying he would kill me so that I couldn't come for him anymore. I begged and told him I was only Huck, but he laughed with such a screechy laugh, and roared and cursed, and kept on chasing me. Once when I turned quickly and dodged under his arm he made a grab and caught me by the jacket between my shoulders, and I thought I was finished; but I slipped out of the jacket as quick as lightning and saved myself. Soon he was completely tired out and dropped down with his back against the door, saying he would rest a minute and then kill me. He put his knife under him and said he would sleep and get strong, and then he would see who was who.

So he fell asleep fairly quickly. After a while, I grabbed the old split-bottom chair and climbed up as quietly as I could to avoid making any sound, and took down the gun. I slid the ramrod down the barrel to confirm it was loaded, then I rested it across the turnip barrel with it aimed toward pap, and sat down behind it to wait for him to move. And how slowly and quietly the time crawled by.

Chapter VII.

"Get up! What are you doing?"

I opened my eyes and looked around, trying to figure out where I was. It was after sunrise, and I had been sleeping deeply. Dad was standing over me looking angry and sick as well. He said:

"What are you doing with this gun?"

I figured he didn't know anything about what he had been doing, so I said:

"Someone tried to break in, so I was waiting for him."

"Why didn't you wake me up?"

"Well, I tried to, but I couldn't; I couldn't budge you."

"Well, all right. Don't stand there chattering all day, but get going and see if there's a fish on the lines for breakfast. I'll be along in a minute."

He unlocked the door, and I hurried away up the riverbank. I saw some pieces of branches and similar debris floating downstream, along with scattered bark, so I knew the river had started to rise. I figured I would have wonderful opportunities now if I could get over to the town. The June flood had always brought me good fortune in the past because as soon as that water level begins to climb, cordwood comes floating down the river, along with sections of log rafts—sometimes a dozen logs bundled together. All you had to do was catch them and sell them to the lumber yards and the sawmill.

I walked along the riverbank keeping one eye out for my father and the other watching for whatever the flood might bring downstream. Suddenly, a canoe appeared—a real beauty, about thirteen or fourteen feet long, floating high on the water like a duck. I dove headfirst off the bank like a frog, fully clothed, and swam toward the canoe. I expected someone would be lying down inside it, since people often did that to trick others—when someone had nearly reached the boat, they'd sit up and laugh at them. But that wasn't the case this time. It was genuinely a drifting canoe, and I climbed in and paddled it to shore. I thought to myself that the old man would be pleased when he saw this—it was worth ten dollars. But when I reached the shore, my father was nowhere to be seen, and as I was steering the canoe into a small creek that looked like a ravine, completely covered with hanging vines and willows, another idea struck me: I decided I'd hide it well, and then, instead of heading into the woods when I ran away, I'd travel down the river about fifty miles and set up a permanent camp in one spot, avoiding the hardship of walking on foot.

It was quite close to the shack, and I kept thinking I heard the old man approaching; but I managed to hide it; and then I stepped out and peered around a cluster of willow trees, and there was the old man further down the path taking aim at a bird with his rifle. So he hadn't noticed anything.

When he returned, I was working hard pulling up a fishing line with multiple hooks. He criticized me a bit for taking so long, but I explained that I had fallen into the river, which was why I was delayed. I knew he would notice I was soaked, and then he would start asking questions. We caught five catfish from the lines and headed home.

While we settled down after breakfast to catch up on sleep, both of us being completely exhausted, I started thinking that if I could figure out some way to prevent my father and the widow from trying to follow me, it would be more reliable than depending on luck to get far enough away before they noticed I was missing; you see, all sorts of things could go wrong. Well, I couldn't think of any solution for a while, but eventually my father sat up for a moment to drink another large amount of water, and he said:

"If another man comes prowling around here, you wake me up, do you understand? That man wasn't here for any good reason. I would have shot him. Next time, you wake me up, do you hear me?"

Then he lay back down and fell asleep again; but what he had been saying gave me exactly the idea I needed. I said to myself, I can arrange things now so that nobody will think of following me.

Around noon we got up and walked along the riverbank. The river was rising pretty quickly, and lots of driftwood was floating by with the current. After a while, part of a log raft came floating down—nine logs tied together. We took the small boat out and pulled it to shore. Then we ate dinner. Anyone except my father would have waited and stayed through the day to catch more stuff, but that wasn't my father's way. Nine logs were enough for one trip; he had to head straight to town and sell them. So he locked me inside and took the small boat, and left towing the raft around three-thirty. I figured he wouldn't return that night. I waited until I thought he had gotten a good head start; then I pulled out my saw and got back to work on that log. Before he reached the other side of the river, I was out of the hole; he and his raft were just a tiny dot on the water far off in the distance.

I grabbed the sack of cornmeal and carried it to where I had hidden the canoe, pushed aside the vines and branches, and placed it inside. Then I did the same thing with the side of bacon, followed by the whiskey jug. I gathered all the coffee and sugar that was there, along with all the ammunition. I took the wadding, the bucket and gourd, a dipper and a tin cup, my old saw and two blankets, plus the skillet and coffee pot. I collected fishing lines and matches and other items—everything that had any value at all. I cleared out the entire place. I wanted to take an axe, but there wasn't one available except for the one by the woodpile, and I knew exactly why I had to leave that one behind. I brought out the gun, and then I was finished.

I had worn down the ground quite a bit from crawling out of the hole and dragging out so many items. So I repaired that area as well as I could from the outside by scattering dirt on the spot, which covered up the smooth surface and the sawdust. Then I fitted the piece of log back into its place, and put two rocks underneath it and one against it to hold it in position, because it was warped at that spot and didn't quite touch the ground. If you stood four or five feet away and didn't know it had been sawed, you would never notice it; and besides, this was the back of the cabin, and it wasn't likely that anyone would go around messing with it.

It was all grass leading right up to the canoe, so I hadn't left any tracks behind. I walked around to check and make sure. I stood on the riverbank and looked out across the water. Everything appeared safe. So I picked up the gun and headed a short distance into the woods, searching around for some birds when I spotted a wild pig; hogs quickly turned wild in those lowlands after they had escaped from the prairie farms. I shot this one and carried him back to camp.

I grabbed the axe and broke down the door. I beat it and chopped at it quite a bit while doing this. I brought the pig inside, carried him close to the table and struck his throat with the axe, then laid him on the floor to bleed; I say floor because that's what it was—hard-packed dirt, with no wooden planks. Then I took an old bag and filled it with as many large stones as I could manage to carry, and I dragged it away from the pig, pulled it to the door and through the woods down to the river where I threw it in, and it sank completely out of view. Anyone could easily tell that something had been dragged across the ground. I really wished Tom Sawyer had been there; I knew he would have found this kind of work fascinating, and would have added his own creative flourishes. No one could show off like Tom Sawyer when it came to something like this.

Finally, I pulled out some of my hair and got blood on the axe, then stuck it on the back side and threw the axe in the corner. Then I picked up the pig and held it against my chest with my jacket (so it wouldn't drip) until I got a good distance below the house and then threw it into the river. Then I thought of something else. So I went and got the bag of meal and my old saw out of the canoe, and brought them to the house. I took the bag to where it usually stood, and cut a hole in the bottom of it with the saw, since there weren't any knives and forks in the place— dad did everything with his pocket knife when it came to cooking. Then I carried the sack about a hundred yards across the grass and through the willows east of the house, to a shallow lake that was five miles wide and full of rushes—and ducks too, you could say, during the season. There was a swamp or a creek leading out of it on the other side that went for miles, I don't know where, but it didn't go to the river. The meal spilled out and made a little trail all the way to the lake. I dropped dad's whetstone there too, so it would look like it had been done by accident. Then I tied up the tear in the meal sack with a string, so it wouldn't leak anymore, and took it and my saw back to the canoe.

It was getting dark by now, so I guided the canoe down the river and tucked it under some willows that drooped over the bank, then waited for the moon to come up. I tied the canoe to a willow branch, grabbed something to eat, and after a while stretched out in the canoe to smoke my pipe and figure out what to do next. I told myself that they'd follow the trail of that bag full of rocks right to the shore, then they'd drag the river looking for my body. They'd also follow that flour trail to the lake and search along the creek that flows out of it, trying to find the robbers who supposedly killed me and stole my things. They won't bother searching the river for anything except my dead body. Before long, they'll get tired of that and stop worrying about me altogether. That works perfectly for me—I can settle down wherever I please. Jackson's Island will suit me just fine; I know that island well, and nobody ever goes there. Plus, I can paddle back to town at night, sneak around, and grab whatever I need. Jackson's Island is exactly the right place.

I was quite tired, and before I knew it, I had fallen asleep. When I woke up, I didn't know where I was for a moment. I sat up and looked around, feeling a little scared. Then I remembered. The river looked miles and miles wide. The moon was so bright I could have counted the driftwood logs that went sliding along, black and still, hundreds of yards out from the shore. Everything was completely quiet, and it looked late, and smelled late. You know what I mean—I don't know the words to describe it.

I took a good stretch and was just about to untie the boat and leave when I heard a sound coming from across the water. I listened carefully. Soon I figured out what it was. It was that muffled kind of steady sound that comes from oars working in oarlocks on a quiet night. I peered out through the willow branches, and there it was—a small boat, far across the water. I couldn't tell how many people were in it. It kept coming closer, and when it was directly across from me I could see there was only one man in it. I thought to myself, maybe it's my father, though I wasn't expecting him. He drifted past me with the current, and eventually he came swinging back toward shore in the calmer water, and he passed by so close I could have reached out with the gun and touched him. Well, it was my father, sure enough—and sober, too, judging by the way he handled his oars.

I didn't waste any time. The next minute I was gliding downstream quietly but quickly in the shade of the bank. I traveled two and a half miles, and then headed out a quarter of a mile or more toward the middle of the river, because soon I would be passing the ferry landing, and people might spot me and call out to me. I reached the area among the driftwood, and then lay down in the bottom of the canoe and let it float.

I lay there, enjoying a good rest and smoking my pipe while gazing up at the sky; there wasn't a single cloud in sight. The sky looks incredibly deep when you're lying on your back in the moonlight; I had never noticed that before. And how far you can hear sounds across the water on nights like this! I could hear people talking at the ferry landing. I heard what they were saying too—every single word. One man said it was getting close to the long days and short nights now. The other one said this wasn't one of the short ones, he figured—and then they laughed, and he repeated it again, and they laughed once more; then they woke up another fellow and told him, and laughed, but he didn't laugh; he snapped out something sharp and told them to leave him alone. The first fellow said he planned to tell it to his wife—she would think it was pretty funny; but he said that was nothing compared to some things he had said in his time. I heard one man say it was nearly three o'clock, and he hoped daylight wouldn't take more than about a week longer to come. After that the conversation grew more and more distant, and I couldn't make out the words anymore; but I could hear the murmur, and occasionally a laugh too, but it seemed very far away.

I was now downstream from the ferry. I stood up, and there was Jackson's Island, about two and a half miles downstream, heavily forested and rising up from the middle of the river, large and dark and solid, like a steamboat without any lights. There were no signs of the sandbar at the head—it was all underwater now.

It didn't take me long to reach my destination. I flew past the head of the island at an incredible speed because the current was so strong, and then I entered the calm water and came ashore on the Illinois side. I steered the canoe into a deep hollow in the bank that I knew about; I had to push through the willow branches to get inside; and once I secured it, no one could have spotted the canoe from the outside.

I walked up and sat down on a log at the head of the island, and looked out at the wide river and the black driftwood and across to the town, three miles away, where there were three or four lights twinkling. An enormous lumber raft was about a mile upstream, floating down toward me, with a lantern in the middle of it. I watched it drift slowly down, and when it was almost directly across from where I stood I heard a man say, "Stern oars, there! turn her head to starboard!" I heard that just as clearly as if the man was right beside me.

There was a hint of gray light in the sky now, so I walked into the woods and lay down for a nap before breakfast.

Chapter VIII.

The sun was positioned so high when I woke up that I figured it must have been after eight o'clock. I lay there in the grass and cool shade thinking about various things, feeling rested and quite comfortable and content. I could glimpse the sun through one or two openings, but mostly there were large trees all around, creating a dim atmosphere among them. There were dappled spots on the ground where the light filtered down through the leaves, and these dappled areas shifted around slightly, indicating there was a gentle breeze above. A pair of squirrels perched on a branch and chattered at me in a very friendly manner.

I was feeling incredibly lazy and comfortable—I didn't want to get up and make breakfast. Well, I was starting to doze off again when I thought I heard a deep "boom!" sound coming from up the river. I sat up and leaned on my elbow to listen; soon enough

I heard it again. I jumped up and went to look through a gap in the leaves, and I could see a cloud of smoke hanging over the water far upstream—roughly level with the ferry landing. There was the ferryboat packed with people floating down the river. I understood what was happening now. "Boom!" I watched the white smoke shoot out from the side of the ferryboat. You see, they were firing cannons over the water, trying to make my dead body float to the surface.

I was pretty hungry, but it wouldn't be smart for me to start a fire, because they might see the smoke. So I sat there and watched the cannon smoke and listened to the booming sound. The river was a mile wide at that spot, and it always looks beautiful on a summer morning—so I was having a good enough time watching them hunt for my remains, if only I had something to eat. Well, then I happened to think about how they always put mercury in loaves of bread and float them downstream, because they always drift right to the drowned body and stop there. So I said to myself, I'll keep watch, and if any of them are floating around looking for me, I'll give them a show. I moved to the Illinois side of the island to see what luck I might have, and I wasn't disappointed. A big double loaf came along, and I almost caught it with a long stick, but my foot slipped and it floated out further. Of course I was positioned where the current flowed closest to the shore—I knew enough for that. But after a while another one came along, and this time I succeeded. I pulled out the plug and shook out the little bit of mercury, and sank my teeth into it. It was baker's bread—the kind that wealthy people eat; not your cheap cornbread.

I found a good spot among the leaves and sat there on a log, eating the bread and watching the ferry-boat, feeling very satisfied. Then something occurred to me. I thought to myself, I suppose the widow or the parson or someone prayed that this bread would find me, and here it has gone and done exactly that. So there's no doubt that there's something to that practice—that is, there's something to it when a person like the widow or the parson prays, but it doesn't work for me, and I figure it only works for just the right kind of people.

I lit my pipe and enjoyed a long, satisfying smoke while continuing to watch. The ferry boat drifted along with the current, and I figured I'd get a chance to see who was on board when it came by, since it would pass close to shore where the bread had floated in. When the boat had moved fairly far downstream toward my position, I put out my pipe and walked over to the spot where I had retrieved the bread, then lay down behind a fallen log on the bank in a small clearing. At the place where the log split into two branches, I could peek through and observe.

Soon she came along, and she drifted in so close that they could have run out a plank and walked ashore. Almost everyone was on the boat. Pap, and Judge Thatcher, and Bessie Thatcher, and Jo Harper, and Tom Sawyer, and his old Aunt Polly, and Sid and Mary, and plenty more. Everyone was talking about the murder, but the captain interrupted and said:

"Pay attention now; the current flows strongest right here, and he might have washed up on shore and gotten caught in the bushes along the water's edge. I hope that's what happened, at least."

I didn't think so. They all gathered together and leaned over the railings, almost right in my face, and stayed quiet, watching as intently as they could. I could see them perfectly, but they couldn't see me. Then the captain called out:

"Stand away!" and the cannon fired such a blast right in front of me that it made me deaf with the noise and nearly blind with the smoke, and I thought I was done for. If they had loaded some bullets in there, I believe they would have gotten the corpse they were looking for. Well, I could see I wasn't hurt, thank goodness. The boat drifted on and disappeared from view around the bend of the island. I could hear the booming now and then, getting farther and farther away, and eventually, after about an hour, I

49

couldn't hear it anymore. The island was three miles long. I figured they had reached the far end and were giving up the search. But they weren't finished just yet. They turned around the foot of the island and started up the channel on the Missouri side, under steam power, firing their cannon occasionally as they went. I crossed over to that side and watched them. When they drew even with the head of the island they stopped shooting and moved over to the Missouri shore and headed home to the town.

I knew I was safe now. Nobody else would come looking for me. I got my supplies out of the canoe and set up a good camp in the dense woods. I made a kind of tent out of my blankets to put my things under so the rain couldn't reach them. I caught a catfish and cut it open with my saw, and toward sunset I started my campfire and had dinner. Then I set out a fishing line to catch some fish for breakfast.

When darkness fell, I sat by my campfire smoking and feeling quite satisfied with myself. But after a while, loneliness began to creep in, so I walked over and sat on the riverbank, listening to the current rushing past. I counted the stars overhead and watched the drifting logs and rafts floating downstream, then finally went to bed. There's no better way to spend time when you're feeling lonely—you can't stay that way for long, and you'll soon get over it.

And so it continued for three days and nights. Nothing changed—just the same routine. But the next day I went exploring down through the island. I was in charge of it; it all belonged to me, you could say, and I wanted to learn everything about it; but mostly I wanted to pass the time. I found plenty of strawberries, ripe and perfect; and green summer grapes, and green raspberries; and the green blackberries were just starting to appear. They would all come in handy later on, I figured.

I wandered through the thick woods until I figured I was close to the bottom end of the island. I carried my gun with me, but I hadn't shot anything yet; it was just for protection, though I thought I might hunt some game near home. Around this time I almost stepped on a large snake, and it slithered away through the grass and flowers while I followed it, trying to get a shot. I moved quickly along, and suddenly I stumbled right onto the ashes of a campfire that was still smoking.

My heart leaped up into my chest. I didn't wait to look any further, but uncocked my gun and went sneaking back on my tiptoes as fast as I could. Every now and then I stopped for a second among the thick leaves and listened, but my breathing came so hard I couldn't hear anything else. I crept along a little further, then listened again; and so on, and so on. If I saw a stump, I mistook it for a man; if I stepped on a stick and broke it, it made me feel like someone had cut one of my breaths in two and I only got half, and the short half, too.

When I reached the camp, I wasn't feeling very confident, and there wasn't much courage left in me; but I told myself, this isn't the time to be messing around. So I loaded all my belongings back into my canoe to keep them hidden from view, and I extinguished the fire and spread the ashes around to make it look like an old campsite from the previous year, and then I climbed up a tree.

I figure I was up in that tree for about two hours, but I didn't see anything or hear anything—I just imagined I was hearing and seeing a thousand different things. Well, I couldn't stay up there forever, so eventually I climbed down, but I stayed hidden in the dense woods and remained alert the whole time. All I could find to eat were berries and whatever leftovers remained from breakfast.

By the time night fell, I was quite hungry. So when it was completely dark, I slipped away from the shore before the moon came up and paddled across to the Illinois side—roughly a quarter mile away. I headed into the woods and prepared myself a meal, and I had nearly decided to spend the entire night there when I heard a clip-clop, clip-clop sound, and I thought to myself, horses approaching; then I heard people talking. I gathered everything into the canoe as quickly as possible, and then crept through the woods to see what I could discover. I hadn't gone very far when I heard a man speaking:

"We should set up camp here if we can find a suitable spot; the horses are nearly exhausted. Let's scout the area."

I didn't wait around, but pushed off and paddled away with ease. I tied up at the familiar spot, and figured I would sleep in the canoe.

I didn't sleep much. I couldn't, somehow, because I kept thinking. And every time I woke up I thought somebody had grabbed me by the neck. So the sleep didn't do me any good. After a while I said to myself, I can't live this way; I'm going to find out who it is that's here on the island with me; I'll find it out or die trying. Well, I felt better right away.

So I grabbed my paddle and pushed out from the shore just a step or two, then let the canoe drift down among the shadows. The moon was shining bright, and outside those shadows it was almost as light as day. I paddled along for nearly an hour, with everything as still as stone and fast asleep. By this time I had nearly reached the bottom end of the island. A gentle, cool breeze started to blow, which was like nature's way of saying the night was almost over. I turned the canoe with my paddle and brought its front end to shore; then I grabbed my gun and slipped out into the edge of the woods. I sat down on a fallen log and peered out through the leaves. I watched the moon finish its watch, and darkness began to cover the river. But after a short while I saw a pale streak above the treetops, and I knew daybreak was coming. So I took my gun and crept off toward where I had come across that campfire earlier, stopping every minute or two to listen. But I wasn't having any luck somehow; I couldn't seem to locate the spot. But eventually, sure enough, I caught sight of firelight flickering through the trees.

I headed toward it, careful and slow. Soon I was close enough to get a good look, and there was a man lying on the ground. It nearly scared me to death. He had a blanket wrapped around his head, and his head was almost touching the fire. I crouched there behind a cluster of bushes, about six feet away from him, and kept my eyes fixed on him steadily. Gray daylight was breaking now. Before long he yawned and stretched himself and threw off the blanket, and it was Miss Watson's Jim! I was so happy to see him. I said:

"Hello, Jim!" and skipped out.

He jumped up and stared at me with wild eyes. Then he dropped down on his knees, put his hands together and said:

"Don't hurt me—don't! I haven't ever done any harm to a ghost. I always liked dead people, and did all I could for them. You go and get in the river again, where you belong, and don't do nothing to Old Jim, who was always your friend."

Well, it didn't take me long to make him understand I wasn't dead. I was so glad to see Jim. I wasn't lonely anymore. I told him I wasn't afraid of him telling people where I was. I kept talking, but he just sat there and looked at me without saying anything. Then I said:

"It's broad daylight. Let's get breakfast. Build up your campfire properly."

"What's the use of making up the campfire to cook strawberries and such stuff? But you got a gun, haven't you? Then we can get something better than strawberries."

"Strawberries and that kind of stuff," I said. "Is that what you live on?"

"I couldn't get anything else," he says.

"Tell me, Jim, how long have you been on this island?"

"I came here the night after you were killed."

"What, all that time?"

"Yes—indeedy."

"And haven't you had anything but that kind of garbage to eat?"

"No, sir—nothing else."

"Well, you must be absolutely starving, aren't you?"

"I reckon I could eat a horse. I think I could. How long have you been on the island?"

"Since the night I got killed."

"No! Why, what have you been living on? But you have a gun. Oh, yes, you have a gun. That's good. Now you kill something and I'll build up the fire."

So we walked over to where the canoe was, and while he built a fire in a grassy clearing among the trees, I brought meal and bacon and coffee, along with the coffee pot and frying pan, plus sugar and tin cups, and the man was quite amazed, because he thought it was all accomplished through magic. I caught a good big catfish as well, and Jim cleaned it with his knife and fried it.

When breakfast was ready, we sprawled on the grass and ate it while it was still steaming hot. Jim ate with tremendous enthusiasm because he was nearly starving. After we had eaten our fill, we stretched out and relaxed. Eventually Jim said:

"But look here, Huck, who was it that was killed in that shack if it wasn't you?"

Then I told him everything, and he said it was clever. He said Tom Sawyer couldn't come up with a better plan than what I had. Then I said:

"How did you end up here, Jim, and how did you get here?"

He looked quite uncomfortable and didn't say anything for a minute. Then he said:

"Maybe I better not tell."

"Why, Jim?"

"Well, there are reasons. But you wouldn't tell on me if I were to tell you, would you, Huck?"

"I sure wouldn't, Jim."

"Well, I believe you, Huck. I—I ran away."

"Jim!"

"But remember, you promised you wouldn't tell—you know you said you wouldn't tell, Huck."

"Well, I did. I said I wouldn't, and I'll stick to it. I swear I will. People would call me a lowdown abolitionist and look down on me for keeping quiet—but that doesn't make any difference. I'm not going to tell, and I'm not going back there anyway. So now, let's hear all about it."

"Well, you see, it was like this. Old missus—that's Miss Watson—she nags me all the time, and treats me pretty rough, but she always said she wouldn't sell me down to Orleans. But I noticed there was a slave trader around the place quite a bit lately, and I began to get uneasy. Well, one night I crept to the door pretty late, and the door wasn't quite shut, and I heard old missus tell the widow she was going to sell me down to Orleans, but she didn't want to, but she could get eight hundred dollars for me, and it was such a big stack of money she couldn't resist. The widow tried to get her to say she wouldn't do it, but I never waited to hear the rest. I took off mighty quick, I tell you."

"I took off and ran down the hill, planning to steal a boat somewhere along the shore above the town, but there were still people moving around, so I hid in the old run-down barrel-maker's shop on the bank to wait for everyone to leave. Well, I was there all night. There was always somebody around. Around six in the morning boats started going by, and about eight or nine o'clock every boat that passed was talking about how your father came over to the town and said you were killed. These later boats were full of ladies and gentlemen going over to see the place. Sometimes they'd pull up at the shore and take a rest before they started across, so from their talk I learned all about the killing. I was terribly sorry you were killed, Huck, but I'm not anymore now."

I stayed hidden under the wood shavings all day. I was hungry, but I wasn't afraid, because I knew the old mistress and the widow were going to leave for the camp meeting right after breakfast and be gone all day, and they know I go off with the cattle around daylight, so they wouldn't expect to see me around the place, and so they wouldn't miss me until after dark in the evening. The other servants wouldn't miss me either, because they'd slip away and take a holiday as soon as the old folks were out of the way.

"Well, when it got dark I headed out on the river road, and went about two miles or more to where there weren't any houses. I'd made up my mind about what I was going to do. You see, if I kept on trying to get away on foot, the dogs would track me; if I stole a boat to cross over, they'd miss that boat, you see, and they'd know about where I'd land on the other side, and where to pick up my trail. So I said to myself, a raft is what I'm after; it doesn't leave any tracks.

"I saw a light coming around the point after a while, so I waded in and pushed a log ahead of me and swam more than halfway across the river, and got in among the driftwood, and kept my head down low, and sort of swam against the current until the raft came along. Then I swam to the stern of it and took hold. It clouded up and was pretty dark for a little while. So I climbed up and lay down on the planks. The men were all way over there in the middle, where the lantern was. The river was rising, and there was a good current; so I figured that by four in the morning I'd be twenty-five miles down the river, and then I'd slip in just before daylight and swim ashore, and take to the woods on the Illinois side."

"But I didn't have any luck. When we were almost down to the head of the island, a man began to come toward the back with the lantern. I saw it wasn't any use to wait, so I slipped overboard and struck out for the island. Well, I had an idea I could land most anywhere, but I couldn't—the bank was too steep. I was almost to the foot of the island before I found a good place. I went into the woods and figured I wouldn't fool with rafts anymore, as long as they moved the lantern around like that. I had my pipe and a plug of tobacco, and some matches in my cap, and they weren't wet, so I was all right."

"So you haven't had any meat or bread to eat this whole time? Why didn't you catch mud turtles?"

"How are you going to catch them? You can't sneak up on them and grab them; and how is someone going to hit them with a rock? How could anyone do it at night? And I wasn't going to show myself on the bank during the daytime."

"Well, that's true. You've had to stay hidden in the woods the whole time, naturally. Did you hear them firing the cannon?"

"Oh, yes. I knew they were after you. I saw them go by here— watched them through the bushes."

Some young birds came along, flying a yard or two at a time before landing. Jim said it was a sign that it was going to rain. He said it was a sign when young chickens flew that way, and so he figured it was the same way when young birds did it. I was going to catch some of them, but Jim wouldn't let me. He said it meant death. He said his father was very sick once, and some of them caught a bird, and his old grandmother said his father would die, and he did.

Jim told me you shouldn't count the ingredients you plan to cook for dinner because it would bring bad luck. The same rule applied if you shook out the tablecloth after sunset. He also explained that if someone who owned a beehive passed away, the bees had to be informed before sunrise the following morning, or they would grow weak, stop working, and eventually die. Jim claimed that bees never sting foolish people, but I wasn't convinced of that theory since I had tested it on myself many times, and they never stung me.

I had heard about some of these things before, but not all of them. Jim knew all kinds of signs. He said he knew almost everything. I said it looked to me like all the signs were about bad luck, so I asked him if there weren't any good-luck signs. He says:

"Very few—and they're no use to anyone. Why would you want to know when good luck is coming? Do you want to keep it away?" And he said: "If you have hairy arms and a hairy chest, it's a sign that you're going to be rich. Well, there's some use in a sign like that, because it's so far ahead. You see, maybe you have to be poor for a long time first, and so you might get discouraged and kill yourself if you didn't know by the sign that you're going to be rich eventually."

"Do you have hairy arms and a hairy chest, Jim?"

"What's the use of asking that question? Don't you see I have?"

"Well, are you rich?"

"No, but I was rich once, and I'm going to be rich again. Once I had fourteen dollars, but I took to speculating, and got wiped out."

"What did you invest in, Jim?"

"Well, first I tried my hand at stocks."

"What kind of stock?"

"Why, livestock—cattle, you know. I put ten dollars into a cow. But I'm not going to risk any more money in stock. The cow up and died on me."

"So you lost the ten dollars."

"No, I didn't lose it all. I only lost about nine dollars of it. I sold the hide and tallow for a dollar and ten cents."

"You had five dollars and ten cents remaining. Did you engage in any more speculation?"

"Yes. You know that one-legged black man who belongs to old Mr. Bradish? Well, he set up a bank, and said anybody who put in a dollar would get four dollars more at the end of the year. Well, all the black folks went in, but they didn't have much. I was the only one who had much. So I held out for more than four dollars, and I said if I didn't get it I'd start a bank myself. Well, of course that man wanted to keep me out of the business, because he says there wasn't business enough for two banks, so he said I could put in my five dollars and he'd pay me thirty-five at the end of the year."

"So I did it. Then I figured I'd invest the thirty-five dollars right away and keep things moving. There was a black man named Bob who had caught a wood-flat, and his master didn't know about it; and I bought it from him and told him to take the thirty-five dollars when the end of the year came; but somebody stole the wood-flat that night, and the next day the one-legged black man said the bank had failed. So none of us got any money."

"What did you do with the ten cents, Jim?"

"Well, I was going to spend it, but I had a dream, and the dream told me to give it to a black man named Balum—Balum's Ass they call him for short; he's one of those fools, you know. But he's lucky, they say, and I could see I wasn't lucky. The dream said let Balum invest the ten cents and he'd make a profit for me. Well, Balum he took the money, and when he was in church he heard the preacher say that whoever gives to the poor lends to the Lord, and is bound to get his money back a hundred times. So Balum he took and gave the ten cents to the poor, and laid low to see what was going to come of it."

"Well, what did come of it, Jim?"

"Nothing ever came of it. I couldn't manage to collect that money in any way, and Balum couldn't either. I'm not going to lend any more money unless I see the security. Bound to get your money back a hundred times, the preacher says! If I could get the ten cents back, I'd call it square and be glad of the chance."

"Well, it's all right anyway, Jim, as long as you're going to be rich again sometime or other."

"Yes, and I'm rich now, when you think about it. I own myself, and I'm worth eight hundred dollars. I wish I had the money—I wouldn't want anything more."

———————————

Chapter IX.

I wanted to visit a spot near the center of the island that I had discovered during my earlier exploration, so we set off and quickly reached it, since the island was just three miles long and a quarter of a mile wide.

This place was a reasonably long, steep hill or ridge about forty feet high. We had a difficult time reaching the top because the sides were so steep and the bushes so thick. We walked and climbed around all over it, and eventually found a good large cave in the rock, almost at the top on the side facing Illinois. The cave was as big as two or three rooms put together, and Jim could stand up straight in it. It was cool inside. Jim wanted to put our supplies in there right away, but I said we didn't want to be climbing up and down there all the time.

Jim said that if we kept the canoe hidden in a good spot and stored all our supplies in the cave, we could quickly escape there if anyone came to the island, and they would never find us without dogs. Besides, he pointed out that those little birds had indicated it was going to rain, and did I want our things to get soaked?

So we returned and retrieved the canoe, then paddled upstream alongside the cave and hauled all our supplies up there. After that, we searched for a nearby spot to conceal the canoe among the dense willow trees. We removed some fish from the fishing lines and reset them, then started preparing for our meal.

The cave entrance was large enough to roll a barrel through, and beside the doorway the ground extended outward slightly, creating a flat surface that made an ideal spot for a fire. We built our fire there and prepared our meal.

We spread the blankets inside to use as a carpet and ate our dinner in there. We put all the other things within easy reach at the back of the cave. Soon it grew dark and began to thunder and lightning started flashing, so the birds had been right about the coming storm. Then it started to rain, and it poured down furiously—I had never seen the wind blow so hard. It was one of those typical summer storms. It would get so dark that everything outside looked blue-black and beautiful, and the rain would come down so heavily that the trees a short distance away appeared dim and hazy like spider webs. Then a blast of wind would come that bent the trees down and flipped up the pale undersides of the leaves, followed by a tremendous gust that set the branches swaying and thrashing as if they had gone wild. Next, when everything was at its darkest and most blue-black—flash! It became as bright as heaven, and you'd catch a quick glimpse of treetops tossing about far off in the storm, hundreds of yards farther than you could see before. Then it would turn dark as night again in an instant, and you'd hear the thunder crash with a terrible sound before rumbling, grumbling, and tumbling down the sky toward the far side of the world, like empty barrels rolling down a long staircase where they bounce quite a bit.

"Jim, this is wonderful," I said. "I wouldn't want to be anywhere else but here. Pass me another piece of fish and some hot cornbread."

"Well, you wouldn't have been here if it hadn't been for Jim. You would have been down there in the woods without any dinner, and getting almost drowned, too; that you would, honey. Chickens know when it's going to rain, and so do the birds, child."

The river kept rising and rising for ten or twelve days, until it finally overflowed its banks. The water reached three or four feet deep on the island in the low-lying areas and across the Illinois floodplain. On that side, it stretched for many miles, but on the Missouri side it remained the same distance across—about half a mile—because the Missouri shore formed a wall of high bluffs.

During the day, we paddled our canoe all around the island. The deep woods were wonderfully cool and shaded, even when the sun was burning hot outside. We weaved in and out between the trees, and sometimes the vines were so thick we had to turn back and find another route. On every old fallen tree, you could spot rabbits, snakes, and other creatures. After the island had been flooded for a day or two, these animals became so tame from hunger that you could paddle right up to them and touch them with your hand if you wanted to—except for the snakes and turtles, which would slip away into the water. The ridge where our cave was located was full of these animals. We could have had plenty of pets if we had wanted them.

One night we caught a small section of a lumber raft—made of nice pine planks. It was twelve feet wide and about fifteen or sixteen feet long, and the top rose above the water six or seven inches—creating a solid, level floor. We could see saw-logs floating by during the daylight sometimes, but we let them pass; we didn't reveal ourselves in daylight.

Another night when we were up at the head of the island, just before dawn, a frame house came floating down on the west side. It was a two-story house, tilted over quite a bit. We paddled out and climbed aboard through an upstairs window. But it was still too dark to see anything, so we tied up the canoe and sat inside to wait for daylight.

The light started to appear before we reached the bottom of the island. Then we peered through the window. We could see a bed, a table, and two old chairs, along with many items scattered across the floor, and there were clothes hanging on the wall. There was something lying on the floor in the far corner that looked like a man. So Jim says:

"Hello, you!"

But it didn't move. So I yelled again, and then Jim says:

"The man isn't asleep—he's dead. You stay put—I'll go and see."

He went over, bent down to look, and said:

"It's a dead man. Yes, indeed; naked, too. He's been shot in the back. I reckon he's been dead two or three days. Come in, Huck, but don't look at his face—it's too ghastly."

I didn't look at him at all. Jim threw some old rags over him, but he didn't need to do it; I didn't want to see him. There were heaps of old greasy cards scattered around over the floor, and old whiskey bottles, and a couple of masks made out of black cloth; and all over the walls were the most ignorant kind of words and pictures made with charcoal. There were two old dirty calico dresses, and a sun-bonnet, and some women's underclothes hanging against the wall, and some men's clothing, too. We put the lot into the canoe—it might come in handy. There was a boy's old speckled straw hat on the floor; I took that, too. And there was a bottle that had had milk in it, and it had a rag stopper for a baby to suck. We would have taken the bottle, but it was broken. There was a shabby old chest, and an old hair trunk with the hinges broken. They stood open, but there wasn't anything left in them that was worth anything. The way things were scattered about we figured the people left in a hurry, and weren't prepared to carry off most of their stuff.

We found an old tin lantern, a butcher knife without a handle, and a brand-new Barlow knife worth twenty-five cents in any store, along with plenty of tallow candles, a tin candlestick, a gourd, and a tin cup, plus a worn-out old bedquilt from the bed, and a small bag containing needles and pins and beeswax and buttons and thread and all sorts of similar items, and a hatchet and some nails, and a fishing line as thick as my little finger with some enormous hooks attached to it, and a roll of buckskin, and a leather dog collar, and a horseshoe, and some bottles of medicine that had no labels on them; and just as we were about to leave I discovered a reasonably good curry comb, and Jim found a worn-out old fiddle bow, and a wooden leg. The straps had broken off of it, but aside from that, it was a decent enough leg, although it was too long for me and not long enough for Jim, and we couldn't locate the other one, even though we searched everywhere.

And so, taking everything into account, we made a good haul. When we were ready to push off we were a quarter of a mile below the island, and it was pretty broad daylight; so I made Jim lie down in the canoe and cover up with the quilt, because if he sat up people could tell he was Black from a good distance away. I paddled over to the Illinois shore, and drifted down almost half a mile doing it. I crept up the still water under the bank, and had no accidents and didn't see anybody. We got home all safe.

Chapter X.

After breakfast I wanted to talk about the dead man and figure out how he came to be killed, but Jim didn't want to. He said it would bring bad luck; and besides, he said, the man might come and haunt us; he said a man that wasn't buried was more likely to go haunting around than one that was properly laid to rest and comfortable. That sounded pretty reasonable, so I didn't say anything more; but I couldn't keep from thinking about it and wishing I knew who shot the man, and what they did it for.

We searched through the clothes we had taken and discovered eight dollars in silver coins sewn into the lining of an old blanket overcoat. Jim said he figured the people in that house had stolen the coat, because if they had known the money was there they wouldn't have left it behind. I said I thought they had killed him too, but Jim didn't want to discuss that. I said:

"Now you think it's bad luck; but what did you say when I brought in the snakeskin that I found on top of the ridge the day before yesterday? You said it was the worst bad luck in the world to touch a snakeskin with my hands. Well, here's your bad luck! We've gathered all this stuff and eight dollars on top of it. I wish we could have some bad luck like this every day, Jim."

"Don't worry about it, honey, don't worry about it. Don't get too bold. It's coming. Remember what I'm telling you, it's coming."

It did happen, too. It was on a Tuesday that we had that conversation. Well, after dinner on Friday we were lying around in the grass at the upper end of the ridge, and we ran out of tobacco. I went to the cave to get some, and discovered a rattlesnake in there. I killed it, and coiled it up on the foot of Jim's blanket, making it look very natural, thinking there would be some fun when Jim found it there. Well, by nighttime I had completely forgotten about the snake, and when Jim threw himself down on the blanket while I lit a light, the snake's mate was there, and it bit him.

He jumped up shouting, and the first thing the light revealed was the snake coiled up and ready to strike again. I killed it instantly with a stick, and Jim grabbed my father's whiskey jug and started pouring it down.

He was barefooted, and the snake bit him right on the heel. All of this happened because I was foolish enough to forget that wherever you leave a dead snake, its mate always comes there and coils around it. Jim told me to cut off the snake's head and throw it away, and then skin the body and roast a piece of it. I did it, and he ate it and said it would help cure him. He made me take off the rattles and tie them around his wrist, too. He said that would help. Then I quietly slipped out and threw the snakes far away among the bushes; I wasn't going to let Jim find out it was all my fault, not if I could help it.

Jim kept drinking from the jug over and over, and occasionally he became delirious and thrashed around while shouting; but each time he regained consciousness he returned to drinking from the jug again. His foot swelled up quite large, and his leg did too; but eventually the intoxication began to take effect, so I figured he would be okay; however, I would have preferred being bitten by a snake rather than drinking pap's whiskey.

Jim was bedridden for four days and nights. Then the swelling completely disappeared and he was up and about again. I decided I would never touch a snake skin again with my bare hands, now that I had seen what came of it. Jim said he figured I would believe him next time. And he said that handling a snake skin brought such terrible bad luck that maybe we hadn't reached the end of it yet. He said he would rather see the new moon over his left shoulder a thousand times than pick up a snake skin with his hand. Well, I was starting to feel the same way, though I had always thought that looking at the new moon over your left shoulder was one of the most careless and foolish things a person could do. Old Hank Bunker did it once, and boasted about it; and in less than two years he got drunk and fell off the shot tower, and flattened himself out so that he was just like a pancake, you might say; and they slid him sideways between two barn doors to use as a coffin, and buried him that way, so they say, but I didn't witness it. My father told me about it. But regardless, it all resulted from looking at the moon that way, like a fool.

Well, the days passed by, and the river receded back between its banks; and one of the first things we did was bait one of the large hooks with a skinned rabbit, set it out, and catch a catfish that was as big as a man—six feet two inches long and weighing over two hundred pounds. We couldn't handle it, of course; it would have thrown us clear into Illinois. We just sat there and watched it thrash and struggle around until it drowned. We found a brass button in its stomach along with a round ball and lots of debris. We split the ball open with the hatchet, and there was a spool inside it. Jim said it had been there a long time, getting coated over to form a ball around it. It was probably the biggest fish ever caught in the Mississippi, I figure. Jim said he had never seen a larger one. It would have been worth quite a bit of money back at the village. They sell fish like that by the pound at the market there; everyone buys some of it; the meat is as white as snow and makes excellent eating when fried.

The next morning I said things were getting slow and boring, and I wanted to stir up some excitement somehow. I said I thought I would slip across the river and find out what was happening. Jim liked that idea, but he said I had to go in the dark and be careful. Then he thought it over and said, couldn't I put on some of those old clothes and dress up like a girl? That was a good idea, too. So we shortened one of the cotton dresses, and I rolled up my pant legs to my knees and got into it. Jim fastened it in the back with the hooks, and it fit pretty well. I put on the sunbonnet and tied it under my chin, and then for someone to look in and see my face was like looking down a section of stovepipe. Jim said nobody would recognize me, even in the daytime, hardly. I practiced around all day to get the hang of wearing those clothes, and eventually I could manage pretty well in them, except Jim said I didn't walk like a girl; and he said I had to stop pulling up my dress to reach my pants pocket. I paid attention and did better.

I began paddling along the Illinois shoreline in my canoe right after nightfall.

I began crossing toward the town from just below where the ferry docked, and the current carried me downstream to the lower end of town. I secured my boat and walked along the riverbank. A light was glowing in a small shack that had been empty for quite some time, and I wondered who had moved in there. I crept closer and peered through the window. Inside sat a woman around forty years old, knitting by candlelight at a pine table. Her face was unfamiliar to me; she was clearly a newcomer, since there wasn't a single face in that town I didn't recognize. This turned out to be fortunate, because my confidence was wavering; I was growing worried that coming here had been a mistake, afraid that people might recognize my voice and discover who I really was. However, if this woman had been living in such a small town for even two days, she would be able to tell me everything I needed to know. So I knocked on her door, reminding myself not to forget that I was supposed to be a girl.

Chapter XI.

"Come in," the woman said, and I entered. She told me, "Have a seat."

I did it. She looked me over completely with her small, bright eyes and said:

"What might your name be?"

"Sarah Williams."

"Where do you live? In this neighborhood?"

"No, ma'am. In Hookerville, seven miles down the river. I've walked the entire way and I'm completely exhausted."

"I bet you're hungry too. I'll get you something to eat."

"No ma'am, I'm not hungry. I was so hungry that I had to stop two miles back at a farm, so I'm not hungry anymore. That's what made me so late. My mother is sick in bed, and we're out of money and everything, and I came to tell my uncle Abner Moore. He lives at the upper end of the town, she says. I've never been here before. Do you know him?"

"No, but I don't know everyone yet. I haven't been living here for quite two weeks. It's quite a distance to the upper end of town. You'd better stay here for the night. Take off your hat."

"No," I said; "I'll rest for a while, I think, and then continue on. I'm not afraid of the dark."

She said she wouldn't let me go by myself, but her husband would be home soon, maybe in an hour and a half, and she'd send him along with me. Then she started talking about her husband, and about her relatives up the river, and her relatives down the river, and about how much better off they used to be, and how they weren't sure but they might have made a mistake coming to our town, instead of leaving well enough alone—and so on and so on, until I was afraid I had made a mistake coming to her to find out what was going on in the town; but eventually she moved on to talking about pap and the murder, and then I was pretty willing to let her chatter right along. She told about me and Tom Sawyer finding the six thousand dollars (only she said it was ten) and all about pap and what a difficult person he was, and what a hard life I had, and finally she got down to where I was murdered. I said:

"Who did it? We've heard quite a bit about what's been happening down in Hookerville, but we don't know who it was that killed Huck Finn."

"Well, I think there's a pretty good chance that people around here would like to know who killed him. Some think old Finn did it himself."

"No—is that so?"

"Most everyone thought that at first. He'll never know how close he came to being lynched. But before nightfall they changed their minds and decided it was done by a runaway slave named Jim."

"Why he—"

I stopped. I figured I'd better stay quiet. She kept talking and never noticed that I had spoken up at all:

"The slave ran off the very night Huck Finn was killed. So there's a reward out for him—three hundred dollars. And there's a reward out for old Finn, too—two hundred dollars. You see, he came to town the morning after the murder, and told about it, and was out with them on the ferry-boat hunt, and right away after he up and left. Before night they wanted to lynch him, but he was gone, you see. Well, next day they found out the slave was gone; they found out he hadn't been seen since ten o'clock the night the murder was done. So then they put it on him, you see; and while they were full of it, next day, back comes old Finn, and went crying to Judge Thatcher to get money to hunt for the slave all over Illinois with. The judge gave him some, and that evening he got drunk, and was around till after midnight with a couple of mighty hard-looking strangers, and then went off with them. Well, he hasn't come back since, and they aren't looking for him back till this thing blows over a little, for people think now that he killed his boy and fixed things so folks would think robbers done it, and then he'd get Huck's money without having to bother a long time with a lawsuit. People do say he wasn't any too good to do it. Oh, he's sly, I reckon. If he doesn't come back for a year he'll be all right. You can't prove anything on him, you know; everything will be quieted down then, and he'll walk into Huck's money as easy as nothing."

"Yes, I think so, ma'am. I don't see anything preventing it. Has everyone stopped thinking the Black man did it?"

"Oh, no, not everybody. A good many think he did it. But they'll catch the Black man pretty soon now, and maybe they can scare it out of him."

"Why, are they still chasing him?"

"Well, you're certainly naive, aren't you! Does three hundred dollars just lie around every day for people to find? Some people think the runaway slave isn't far from here. I'm one of them—but I haven't spread it around. A few days ago I was talking with an elderly couple that lives next door in the log cabin, and they happened to mention that hardly anybody ever goes to that island over there that they call Jackson's Island. Doesn't anyone live there? I asked. No, nobody, they said. I didn't say anything more, but I did some thinking. I was pretty nearly certain I'd seen smoke over there, around the head of the island, a day or two before that, so I said to myself, chances are that runaway slave is hiding over there; anyway, I thought, it's worth the effort to search the place. I haven't seen any smoke since, so I figure maybe he's gone, if it was him; but my husband's going over to check—him and another

70

man. He had gone up the river; but he returned today, and I told him as soon as he arrived two hours ago."

I had become so restless I couldn't sit still. I needed to do something with my hands, so I picked up a needle from the table and started threading it. My hands were shaking, and I was doing a terrible job of it. When the woman stopped talking, I looked up and saw she was watching me with curiosity and a slight smile. I set down the needle and thread and pretended to be interested—though I actually was—and said:

"Three hundred dollars is a lot of money. I wish my mother could get it. Is your husband going over there tonight?"

"Oh, yes. He went uptown with the man I was telling you about, to get a boat and see if they could borrow another gun. They'll go over after midnight."

"Couldn't they see better if they waited until daytime?"

"Yes. And couldn't the man see better, too? After midnight he'll likely be asleep, and they can slip around through the woods and hunt up his camp fire all the better for the dark, if he's got one."

"I didn't think of that."

The woman continued staring at me with obvious curiosity, and I felt completely uncomfortable. Before long, she said,

"What did you say your name was, honey?"

"M—Mary Williams."

Somehow it didn't feel like I had said it was Mary earlier, so I didn't look up—it seemed to me I had said it was Sarah; so I felt kind of trapped, and was afraid maybe I was showing it, too. I wished the woman would say something more; the longer she sat quietly the more uncomfortable I became. But then she says:

"Honey, I thought you said it was Sarah when you first came in?"

"Oh, yes ma'am, I did. Sarah Mary Williams. Sarah's my first name. Some people call me Sarah, some call me Mary."

"Oh, so that's how it is?"

"Yes'm."

I was feeling better at that point, but I still wanted to get out of there. I couldn't bring myself to look up yet.

Well, the woman started talking about how difficult times were, and how poorly they had to live, and how the rats acted as if they owned the place, and so on and so forth, and then I felt comfortable again. She was right about the rats. You'd see one poke his nose out of a hole in the corner every now and then. She said she had to keep things nearby to throw at them when she was alone, or they wouldn't give her any peace. She showed me a bar of lead twisted up into a knot, and said she was usually a good shot with it, but she'd hurt her arm a day or two ago, and didn't know whether she could throw accurately now. But she waited for an opportunity, and suddenly threw it at a rat; but she missed him by a wide margin, and said "Ouch!" it hurt her arm so much. Then she told me to try for the next one. I wanted to be leaving before the old man returned, but of course I didn't show it. I picked up the thing, and the first rat that showed his nose I threw it, and if he'd stayed where he was he would have been a very sick rat. She said that was excellent, and she figured I would get the next one. She went and retrieved the lump of lead and brought it back, and brought along a ball of yarn which she wanted me to help her with. I held up my two hands and she put the ball over them, and continued talking about her and her husband's affairs. But she stopped to say:

"Keep your eye on the rats. You better have the lead in your lap, handy."

So she dropped the lump right into my lap at that exact moment, and I quickly pressed my legs together to hold it while she continued talking. But she only kept going for about a minute. Then she removed the hank and looked directly at me, appearing very pleasant, and said:

"Come on, what's your actual name?"

"What—what, mom?"

"What's your real name? Is it Bill, or Tom, or Bob?—or what is it?"

I think I was shaking like a leaf, and I barely knew what to do. But I said:

"Please don't make fun of a poor girl like me, ma'am. If I'm in the way here, I'll—"

"No, you won't. Sit down and stay where you are. I'm not going to hurt you, and I'm not going to tell on you, either. You just tell me your secret, and trust me. I'll keep it; and, what's more, I'll help you. So will my husband if you want him to. You see, you're a runaway apprentice, that's all. It's nothing. There's no harm in it. You've been treated badly, and you made up your mind to leave. Bless you, child, I wouldn't tell on you. Tell me all about it now, that's a good boy."

So I said it wouldn't be any use to try to keep pretending any longer, and I would just come clean and tell her everything, but she mustn't break her promise. Then I told her my father and mother were dead, and the law had assigned me to a cruel old farmer in the country thirty miles back from the river, and he treated me so badly I couldn't stand it any longer; he went away to be gone a couple of days, and so I took my chance and stole some of his daughter's old clothes and ran away, and I had been three nights traveling the thirty miles. I traveled at night, and hid during the day and slept, and the bag of bread and meat I carried from home lasted me the whole way, and I had plenty. I said I believed my uncle Abner Moore would take care of me, and so that was why I headed out for this town of Goshen.

"Goshen, child? This isn't Goshen. This is St. Petersburg. Goshen's ten miles further up the river. Who told you this was Goshen?"

"Well, I met a man at dawn this morning, right as I was about to head into the woods for my usual rest. He told me that when the roads split, I should take the right path, and walking five miles would get me to Goshen."

"He was drunk, I think. He told you completely wrong."

"Well, he did act like he was drunk, but it doesn't matter now. I need to get moving. I'll reach Goshen before daylight."

"Wait a moment. I'll prepare you something to eat. You might need it."

So she prepared a snack for me and said:

"Tell me, when a cow is lying down, which end of her stands up first? Answer quickly now—don't take time to think about it. Which end gets up first?"

"The back end, ma'am."

"Well, then, a horse?"

"The front end, ma'am."

"Which side of a tree does moss grow on?"

"North side."

"If fifteen cows are grazing on a hillside, how many of them eat with their heads pointing in the same direction?"

"All fifteen of them, ma'am."

"Well, I figure you've lived in the countryside. I thought maybe you were trying to trick me again. What's your real name, anyway?"

"George Peters, ma'am."

"Well, try to remember it, George. Don't forget and tell me it's Alexander before you leave, and then get out of it by saying it's George Alexander when I catch you. And don't go around women in that old cotton dress. You make a pretty poor girl, but you might fool men, perhaps. Bless you, child, when you set out to thread a needle don't hold the thread still and bring the needle up to it; hold the needle still and push the thread at it; that's the way a woman almost always does it, but a man always does it the other way. And when you throw at a rat or anything, lift yourself up on your tiptoes and bring your hand up over your head as awkwardly as you can, and miss your rat by about six or seven feet. Throw stiff-armed from the shoulder, like there's a pivot there for it to turn on, like a girl; not from the wrist and elbow, with your arm out to one side, like a boy. And, mind you, when a girl tries to catch anything in her lap she spreads her knees apart; she doesn't clap them together, the way you did when you caught the lump of lead. Why, I spotted you for a boy when you were threading the needle; and I planned the other things just to make certain. Now run along to your uncle, Sarah Mary Williams George Alexander Peters, and if you get into trouble you send word to Mrs. Judith Loftus, which is me, and I'll do what I can to get you out of it. Keep to the river road all the way, and next time you travel take shoes and socks with you. The river road's a rocky one, and your feet will be in bad shape when you get to Goshen, I expect."

I walked up the riverbank about fifty yards, then doubled back on my path and quietly returned to where my canoe was positioned, a good distance below the house. I jumped in and took off quickly. I paddled upstream far enough to reach the head of the island, then started across. I removed the sun-bonnet because I didn't want anything blocking my vision at that moment. When I reached about the middle of the crossing, I heard the clock begin to strike, so I stopped and listened; the sound came faintly over the water but clearly—eleven strikes. When I reached the head of the island, I didn't pause to catch my breath, even though I was nearly out of wind, but I pushed straight into the woods where my old campsite used to be and built a good fire there on a high and dry spot.

Then I jumped into the canoe and paddled as hard as I could toward our hideout, about a mile and a half downstream. I reached the shore and trudged through the woods, up the hill, and into the cave. Jim was lying there, fast asleep on the ground. I woke him up and said:

"Get up and move quickly, Jim! There isn't a minute to lose. They're after us!"

Jim never asked any questions and didn't say a word, but the way he worked for the next half hour showed just how scared he was. By that time everything we owned in the world was on our raft, and she was ready to be pushed out from the willow cove where she was hidden. We put out the campfire at the cavern first thing, and didn't show a candle outside after that.

I paddled the canoe out from the shore a short distance and looked around, but if there was a boat nearby, I couldn't spot it because stars and shadows don't provide good visibility. Then we brought out the raft and quietly drifted down along the shadowy water, past the end of the island in complete silence—not speaking a single word.

Chapter XII.

It must have been close to one o'clock when we finally got below the island, and the raft seemed to move incredibly slowly. If a boat had come along, we were going to take the canoe and head for the Illinois shore; and it was fortunate that no boat came, because we had never thought to put the gun in the canoe, or a fishing line, or anything to eat. We were in far too much of a hurry to think of so many things. It wasn't good judgment to put everything on the raft.

If the men went to the island, I figure they found the campfire I built and watched it all night waiting for Jim to show up. Either way, they stayed away from us, and if my building the fire didn't fool them, it wasn't my fault. I played it as sneaky as I could on them.

When the first light of dawn started to appear, we tied up to a small island in a large bend on the Illinois side, and chopped off cottonwood branches with the hatchet, and covered the raft with them so it looked like there had been a landslide along the bank. A small island is a sandbar that has cottonwoods growing on it as densely packed as the teeth on a harrow.

We had mountains on the Missouri shore and thick forest on the Illinois side, and the main channel ran along the Missouri shore at that spot, so we weren't worried about anyone discovering us. We stayed there all day, watching the rafts and steamboats move down the Missouri shore, while upstream steamboats struggled against the powerful current in the middle of the river. I told Jim everything about my conversation with that woman, and Jim said she was clever, and if she decided to come after us herself, she wouldn't just sit there watching a campfire—no way, she'd bring a dog with her. Well then, I said, why couldn't she tell her husband to bring a dog? Jim said he was sure she thought of it by the time the men were ready to leave, and he believed they must have gone into town to get a dog, which made them lose all that time, or else we wouldn't be sitting here on this small island sixteen or seventeen miles downstream from the village—no sir, we'd be back in that same old town again. So I said I didn't care what the reason was that they didn't catch us, as long as they didn't.

When darkness began to fall, we stuck our heads out of the cottonwood thicket and looked in every direction; there was nothing in sight, so Jim took some of the top planks from the raft and built a cozy shelter to protect us during hot weather and rain, and to keep our belongings dry. Jim constructed a floor for the shelter and raised it a foot or more above the raft's surface, so the blankets and all our supplies would be safe from steamboat waves. Right in the center of the shelter, we created a layer of dirt about five or six inches deep with a frame around it to hold it in place; this would serve as a place to build a fire during wet or cold weather, and the shelter would hide the flames from view. We also made an extra steering paddle, since one of the others might break on a snag or obstacle. We set up a short forked stick to hang the old lantern on, because we always had to light the lantern whenever we spotted a steamboat coming downstream to avoid getting run down; however, we didn't need to light it for upstream boats unless we found ourselves in what's called a "crossing," since the river was still quite high with the low banks partially underwater, so upstream boats didn't always follow the main channel but instead looked for easier water.

On the second night, we traveled for seven to eight hours with a current moving at over four miles per hour. We caught fish and talked, and occasionally took a swim to stay awake. There was something peaceful about drifting down the large, quiet river, lying on our backs and gazing up at the stars. We never felt like speaking loudly, and we rarely laughed—just an occasional soft chuckle. We generally had excellent weather, and nothing eventful happened to us at all—not that night, nor the next, nor the one after that.

Every night we passed towns, some of them perched high up on dark hillsides, appearing as nothing more than a glowing cluster of lights; you couldn't make out a single house. On the fifth night we passed St. Louis, and it looked like the entire world was illuminated. Back in St. Petersburg they used to claim there were twenty or thirty thousand people living in St. Louis, but I never believed it until I saw that amazing expanse of lights at two o'clock on that quiet night. There wasn't a sound to be heard; everyone was fast asleep.

Every night now I would slip ashore around ten o'clock at some small village, and buy ten or fifteen cents' worth of meal or bacon or other food to eat; and sometimes I took a chicken that wasn't roosting comfortably, and brought him along. Pap always said, take a chicken when you get a chance, because if you don't want him yourself you can easily find somebody that does, and a good deed is never forgotten. I never saw pap when he didn't want the chicken himself, but that is what he used to say, anyway.

In the early morning hours before dawn, I would sneak into cornfields and take a watermelon, or a muskmelon, or a pumpkin, or some fresh corn, or similar items. Dad always said there was no harm in borrowing things if you intended to pay them back eventually; but the widow said it was nothing more than a polite word for stealing, and no respectable person would do it. Jim said he thought the widow was partially right and Dad was partially right; so the best approach would be for us to choose two or three items from the list and say we wouldn't borrow them anymore—then he thought it wouldn't be any harm to borrow the rest. So we discussed it throughout one entire night, floating down the river, trying to decide whether to give up the watermelons, or the cantaloupes, or the muskmelons, or what. But toward daylight we got everything settled satisfactorily, and decided to give up crabapples and persimmons. We hadn't been feeling quite right before that, but everything was comfortable now. I was happy with how it turned out, too, because crabapples are never good, and the persimmons wouldn't be ripe for two or three months yet.

We occasionally shot a waterfowl that rose too early in the morning or stayed up too late in the evening. All things considered, we ate quite well.

On our fifth night past St. Louis, we encountered a massive storm after midnight, filled with tremendous thunder and lightning, while rain came down like a solid wall of water. We remained inside the shelter and allowed the raft to drift on its own. When the lightning flashed, we could make out a wide, straight river stretching ahead, bordered by tall, rocky cliffs on either side. After a while, I called out, "Hey there, Jim, look over there!" A steamboat had wrecked itself against a rock. We were floating directly toward it. The lightning illuminated it clearly. The vessel was tilted to one side, with portions of its upper deck still visible above the waterline, and you could see every small smokestack wire perfectly, along with a chair positioned near the large bell, with an old floppy hat draped over its back whenever the lightning struck.

Well, since it was late at night and stormy, and everything felt so mysterious, I felt exactly the way any other boy would have felt when I saw that wreck lying there so sad and lonely in the middle of the river. I wanted to get on board and sneak around a little to see what was there. So I said:

"Let's land on her, Jim."

But Jim was completely opposed to it at first. He said:

"I don't want to go fooling around with any wreck. We're doing perfectly fine, and we'd better leave well enough alone, as the good book says. There's probably a watchman on that wreck."

"Forget about being a watchman," I said; "there's nothing to guard except the upper deck and the pilot-house; and do you think anyone would risk their life for an upper deck and pilot-house on a night like this, when the whole thing could break apart and wash downstream at any moment?" Jim couldn't argue with that logic, so he remained silent. "Besides," I continued, "we could take something valuable from the captain's cabin. Cigars, I'm betting— the kind that cost five cents each in real money. Steamboat captains are always wealthy, earning sixty dollars every month, and they don't worry about what anything costs as long as they want it. Put a candle in your pocket; I can't relax, Jim, until we search through that boat thoroughly. Do you think Tom Sawyer would pass up an opportunity like this? Not a chance. He'd call it an adventure—that's exactly what he'd call it; and he'd board that wreck even if it killed him. And wouldn't he make it dramatic?— wouldn't he put on a show like nobody's business? You'd think he was Christopher Columbus discovering the promised land. I really wish Tom Sawyer were here with us."

Jim grumbled a little, but he gave in. He said we shouldn't talk any more than absolutely necessary, and when we did talk, we had to keep our voices very low. The lightning showed us the wreck again just in time, and we reached the starboard derrick and secured ourselves there.

The deck was elevated up here. We crept down its sloping surface toward the port side, moving through the darkness toward the officers' quarters, carefully feeling our way with our feet and extending our hands to push away the rigging, since it was so dark we couldn't see any trace of it. Soon we reached the front end of the skylight and climbed onto it; the next step brought us in front of the captain's door, which stood open, and by God, far down through the officers' corridor we saw a light! and at that very moment we thought we heard quiet voices coming from that direction!

Jim whispered that he was feeling really sick and told me to come with him. I said all right and was about to head for the raft, but just then I heard a voice cry out and say:

"Oh, please don't, boys; I swear I won't ever tell!"

Another voice spoke up, quite loudly:

"That's a lie, Jim Turner. You've behaved this way before. You always want more than your fair share of the goods, and you've always gotten it, too, because you've sworn that if you didn't get it you'd tell on us. But this time you've said it just one time too many. You're the most mean-spirited, treacherous dog in this entire region."

By this time Jim had left to get the raft. I was burning with curiosity, and I told myself that Tom Sawyer wouldn't back down now, so I wouldn't either; I was going to see what was happening here. So I got down on my hands and knees in the narrow passage and crawled toward the back in the darkness until there was only one stateroom between me and the cross-hall of the texas. Then I saw a man lying stretched out on the floor, tied hand and foot, with two men standing over him. One of them held a dim lantern in his hand, and the other had a pistol. The one with the pistol kept pointing it at the head of the man on the floor, saying:

"I'd like to! And I should, too—what a rotten person I am!"

The man on the floor would shrivel up and say, "Oh, please don't, Bill; I'm never going to tell."

And every time he said that, the man with the lantern would laugh and say:

"You certainly didn't! You never spoke a truer word than that, I guarantee it." And once he said: "Listen to him beg! And yet if we hadn't gotten the better of him and tied him up, he would have killed us both. And for what reason? Just for nothing. Simply because we stood up for our rights—that's why. But I promise you won't be threatening anyone anymore, Jim Turner. Put away that gun, Bill."

Bill says:

"I don't want to, Jake Packard. I'm in favor of killing him—and didn't he kill old Hatfield in exactly the same way—and doesn't he deserve it?"

"But I don't want him killed, and I have my reasons for it."

"Thank you so much for those words, Jake Packard! I'll never forget you as long as I live!" said the man on the floor, sobbing.

Packard didn't pay any attention to that, but hung his lantern on a nail and headed toward where I was hiding in the darkness, gesturing for Bill to follow. I backed away as quickly as I could for about two yards, but the boat was tilted at such an angle that I couldn't move very fast; so to avoid being trampled and caught, I crawled into a stateroom on the upper side. The man came feeling his way through the darkness, and when Packard reached my stateroom, he said:

"Here—come in here."

They came in, with Bill following behind. But before they entered, I had already climbed up to the upper bunk, trapped there and regretting that I had come. They stood below with their hands resting on the edge of the bunk and began talking. I couldn't see them, but I could tell where they were from the smell of whisky they had been drinking. I was grateful I didn't drink whisky, though it wouldn't have made much difference anyway, since most of the time they couldn't have found me because I wasn't breathing. I was too frightened. Besides, a person couldn't breathe and listen to that kind of conversation at the same time. They spoke quietly and seriously. Bill wanted to kill Turner. He said:

"He said he's going to tell, and he will. Even if we gave him both our shares right now, it wouldn't make any difference after the fight and the way we've treated him. As sure as you're born, he'll turn state's evidence; now you listen to me. I'm in favor of putting him out of his misery."

"So am I," says Packard, very quietly.

"Damn it, I was starting to think you weren't coming. Well, then, that's fine. Let's go and do it."

"Wait a minute; I haven't had my say yet. You listen to me. Shooting's good, but there are quieter ways if the thing has to be done. But what I say is this: it isn't good sense to go courting around after a noose if you can get at what you're up to in some way that's just as good and at the same time doesn't bring you into any risks. Isn't that so?"

"You bet it is. But how are you going to manage it this time?"

"Well, here's my idea: we'll search around and collect whatever valuables we've missed in the cabins, then head to shore and hide the loot. Then we'll wait. Now I'm telling you it won't be more than two hours before this wreck breaks apart and gets washed down the river. You see? He'll drown, and he won't have anyone to blame for it except himself. I figure that's a whole lot better than killing him. I'm against killing a man as long as you can avoid it; it doesn't make good sense, and it's not moral. Am I right?"

"Yes, I think you are. But suppose she doesn't break up and wash away?"

"Well, we can wait the two hours anyway and see, can't we?"

"All right, then; come along."

So they began moving, and I took off in a cold sweat, scrambling forward. It was completely dark there, but I called out in a rough whisper, "Jim!" and he responded right next to my elbow with something like a groan, and I said:

"Hurry, Jim, this isn't the time for messing around and complaining; there's a group of murderers over there, and if we don't find their boat and set it floating down the river so these men can't escape from the wreck, one of them is going to be in serious trouble. But if we find their boat we can put all of them in serious trouble—because the Sheriff will catch them. Hurry— move fast! I'll search the left side, you search the right side. You start at the raft, and—"

"Oh, my Lord, my Lord! The raft? There isn't any raft anymore; it broke loose and went away—and here we are!"

Chapter XIII.

Well, I caught my breath and nearly fainted. Trapped on a wreck with a gang like that! But this wasn't the time for getting emotional. We had to find that boat now—we needed it for ourselves. So we went trembling and shaking down the starboard side, and it was slow work too—it felt like a week before we reached the stern. There was no sign of a boat. Jim said he didn't think he could go any farther—he was so scared he barely had any strength left, he said. But I said, come on, if we get stranded on this wreck we're in real trouble. So we kept searching again. We headed for the stern of the texas, found it, and then scrambled forward along the skylight, gripping from shutter to shutter, since the edge of the skylight was underwater. When we got pretty close to the cross-hall door, there was the skiff, sure enough! I could just barely make it out. I felt incredibly grateful. In another second I would have been aboard her, but just then the door opened. One of the men stuck his head out only about two feet from me, and I thought I was finished; but he pulled it back in again, and said:

"Get that blame lantern out of sight, Bill!"

He threw a bag of something into the boat, then climbed in himself and sat down. It was Packard. Then Bill came out and got in. Packard said in a low voice:

"All ready—shove off!"

I could barely hold onto the shutters, I was so weak. But Bill says:

"Wait—did you go through him?"

"No. Didn't you?"

"No. So he still has his share of the money."

"Well, then, come on; there's no point in taking the goods and leaving the money behind."

"Say, won't he suspect what we're up to?"

"Maybe he won't. But we have to get it anyway. Come on."

So they got out and went in.

The door slammed shut because it was on the tilted side, and within half a second I was in the boat, with Jim tumbling in after me. I pulled out my knife and cut the rope, and off we went!

We didn't touch an oar, and we didn't speak or whisper, or hardly even breathe. We glided swiftly along in complete silence, past the tip of the paddle-box and past the stern; then within a second or two we were a hundred yards below the wreck, and the darkness swallowed her up completely, every last trace of her, and we were safe, and we knew it.

When we were three or four hundred yards downstream, we saw the lantern appear like a small spark at the texas door for just a moment, and we knew from that sight that those criminals had missed their boat and were starting to realize they were now in just as much trouble as Jim Turner was.

Then Jim took hold of the oars, and we went after our raft. This was the first time I started to worry about those men—I suppose I hadn't had time to before. I started to think about how terrible it was, even for murderers, to be in such a situation. I said to myself, there's no way to know if I might become a murderer myself someday, and then how would I feel about it? So I said to Jim:

"The first light we spot, we'll come ashore about a hundred yards either below or above it, somewhere that provides good cover for you and the boat, and then I'll go make up some story and find someone to go after that gang and rescue them from their predicament, so they can face the gallows when their time arrives."

But that plan didn't work out; before long it started storming again, and this time it was worse than before. The rain came down hard, and there wasn't a single light visible anywhere; I figured everyone was asleep. We rushed along down the river, looking for lights and searching for our raft. After quite a while the rain stopped, but the clouds remained, and the lightning continued flickering weakly, and eventually a flash revealed a dark object ahead of us, floating, and we headed toward it.

It was the raft, and we were extremely glad to get back on board. We saw a light far down to the right, on the shore. So I said I would go toward it. The small boat was half full of stolen goods that the gang had taken from the wreck. We hurriedly loaded everything onto the raft in a pile, and I told Jim to float downstream and show a light when he thought he had traveled about two miles, keeping it burning until I returned; then I took up my oars and headed toward the light. As I approached it, three or four more lights appeared on a hillside. It was a village. I moved in above the shore light, rested my oars, and drifted. As I passed by, I saw it was a lantern hanging on the flagstaff of a double-hulled ferry boat. I searched around for the watchman, wondering where he might be sleeping; and eventually I found him sitting on the posts at the front of the boat, with his head down between his knees. I gave his shoulder two or three gentle pushes and began to cry.

He woke up suddenly, in a startled way; but when he saw it was only me, he took a big yawn and stretch, and then he said:

"Hello, what's going on? Don't cry, buddy. What's wrong?"

I said:

"Dad, and mom, and sis, and—"

Then I broke down. He says:

"Oh, come on now, don't get so upset; we all have to deal with our problems, and this one will work out fine. What's wrong with them?"

"They're—they're—are you the boat's watchman?"

"Yes," he says, sounding quite satisfied with himself. "I'm the captain and the owner and the mate and the pilot and watchman and head deck-hand; and sometimes I'm the freight and passengers. I'm not as rich as old Jim Hornback, and I can't be so incredibly generous and good to everyone like he is, and throw money around the way he does; but I've told him many times that I wouldn't trade places with him; because, I say, a sailor's life is the life for me, and I'll be damned if I'd live two miles out of town, where there's nothing ever going on, not for all his money and twice as much more on top of it. I say—"

I interrupted and said:

"They're in a terrible amount of trouble, and—"

"Who is?"

"Why, dad and mom and sis and Miss Hooker; and if you'd take your ferry-boat and go up there—"

"Up where? Where are they?"

"On the wreck."

"What wreck?"

"Why, there's only one."

"What, you don't mean the Walter Scott?"

"Yes."

"Good heavens! What are they doing there, for goodness' sake?"

"Well, they didn't go there on purpose."

"I bet they didn't! My goodness, they don't have any chance if they don't get out of there really fast! How on earth did they ever get into such trouble?"

"Easy enough. Miss Hooker was visiting up there in the town—"

"Yes, Booth's Landing—continue."

"She was visiting there at Booth's Landing, and just as evening was beginning she started across with her servant woman on the horse-ferry to spend the night at her friend's house, Miss What-you-may-call-her—I can't remember her name—and they lost their steering-oar, and swung around and went floating down, stern first, about two miles, and crashed into the wreck, and the ferryman and the servant woman and the horses were all lost, but Miss Hooker she grabbed hold and got aboard the wreck. Well, about an hour after dark we came along down in our trading-boat, and it was so dark we didn't notice the wreck until we were right on it; and so we crashed into it; but all of us were saved except Bill Whipple—and oh, he was the finest person!—I almost wish it had been me, I do."

"My God! It's the strangest thing I've ever come across. So what did you all do then?"

"Well, we shouted and carried on, but it's so wide there that we couldn't make anyone hear us. So dad said somebody had to get to shore and get help somehow. I was the only one who could swim, so I made a run for it, and Miss Hooker told me that if I didn't find help sooner, I should come here and look up her uncle, and he'd take care of things. I reached land about a mile downstream, and I've been wandering around ever since, trying to get people to do something, but they said, 'What, on a night like this and in such a current? There's no point in it; go get the steam ferry.' Now if you'll go and—"

"By Jackson, I'd like to, and damn it, I don't know but I will; but who the hell is going to pay for it? Do you think your father"

"Why that's perfectly fine. Miss Hooker told me specifically that her uncle Hornback—"

"Good heavens! Is he her uncle? Listen here, you head for that light over there, and turn west when you get there, and about a quarter of a mile out you'll come to the tavern. Tell them to rush you out to Jim Hornback's, and he'll pay for it. And don't waste any time, because he'll want to know what happened. Tell him I'll have his niece safe before he can get to town. Hurry up now; I'm going around the corner here to find my engineer."

I headed toward the light, but as soon as he turned the corner I went back and got into my boat and bailed the water out of it, and then rowed upstream in the calm water about six hundred yards, and hid myself among some lumber boats; I couldn't relax until I could see the ferry boat leave. But all things considered, I was feeling pretty good about going to all this trouble for that gang, since not many people would have done it. I wished the widow knew about it. I figured she would be proud of me for helping these scoundrels, because scoundrels and good-for-nothings are the kind of people the widow and other good people care most about.

Soon enough, the wreck appeared, dark and shadowy, drifting downstream! A cold chill ran through me, and then I headed toward it. The boat was sitting very low in the water, and I could tell right away that there wasn't much hope of finding anyone alive aboard. I paddled all around it and called out a few times, but there was no response; everything was completely silent. I felt somewhat sad about the gang, but not too much, because I figured if they could handle it, so could I.

Then the ferry-boat arrived, so I pushed toward the middle of the river at a long downstream angle. When I figured I was beyond their sight, I rested my oars and looked back to watch them search around the wreck for Miss Hooker's remains, since the captain knew her uncle Hornback would want them. Before long, the ferry-boat gave up and headed for shore, while I got back to my rowing and went racing down the river.

It felt like an incredibly long time before Jim's light appeared; and when it finally did appear, it seemed like it was a thousand miles away. By the time I reached there, the sky was starting to turn slightly gray in the east; so we headed for an island, hid the raft, sank the small boat, and went to sleep and slept like we were dead.

Chapter XIV.

Later, when we woke up, we went through the supplies the gang had stolen from the wreck, and discovered boots, blankets, clothes, and all kinds of other items, plus a bunch of books, a telescope, and three boxes of cigars. Neither of us had ever been this wealthy before in our entire lives. The cigars were excellent quality. We spent the whole afternoon relaxing in the woods, talking and with me reading the books, just having a really good time. I told Jim everything that had happened inside the wreck and at the ferry-boat, and I explained that these types of experiences were adventures; but he said he didn't want any more adventures. He explained that when I went into the officers' quarters and he crawled back to get on the raft only to find it missing, he almost died from fear; because he figured it was over for him no matter how things worked out; since if he didn't get rescued he would drown; and if he did get rescued, whoever saved him would send him back home to collect the reward, and then Miss Watson would definitely sell him to the Deep South. Well, he was correct; he was almost always correct; he had an unusually sharp mind, for a Black man.

I read quite a bit to Jim about kings, dukes, earls, and other nobility, describing how extravagantly they dressed, how much ceremony they displayed, and how they addressed each other as "your majesty," "your grace," and "your lordship" instead of simply "mister." Jim's eyes widened with amazement, and he was completely fascinated. He said:

"I didn't know there were so many of them. I haven't heard about any of them, hardly, except old King Solomon, unless you count those kings that are in a pack of cards. How much does a king get?"

"Get?" I said. "Why, they earn a thousand dollars a month if they want it. They can have as much as they want. Everything belongs to them."

"Isn't that wonderful? And what do they have to do, Huck?"

"They don't do anything! What are you talking about! They just sit around."

"No; is that so?"

"Of course it is. They just sit around—except, maybe, when there's a war; then they go to the war. But other times they just lounge around; or go hawking—just hawking and sp— Sh!—did you hear a noise?"

We slipped out and took a look, but it was nothing more than the churning of a steamboat's paddle wheel in the distance, coming around the bend, so we returned.

"Yes," I said, "and at other times, when things get boring, they mess around with the parliament; and if everyone doesn't do exactly what he wants, he cuts their heads off. But most of the time they just hang around the harem."

"Around which one?"

"Harem."

"What's the harem?"

"The place where he keeps his wives. Don't you know about the harem? Solomon had one; he had about a million wives."

"Why, yes, that's so; I—I'd forgotten about it. A harem's a boarding house, I reckon. Most likely they have noisy times in the nursery. And I reckon the wives quarrel considerably; and that increases the racket. Yet they say Solomon was the wisest man that ever lived. I don't put any stock in that. Because why: would a wise man want to live in the midst of such a commotion all the time? No—indeed he wouldn't. A wise man would take and build a boiler factory; and then he could shut down the boiler factory when he wants to rest."

"Well, he was the wisest man anyway, because the widow told me so herself."

"I don't care what the widow says, he wasn't a wise man either. He had some of the most foolish ways I ever saw. Do you know about that child that he was going to chop in two?"

"Yes, the widow told me everything about it."

"Well, then! Wasn't that the most foolish idea in the world? You just take and look at it for a minute. There's the stump, there—that's one of the women; here's you—that's the other one; I'm Solomon; and this here dollar bill is the child. Both of you claim it. What do I do? Do I go around among the neighbors and find out which one of you the bill really belongs to, and hand it over to the right one, all safe and sound, the way that anybody who had any sense would? No; I take and split the bill in two, and give half of it to you, and the other half to the other woman. That's the way Solomon was going to do with the child. Now I want to ask you: what's the use of that half a bill?—can't buy nothing with it. And what use is half a child? I wouldn't give a damn for a million of them."

"But damn it, Jim, you've completely missed the point—blast it, you've missed it by a thousand miles."

"Who? Me? Go on. Don't talk to me about your points. I reckon I know sense when I see it, and there ain't no sense in such doings as that. The dispute wasn't about a half a child, the dispute was about a whole child; and the man that thinks he can settle a dispute about a whole child with a half a child doesn't know enough to come in out of the rain. Don't talk to me about Solomon, Huck, I know him by the back."

"But I'm telling you that you're missing the point."

"Forget the point! I reckon I know what I know. And mind you, the real point goes much deeper than that. It lies in the way Solomon was raised. You take a man who's only got one or two children; is that man going to be wasteful with children? No, he isn't; he can't afford to be. He knows how to value them. But you take a man who's got about five million children running around the house, and it's different. He'd just as soon chop a child in two as he would a cat. There's plenty more where they came from. A child or two, more or less, didn't mean anything to Solomon, darn him!"

I never encountered such a person. Once he formed an opinion, there was no changing his mind. He was more critical of Solomon than anyone I had ever met. So I started discussing other kings and dropped the subject of Solomon. I told him about Louis the Sixteenth who was executed in France long ago, and about his young son the dauphin, who should have become king, but they imprisoned him, and some say he died in that jail.

"Poor little guy."

"But some people say he escaped and got away, and came to America."

"That's good! But he'll be pretty lonesome—there aren't any kings here, are there, Huck?"

"No."

"Then he can't get any job. What is he going to do?"

"Well, I don't know. Some of them become police officers, and some of them teach people how to speak French."

"Why, Huck, don't French people talk the same way we do?"

"No, Jim; you wouldn't be able to understand a single word they said—not one word."

"Well, I'll be damned! How did that happen?"

"I don't know, but that's just how it is. I picked up some of their foreign talk from a book. Suppose someone came up to you and said 'Polly-voo-franzy'—what would you think?"

"I wouldn't think twice about it; I'd take and hit him over the head—that is, if he wasn't white. I wouldn't allow any Black person to call me that."

"Come on, it's not calling you anything. It's just asking if you know how to speak French."

"Well, then, why couldn't he say it?"

"Why, he is saying it. That's how a Frenchman says it."

"Well, it's a completely ridiculous way, and I don't want to hear any more about it. There's no sense in it."

"Look here, Jim; does a cat talk like we do?"

"No, a cat doesn't."

"Well, does a cow?"

"No, a cow doesn't either."

"Does a cat talk like a cow, or a cow talk like a cat?"

"No, they don't."

"It's natural and right for them to talk differently from each other, isn't it?"

"'Course."

"And isn't it natural and right for a cat and a cow to talk differently from us?"

"Why, most surely it is."

"Well, then, why isn't it natural and right for a Frenchman to talk different from us? You answer me that."

"Is a cat a man, Huck?"

"No."

"Well, then, there's no sense in a cat talking like a man. Is a cow a man?—or is a cow a cat?"

"No, she isn't either of them."

"Well, then, she has no business talking like either one of them. Is a Frenchman a man?"

"Yes."

"Well, then! Darn it, why doesn't he talk like a man? You answer me that!"

I could see there was no point in wasting words—you can't teach someone to argue when they're set in their ways. So I gave up.

Chapter XV.

We figured that three more nights would bring us to Cairo, at the southern tip of Illinois, where the Ohio River meets the Mississippi, and that was our destination. We would sell the raft and board a steamboat to travel up the Ohio River into the free states, and then we would be safe from trouble.

Well, on the second night a fog started to roll in, and we headed for a small island to tie up to, since it wouldn't be safe to try navigating in fog; but when I paddled ahead in the canoe with the rope to secure it, there was nothing but small young trees to tie to. I wrapped the line around one of them right at the edge of the steep bank, but there was a strong current, and the raft came rushing down so fast that it tore the tree out by the roots and drifted away. I saw the fog settling in, and it made me feel so sick and frightened I couldn't move for what felt like almost half a minute—and then the raft was nowhere to be seen; you couldn't see twenty yards ahead. I jumped into the canoe and rushed back to the rear, grabbed the paddle and tried to push back with a stroke.

But it wouldn't move. I was in such a rush I hadn't untied it. I stood up and tried to untie it, but I was so panicked my hands were shaking so badly I could barely do anything with them.

As soon as I began, I chased after the raft with intense determination, heading straight down the small island. That worked fine for as long as it lasted, but the island wasn't even sixty yards long, and the moment I raced past the end of it, I burst into the thick white fog and had no more sense of direction than a corpse.

I thought to myself that paddling wouldn't work; before I knew it, I'd crash into the riverbank or a sandbar or something else. I had to stay still and just drift with the current, but it was incredibly nerve-wracking to keep my hands motionless at a time like this. I called out and listened carefully. Far off in the distance, I heard a faint call in response, and my hopes lifted. I rushed toward the sound, straining to hear it again. When it came the next time, I realized I wasn't heading directly toward it, but was actually moving away to the right of it. The time after that, I was drifting away to the left of it—and I wasn't getting any closer either, because I was spinning around in all directions while the sound kept moving straight ahead the whole time.

I really wished that fool would think to bang a tin pan and keep banging it constantly, but he never did, and it was the quiet moments between the shouts that were causing me problems. Well, I struggled forward, and then I heard the shout behind me. I was completely confused now. That was someone else's shout, or I had gotten turned around.

I threw the paddle down. I heard the whoop again; it was behind me still, but in a different place; it kept coming, and kept changing its location, and I kept answering, until eventually it was in front of me again, and I knew the current had swung the canoe's head downstream, and I was all right if that was Jim and not some other raftsman shouting. I couldn't tell anything about voices in a fog, for nothing looks natural or sounds natural in a fog.

The whooping continued, and in about a minute I came rushing down toward a steep riverbank with the shadowy outlines of large trees on it, and the current threw me off to the left and shot past, among a bunch of fallen logs that practically roared as the current tore past them so quickly.

In another moment or two, everything was solid white and motionless again. I sat completely still then, listening to my heart pound, and I think I didn't take a breath while it beat a hundred times.

I just gave up then. I knew what the problem was. That steep bank was an island, and Jim had gone down the other side of it. It wasn't a small sandbar that you could float past in ten minutes. It had the large trees of a regular island; it might be five or six miles long and more than half a mile wide.

I stayed silent, listening carefully, for about fifteen minutes, I estimate. I was drifting along, naturally, at four or five miles per hour; but you never really think about that. No, you feel like you're lying completely motionless on the water; and if you catch a brief glimpse of a fallen tree passing by, you don't think about how fast you're moving, but you gasp and think, wow! how quickly that tree is rushing past. If you think it isn't gloomy and lonely out in fog like that by yourself at night, you should try it once—you'll find out.

Next, for about half an hour, I called out now and then; finally I heard an answer from far away, and tried to follow it, but I couldn't manage it, and soon I realized I'd gotten into a cluster of small islands, because I caught brief glimpses of them on both sides of me—sometimes just a narrow channel between them, and others that I couldn't see I knew were there because I'd hear the sound of the current against the old dead brush and debris that hung over the banks. Well, I wasn't long before I lost track of the calls down among the small islands; and I only tried to chase them for a little while, anyway, because it was worse than chasing a will-o'-the-wisp. You never knew a sound could dodge around so much, and change places so quickly and so often.

I had to paddle away from the shore quite quickly four or five times to avoid crashing into the islands in the river, so I figured the raft must be bumping into the bank now and then, or else it would have gotten farther ahead and moved out of earshot—it was floating a bit faster than I was.

Well, I seemed to be back in the open river again after a while, but I couldn't hear any sign of a whoop anywhere. I figured Jim had gotten caught on a snag, maybe, and it was all over for him. I was really tired, so I lay down in the canoe and said I wouldn't worry about it anymore. I didn't want to fall asleep, of course; but I was so sleepy I couldn't help it; so I thought I would take just one little nap.

But I think it was more than just a brief nap, because when I woke up the stars were shining brightly, the fog had completely disappeared, and I was drifting down a large bend backwards. At first I didn't know where I was; I thought I was dreaming; and when memories started returning to me they seemed to emerge hazily from what felt like last week.

It was an enormous river here, with the tallest and thickest trees on both sides; just a solid wall, as far as I could see by the stars. I looked downstream and saw a black spot on the water. I went after it, but when I reached it, it was nothing but a couple of logs tied together. Then I saw another spot and chased that one; then another, and this time I was right. It was the raft.

When I reached the raft, Jim was sitting there with his head hanging down between his knees, fast asleep, his right arm draped over the steering oar. The other oar had been broken off completely, and the raft was covered with leaves, branches, and dirt. It was clear she had been through a rough time.

I quickly secured the raft and lay down right under Jim's nose, then started to yawn and stretch my fists out toward Jim, saying:

"Hello, Jim, have I been sleeping? Why didn't you wake me up?"

"Good heavens, is that you, Huck? And you're not dead—you didn't drown—you're back again? It's too good to be true, honey, it's too good to be true. Let me look at you, child, let me touch you. No, you're not dead! You're back again, alive and well, just the same old Huck—the same old Huck, thank goodness!"

"What's wrong with you, Jim? Have you been drinking?"

"Drinking? Have I been drinking? Have I had a chance to be drinking?"

"Well, then, what makes you talk so wildly?"

"How do I talk wild?"

"How? Why, haven't you been talking about my coming back, and all that stuff, as if I'd been gone away?"

"Huck—Huck Finn, you look me in the eye; look me in the eye. Haven't you been gone away?"

"Gone away? Why, what on earth do you mean? I haven't been gone anywhere. Where would I go to?"

"Well, look here, boss, there's something wrong, there is. Am I me, or who am I? Am I here, or where am I? Now that's what I want to know."

"Well, I think you're here, that's obvious enough, but I think you're a confused old fool, Jim."

"Am I, is that me? Well, you answer me this: Didn't you carry out the rope in the canoe to tie it to the sandbar?"

"No, I didn't. What sandbar? I haven't seen any sandbar."

"Haven't you seen any small island? Look here, didn't the rope break loose and the raft go rushing down the river, leaving you and the canoe behind in the fog?"

"What fog?"

"Why, the fog!—the fog that's been around all night. And didn't you shout, and didn't I shout, until we got mixed up in the islands and one of us got lost and the other one was just as good as lost, because he didn't know where he was? And didn't I crash into a lot of those islands and have a terrible time and almost get drowned? Now isn't that so, boss—isn't it so? You answer me that."

"Well, this is too much for me, Jim. I haven't seen any fog, or any islands, or any troubles, or anything. I've been sitting here talking with you all night until you went to sleep about ten minutes ago, and I think I did the same. You couldn't have gotten drunk in that time, so of course you've been dreaming."

"Darn it, how am I going to dream all that in ten minutes?"

"Well, damn it all, you did dream it, because none of it actually happened."

"But, Huck, it's all just as plain to me as—"

"It doesn't matter how obvious it seems; there's nothing to it. I know this because I've been here the entire time."

Jim didn't say anything for about five minutes, but sat there thinking it over. Then he said:

"Well, then, I guess I did dream it, Huck; but I'll be darned if it isn't the most powerful dream I've ever had. And I've never had a dream before that's tired me out like this one has."

"Oh, well, that's perfectly fine, because a dream can really wear a person out sometimes. But this one was an incredible dream; tell me everything about it, Jim."

So Jim got to work and told me the entire story from beginning to end, exactly as it had happened, except he embellished it quite a bit. Then he said he had to start interpreting it, because it was sent as a warning. He explained that the first sandbar represented a man who would try to help us, but the current was another man who would pull us away from him. The shouts were warnings that would reach us from time to time, and if we didn't work hard to understand them, they would lead us into bad luck instead of protecting us from it. All those sandbars represented troubles we were going to face with argumentative people and all sorts of cruel folks, but if we kept to ourselves and didn't argue back or provoke them, we would make it through and escape the fog into the big clear river, which represented the free States, and we wouldn't have any more trouble.

It had gotten pretty dark with clouds right after I climbed onto the raft, but the sky was clearing up again now.

"Oh, well, that's all interpreted well enough as far as it goes, Jim," I said, "but what do these things stand for?"

It was the leaves and debris on the raft and the broken oar. You could see them perfectly clearly now.

Jim glanced at the debris, then turned his gaze to me, and looked back at the wreckage once more. The dream had become so deeply embedded in his mind that he couldn't seem to dislodge it and immediately restore reality to its proper place. However, once he managed to sort things out, he stared at me intently without any trace of a smile and said:

"What do they stand for? I'm going to tell you. When I got all worn out with work, and with calling for you, and went to sleep, my heart was almost broken because you were lost, and I didn't care anymore what became of me and the raft. And when I woke up and found you back again, all safe and sound, the tears came, and I could have gotten down on my knees and kissed your foot, I was so thankful. And all you were thinking about was how you could make a fool of old Jim with a lie. That junk there is trash; and trash is what people are who put dirt on the heads of their friends and make them ashamed."

Then he stood up slowly and walked to the shelter, going inside without saying anything more than that. But those words were enough. They made me feel so terrible I could have almost kissed his foot to get him to take it back.

It took me fifteen minutes before I could bring myself to go and apologize to a Black man; but I did it, and I was never sorry for it afterward, either. I didn't play any more cruel tricks on him, and I wouldn't have done that one if I had known it would make him feel that way.

Chapter XVI.

We slept almost the entire day and set out at night, following a short distance behind an enormous raft that took as long to pass by as a parade. It had four long oars at each end, so we figured it probably carried around thirty men. The raft had five large tents spaced far apart, an open campfire in the center, and a tall flagpole at each end. There was something impressive and stylish about it. Being a raftsman on a vessel like that really meant something.

We drifted down into a large bend, and the night became cloudy and hot. The river was extremely wide and lined with dense forest on both sides; you could barely see any break in the trees or a single light. We discussed Cairo and wondered if we would recognize it when we reached it. I said we probably wouldn't, since I had heard there were only about a dozen houses there, and if they didn't have their lights on, how would we know we were passing a town? Jim said that if the two large rivers came together there, that would be our sign. But I suggested that we might think we were just passing the end of an island and entering the same river again. This worried Jim—and me as well. So the question was, what should we do? I suggested we paddle to shore the first time we saw a light and tell them that my father was behind us, coming along with a trading boat, and that he was inexperienced at this work and wanted to know how far it was to Cairo. Jim thought this was a good plan, so we smoked our pipes and waited.

There was nothing to do now but to watch carefully for the town and make sure not to pass it without seeing it. He said he would definitely see it, because he would be a free man the moment he spotted it, but if he missed it he would be back in slave territory with no more chance for freedom. Every little while he jumps up and says:

"There she is?"

But it wasn't. It was jack-o'-lanterns, or lightning bugs; so he sat down again, and went back to watching, same as before. Jim said it made him all over shaky and feverish to be so close to freedom. Well, I can tell you it made me all over shaky and feverish, too, to hear him, because I began to get it through my head that he was almost free—and who was to blame for it? Why, me. I couldn't get that out of my conscience, no matter how I tried. It got to troubling me so much I couldn't rest; I couldn't stay still in one place. It had never occurred to me before, what this thing was that I was doing. But now it did; and it stayed with me, and burned me more and more. I tried to convince myself that I wasn't to blame, because I didn't help Jim run away from his rightful owner; but it was no use, conscience spoke up and said, every time, "But you knew he was running for his freedom, and you could have paddled ashore and told somebody." That was true—I couldn't get around that in any way. That was where it hurt. Conscience said to me, "What had poor Miss Watson done to you that you could watch her slave go off right under your eyes and never say one single word? What did that poor old woman do to you that you could treat her so meanly? Why, she tried to teach you your lessons, she tried to teach you your manners, she tried to be good to you every way she knew how. That's what she did."

I started feeling so terrible and miserable that I almost wished I was dead. I paced back and forth on the raft, criticizing myself silently, while Jim was also pacing restlessly beside me. Neither of us could stay still. Every time he jumped around excitedly and said,

103

"That's Cairo!" it hit me like a lightning bolt, and I thought that if it really was Cairo, I believed I would die from sheer misery.

Jim spoke constantly while I was lost in my own thoughts. He was explaining how the first thing he would do when he reached a free state would be to start saving money and never spend a single penny, and when he had saved enough he would purchase his wife, who was enslaved on a farm near where Miss Watson lived; and then they would both work to buy their two children, and if their owner wouldn't sell them, they would find an abolitionist to help them escape.

That kind of talk nearly froze my blood. He had never dared speak like that before in his entire life. You could see what a dramatic change came over him the moment he thought he was close to freedom. It matched the old saying, "Give someone an inch and they'll take a mile." I thought to myself, this is what happens when I don't think things through. Here was this man, whom I had practically helped escape, coming right out and boldly declaring he would steal his children—children who belonged to a man I didn't even know; a man who had never caused me any harm.

I felt bad hearing Jim say that—it really diminished him in my eyes. My conscience started bothering me more intensely than ever, until finally I told myself, "Stop tormenting me—it's not too late yet—I'll paddle to shore at first light and confess everything." I immediately felt relieved, happy, and light as a feather. All my worries disappeared. I began watching carefully for a light, quietly humming to myself. Before long, one appeared. Jim called out:

"We're safe, Huck, we're safe! Jump up and click your heels! That's good old Cairo at last, I just know it!"

I said:

"I'll take the canoe and go check it out, Jim. It might not be what we think, you know."

He jumped up and prepared the canoe, placing his old coat in the bottom for me to sit on, and handed me the paddle; and as I pushed off from shore, he said:

"Pretty soon I'll be shouting for joy, and I'll say, it's all because of Huck; I'm a free man, and I couldn't ever have been free if it hadn't been for Huck; Huck did it. Jim will never forget you, Huck; you're the best friend Jim's ever had; and you're the only friend old Jim has now."

I was paddling away, sweating with eagerness to turn him in; but when he said this, it seemed to completely deflate me. I moved slowly then, and I wasn't entirely sure whether I was glad I had started or whether I wasn't. When I was fifty yards away, Jim says:

"There you go, the same old true Huck; the only white gentleman who ever kept his promise to old Jim."

Well, I just felt sick to my stomach. But I told myself, I have to do this—there's no way I can get out of it. Right at that moment, a small boat came along with two men carrying guns, and they stopped, so I stopped too. One of them said:

"What's that over there?"

"A piece of a raft," I said.

"Do you belong on it?"

"Yes, sir."

"Are there any men on it?"

"Only one, sir."

"Well, there are five Black men who ran away tonight up there, above the head of the bend. Is your man white or Black?"

I didn't respond right away. I tried to, but the words wouldn't come out. I attempted for a moment or two to gather my courage and speak up, but I wasn't brave enough—I didn't have the courage of a rabbit. I could see I was losing my nerve, so I just gave up trying and finally said:

"He's white."

"I think we'll go and see for ourselves."

"I really wish you would," I said, "because that's my father over there, and maybe you could help me pull the raft to shore where the light is. He's sick—and so are my mother and Mary Ann."

"Oh, damn! We're in a hurry, boy. But I suppose we have to. Come on, grab your paddle, and let's get moving."

I gripped my paddle tightly and they took hold of their oars. After we had taken a stroke or two, I said:

"Dad will be really grateful to you, I can tell you that. Everyone leaves when I need them to help me pull the raft to shore, and I can't manage it by myself."

"Well, that's incredibly cruel. Strange, too. Tell me, boy, what's wrong with your father?"

"It's the—uh—the—well, it isn't anything much."

They stopped pulling. It was only a very short distance to the raft now. One of them says:

"Kid, that's not true. What's wrong with your father? Give me a straight answer right now, and things will go better for you."

"I will, sir, I will, I promise—but please don't leave us. It's the—the—gentlemen, if you'll just row forward and let me throw you the rope, you won't have to come close to the raft—please do."

"Turn the boat around, John, turn it around!" one of them shouts. They started rowing backward. "Stay away, boy—keep to the left side. Damn it, I bet the wind has blown it our way. Your father has smallpox, and you know it perfectly well. Why didn't you come out and tell us? Do you want it to spread everywhere?"

"Well," I said, crying, "I've told everyone before, and they just went away and left us."

"Poor fellow, there's some truth to that. We genuinely feel sorry for you, but we—well, darn it, we don't want to catch smallpox, you understand. Listen, I'll tell you what you should do.

Don't try to come ashore by yourself, or you'll wreck everything. Keep floating downstream for about twenty miles, and you'll reach a town on the left side of the river. It'll be well past sunrise by then, and when you ask for help, tell them your family is all sick with chills and fever. Don't be foolish again and let people figure out what's really wrong. Now we're trying to help you out; so just keep twenty miles between us, that's a good fellow. It wouldn't help to land over there where the light is—that's just a lumber yard. Listen, I figure your father is poor, and I have to admit he's having some really tough luck. Here, I'll place a twenty-dollar gold coin on this plank, and you can grab it when it floats past. I feel terrible about leaving you; but good heavens! you can't mess around with smallpox, don't you understand?"

"Wait a minute, Parker," the other man says, "here's a twenty-dollar bill to put on the board for me. Goodbye, son; do what Mr. Parker tells you, and you'll be fine."

"That's right, my boy—goodbye, goodbye. If you see any escaped slaves, get help and catch them, and you can make some money from it."

"Goodbye, sir," I said; "I won't let any runaway slaves get past me if I can help it."

They left and I climbed onto the raft, feeling terrible and dejected, because I knew very well I had done wrong, and I could see it was no use for me to try to learn to do right; a person who doesn't get started right when he's young doesn't have a chance—when the crisis comes there's nothing to support him and keep him on track, and so he gets defeated. Then I thought for a minute, and said to myself, wait; suppose you had done right and turned Jim in, would you have felt better than you do now? No, I said, I would feel bad—I would feel exactly the same way I do now. Well, then, I said, what's the point of learning to do right when it's difficult to do right and no trouble to do wrong, and the reward is exactly the same? I was stumped. I couldn't answer that. So I figured I wouldn't worry about it anymore, but from now on always do whatever seemed most convenient at the time.

I went into the wigwam; Jim wasn't there. I looked all around; he wasn't anywhere. I said:

"Jim!"

"Here I am, Huck. Are they out of sight yet? Don't talk loud."

He was in the river beneath the back oar, with only his nose above water. I told him they were out of sight, so he climbed aboard. He says:

"I was listening to all the talk, and I slipped into the river and was going to push off for sure if they came aboard. Then I was going to swim back to the raft when they were gone. But goodness, how you did fool them, Huck! That was the smartest trick! I tell you, child, I expect it saved old Jim—old Jim isn't going to forget you for that, honey."

Then we talked about the money. It was a pretty good raise—twenty dollars each. Jim said we could buy deck passage on a steamboat now, and the money would last us as far as we wanted to go in the free states. He said twenty miles more wasn't far for the raft to go, but he wished we were already there.

Towards daybreak we tied up, and Jim was extremely careful about hiding the raft well. Then he worked all day organizing things into bundles, and getting everything ready to stop rafting.

That night around ten o'clock, we came within sight of the lights from a town located down in a bend to the left.

I paddled out in the canoe to investigate. Before long, I spotted a man in the river with a small boat, setting up a fishing line. I pulled alongside and said:

"Mister, is that town Cairo?"

"Cairo? No. You must be a complete fool."

"What town is this, sir?"

"If you want to know, go and find out. If you stay here bothering me for about half a minute longer, you'll get something you won't want."

I paddled over to the raft. Jim was terribly disappointed, but I told him not to worry about it, since I figured Cairo would be the next place we'd reach.

We passed another town before dawn, and I was planning to go out again, but it was on high ground, so I decided not to. There's no high ground around Cairo, Jim had told me. I had forgotten that detail. We stayed put for the day on a small island fairly close to the left bank. I started to suspect something was wrong. Jim felt the same way. I said:

"Maybe we passed through Cairo in the fog that night."

He says:

"Don't let's talk about it, Huck. Poor Black folks can't have any luck. I always suspected that rattlesnake skin wasn't done with its work."

"I wish I had never seen that snake skin, Jim—I really wish I had never laid eyes on it."

"It's not your fault, Huck; you didn't know. Don't blame yourself about it."

When daylight came, there was the clear Ohio water near the shore, without a doubt, and beyond it was the same old muddy Mississippi! So that was the end of our hopes for Cairo.

We discussed everything thoroughly. Going to shore wasn't an option; we obviously couldn't paddle the raft upstream either. There was no choice but to wait until nightfall and head back in the canoe, taking our chances. So we spent the entire day sleeping among the cottonwood grove to stay rested for what lay ahead, but when we returned to the raft around dark, the canoe had disappeared!

We didn't say a word for quite a while. There wasn't anything to say. We both knew well enough it was more work of the rattlesnake skin; so what was the point of talking about it? It would only seem like we were complaining, and that would be sure to bring more bad luck—and keep bringing it, too, until we knew enough to stay quiet.

Eventually we discussed what we should do, and discovered there was no other option except to continue downstream with the raft until we found an opportunity to purchase a canoe for our return journey. We weren't going to take one when no one was watching, the way father would have done, because that might cause people to come after us.

So we pushed off into the darkness on the raft.

Anyone who still doesn't believe that it's foolish to handle a snake skin, after everything that snake skin has done to us, will believe it now if they keep reading and see what else it did to us.

The place to buy canoes is from rafts moored at the shore. But we didn't see any rafts moored there, so we continued traveling for three hours and more. Well, the night became gray and rather thick, which is almost as bad as fog. You can't make out the shape of the river, and you can't see any distance. It became very late and quiet, and then a steamboat came up the river. We lit the lantern and figured she would see it. Upstream boats generally didn't come close to us; they go out and follow the sandbars and search for easy water under the reefs; but on nights like this they push right up the main channel against the whole river.

We could hear her thundering toward us, but we couldn't see her clearly until she drew near. She headed straight for us. Ships often do this, trying to see how close they can get without making contact; sometimes the paddle wheel clips a steering oar, and then the pilot pokes his head out and laughs, thinking he's incredibly clever. Well, here she came, and we figured she was going to try to barely miss us; but she didn't appear to be turning away at all. She was enormous, and she was approaching fast, looking like a dark cloud surrounded by rows of fireflies; but suddenly she loomed large and terrifying, with a long line of wide-open furnace doors glowing like red-hot teeth, and her massive bow and protective barriers towering right above us. Someone shouted at us, bells clanged to halt the engines, there was a commotion of swearing and steam whistling—and as Jim jumped overboard on one side and I dove off the other, she came crashing straight through the raft.

I dove down—and I was determined to reach the bottom too, because a thirty-foot paddle wheel was going to pass over me, and I wanted to give it plenty of clearance. I could usually hold my breath underwater for a minute; this time I think I stayed under for a minute and a half. Then I shot up to the surface quickly, because I was nearly out of air. I burst up to my armpits and blew the water out of my nose, and caught my breath for a moment. Naturally there was a strong current; and naturally that steamboat started her engines again ten seconds after she had stopped them, because they never had much concern for raftsmen; so now she was churning her way up the river, out of sight in the heavy weather, though I could still hear her.

I called out for Jim about a dozen times, but I didn't get any response; so I grabbed a plank that bumped into me while I was treading water, and headed for shore, pushing it ahead of me. But I could see that the current was drifting toward the left-hand shore, which meant that I was in a crossing; so I changed direction and went that way.

It was one of those long, diagonal, two-mile crossings, so it took me quite a while to get across. I made it safely to the other side and climbed up the bank. I couldn't see very far ahead, but I kept moving forward over the rough terrain for about a quarter mile or more, and then I came upon a large, old-fashioned double log house before I even noticed it. I was about to rush past it and escape, but a pack of dogs suddenly jumped out and started howling and barking at me, and I knew better than to take another step.

———————————

Chapter XVII.

In about a minute, someone called out from a window without sticking his head outside, saying:

"Stop it, boys! Who's there?"

I said:

"It's me."

"Who's me?"

"George Jackson, sir."

"What do you want?"

"I don't want anything, sir. I just want to pass through, but the dogs won't let me."

"What are you doing sneaking around here at this time of night—hey?"

"I wasn't wandering around, sir, I fell overboard from the steamboat."

"Oh, you did, did you? Light a lamp there, somebody. What did you say your name was?"

"George Jackson, sir. I'm just a boy."

"Listen, if you're being honest, you don't need to worry—no one's going to harm you. But don't try to move; stay exactly where you are. Some of you wake up Bob and Tom, and bring the guns. George Jackson, do you have anyone with you?"

"No, sir, nobody."

I could hear people moving around inside the house now, and I saw a light. The man called out:

"Take that light away, Betsy, you old fool—don't you have any sense? Put it on the floor behind the front door. Bob, if you and Tom are ready, get into your positions."

"All ready."

"Now, George Jackson, do you know the Shepherdsons?"

"No, sir; I never heard of them."

"Well, that might be true, and it might not be. Now, everyone get ready. Step forward, George Jackson. And remember, don't rush—move very slowly. If anyone is with you, make sure they stay back—if they show themselves, they'll get shot. Come on now. Move slowly; push the door open yourself—just enough to slip through, do you hear?"

I didn't rush; I couldn't have even if I'd wanted to. I took one careful step at a time and there wasn't a sound, except I thought I could hear my heart beating. The dogs were as quiet as the people, but they followed a little behind me. When I reached the three log doorsteps I heard them unlocking and removing the bar and unbolting the door. I placed my hand on the door and pushed it open a little and then a little more until somebody said, "There, that's enough—put your head in." I did it, but I figured they would cut it off.

The candle sat on the floor, and there they all were, staring at me while I stared back at them for about fifteen seconds. Three large men had guns aimed directly at me, which definitely made me flinch, I can tell you that much. The eldest man appeared gray-haired and around sixty years old, while the other two looked to be thirty or older—all of them appeared distinguished and good-looking—and there was the kindest old gray-haired woman, with two young women standing behind her whom I couldn't see very clearly. The old gentleman said:

"There; I think it's all right. Come in."

As soon as I was inside with the old gentleman, he locked the door and secured it with both a bar and bolt, then told the young men to bring their guns and come in. They all gathered in a large parlor that had a new rag carpet covering the floor, positioning themselves in a corner that was away from the front windows—there weren't any windows on the side. They held up the candle and examined me carefully, with everyone saying, "Why, he's not a Shepherdson—no, there's nothing Shepherdson about him."

Then the old man said he hoped I wouldn't object to being searched for weapons, explaining that he meant no offense by it—it was simply a precaution. So he didn't dig through my pockets, but just patted me down from the outside with his hands, and declared everything was fine. He told me to relax and make myself comfortable, and to tell them all about myself; but the old lady said:

"Well, bless you, Saul, the poor thing is soaking wet; and don't you think he might be hungry?"

"You're right, Rachel—I forgot."

So the old lady says:

"Betsy" (this was a Black woman), "you hurry around and get him something to eat as quickly as you can, poor thing; and one of you girls go and wake up Buck and tell him—oh, here he is himself. Buck, take this little stranger and get the wet clothes off of him and dress him up in some of your dry clothes."

Buck appeared to be around my age—thirteen or fourteen years old—although he was somewhat larger than me. He wore nothing except a shirt, and his hair was completely disheveled. He entered yawning and rubbing one fist against his eyes, while dragging a gun with his other hand. He said:

"Aren't there any Shepherdsons around?"

They said no, it was a false alarm.

"Well," he says, "if there had been some, I think I would have gotten one."

They all laughed, and Bob says:

"Buck, they could have scalped all of us with how slow you've been getting here."

"Well, nobody comes after me, and it isn't right that I'm always kept down; I don't get any opportunity."

"Don't worry about it, Buck, my boy," the old man says, "you'll get plenty of excitement when the time is right, so don't stress about that. Go on now, and do what your mother told you."

When we went upstairs to his room, he gave me a rough shirt, a jacket, and a pair of his pants, and I put them on. While I was getting dressed, he asked me what my name was, but before I could answer him, he began telling me about a bluejay and a young rabbit he had caught in the woods the day before yesterday, and he asked me where Moses was when the candle went out. I said I didn't know; I had never heard about it before.

"Well, guess," he says.

"How am I supposed to guess," I said, "when I've never heard of it before?"

"But you can guess, can't you? It's just as easy."

"Which candle?" I asked.

"Why, any candle," he says.

"I don't know where he was," I said; "where was he?"

"Why, he was completely in the dark! That's exactly where he was!"

"Well, if you knew where he was, why did you ask me?"

"Well, darn it, it's a puzzle, don't you see? Tell me, how long are you planning to stay here? You have to stay forever. We can have amazing times—there's no school right now. Do you have a dog? I've got a dog—and he'll jump in the river and fetch sticks that you throw in. Do you like getting dressed up on Sundays, and all that kind of nonsense? You bet I don't, but my mother makes me. Darn these old pants! I suppose I should put them on, but I'd rather not, it's so hot. Are you ready? All right. Come on, buddy."

Cold cornbread, cold corned beef, butter and buttermilk—that's what they had waiting for me down there, and I haven't come across anything better since. Buck and his mother and all of them smoked corncob pipes, except the Black woman, who was away, and the two young women. They all smoked and talked, and I ate and talked. The young women had quilts wrapped around them, and their hair hung down their backs. They all asked me questions, and I told them how my father and I and all the family

115

had been living on a small farm down at the bottom of Arkansas, and my sister Mary Ann ran off and got married and was never heard from again, and Bill went to look for them and he wasn't heard from anymore, and Tom and Mort died, and then there wasn't anybody left but just me and my father, and he was worn down to nothing because of his troubles; so when he died I took what was left, because the farm didn't belong to us, and started up the river on deck passage, and fell overboard; and that was how I came to be here. So they said I could have a home there as long as I wanted it. Then it was almost daylight and everybody went to bed, and I went to bed with Buck, and when I woke up in the morning, darn it all, I had forgotten what my name was. So I lay there about an hour trying to think, and when Buck woke up I said:

"Can you spell, Buck?"

"Yes," he says.

"I bet you can't spell my name," I said.

"I bet you whatever you're willing to wager that I can," he says.

"All right," I said, "go ahead."

"G-e-o-r-g-e J-a-x-o-n—there now," he says.

"Well," I said, "you did it, but I didn't think you could. That's not an easy name to spell—right off the bat without studying."

I wrote it down privately, because someone might ask me to spell it next, and I wanted to be ready with it and rattle it off like I was familiar with it.

It was a wonderful family, and a wonderful house, too. I had never seen a house out in the country before that was so nice and had so much elegance. It didn't have an iron latch on the front door, or a wooden one with a leather string, but a brass knob to turn, just like houses in town. There wasn't any bed in the parlor, or any sign of a bed; but many parlors in towns have beds in them. There was a large fireplace that was bricked on the bottom, and the bricks were kept clean and red by pouring water on them and scrubbing them with another brick; sometimes they wash them over with red water-paint that they call Spanish-brown, just like they do in town. They had large brass andirons that could hold up a saw-log. There was a clock on the middle of the mantelpiece, with a picture of a town painted on the bottom half of the glass front, and a round place in the middle of it for the sun, and you could see the pendulum swinging behind it. It was beautiful to hear that clock tick; and sometimes when one of these peddlers had been along and cleaned her up and got her in good shape, she would start in and strike a hundred and fifty times before she got worn out. They wouldn't have taken any money for her.

Well, there was a large exotic parrot on each side of the clock, crafted from something resembling chalk and painted in bright, flashy colors. Next to one of the parrots sat a cat made of pottery, and beside the other stood a ceramic dog; when you pushed down on them they made squeaking sounds, but they didn't open their mouths or appear any different or show any interest. The squeaking came from somewhere underneath. A pair of large wild turkey wing fans were displayed spread out behind these items. On the table in the center of the room sat a beautiful ceramic basket filled with apples, oranges, peaches, and grapes piled high inside it, which appeared much redder and more yellow and prettier than real fruit, but they weren't genuine because you could see where pieces had broken off and revealed the white chalk, or whatever material it was, beneath the surface.

This table was covered with beautiful oilcloth that had a red and blue spread-eagle painted on it, along with a painted border running all the way around the edges. They said it came all the way from Philadelphia. There were also some books stacked up perfectly neat on each corner of the table. One was a large family Bible filled with pictures. Another was Pilgrim's Progress, about a man who left his family, though it didn't explain why. I read quite a bit of it from time to time. The content was interesting, but difficult to understand. Another book was Friendship's Offering, packed with beautiful writing and poetry, though I didn't bother reading the poems. There was also Henry Clay's Speeches, and another called Dr. Gunn's Family Medicine, which explained everything you needed to know about what to do if someone was sick or dead. A hymn book was there too, along with many other books. The room also had nice split-bottom chairs that were in perfect condition—not sagging in the middle and broken like an old basket.

They had pictures hanging on the walls—mostly portraits of Washington and Lafayette, battle scenes, Highland Marys, and one called "Signing the Declaration." There were some they called crayons, which one of the daughters who had died made herself when she was only fifteen years old. They were different from any pictures I had ever seen before—darker, mostly, than usual. One showed a woman in a slim black dress, belted tight under the armpits, with bulges like a cabbage in the middle of the sleeves, and a large black scoop-shovel bonnet with a black veil, and white slim ankles wrapped with black tape, and very small black slippers, like a chisel, and she was leaning thoughtfully on a tombstone with her right elbow, under a weeping willow, and her other hand hanging down her side holding a white handkerchief and a small purse, and underneath the picture it said "Shall I Never See Thee More Alas." Another one showed a young lady with her hair all combed up straight to the top of her head, and knotted there in front of a comb like a chair-back, and she was crying into a handkerchief and had a dead bird lying on its back in her other hand with its feet up, and underneath the picture it said "I Shall Never Hear Thy Sweet Chirrup More Alas." There was one where a young lady was at a window looking up at the moon, and tears running down her cheeks; and she had an open letter in one hand with black sealing wax showing on one edge of it, and she was pressing a locket with a chain to it against her mouth, and underneath the picture it said "And Art Thou Gone Yes Thou Art

Gone Alas." These were all nice pictures, I suppose, but I didn't somehow seem to like them, because whenever I was feeling down a little they always gave me the creeps. Everyone was sorry she died, because she had planned out a lot more of these pictures to make, and a person could see by what she had done what they had lost. But I figured that with her temperament she was having a better time in the graveyard. She was working on what they said was her greatest picture when she got sick, and every day and every night it was her prayer to be allowed to live until she got it finished, but she never got the chance. It was a picture of a young woman in a long white gown, standing on the rail of a bridge all ready to jump off, with her hair all down her back, and looking up to the moon, with the tears running down her face, and she had two arms folded across her chest, and two arms stretched out in front, and two more reaching up towards the moon—and the idea was to see which pair would look best, and then erase all the other arms; but, as I was saying, she died before she made up her mind, and now they kept this picture over the head of the bed in her room, and every time her birthday came they hung flowers on it. Other times it was hidden with a little curtain. The young woman in the picture had a kind of nice sweet face, but there were so many arms it made her look too spider-like, it seemed to me.

This young girl maintained a scrapbook while she was living, and would cut out obituaries, accidents, and stories of patient suffering from the Presbyterian Observer to paste into it, then compose her own poetry inspired by these clippings. Her poetry was quite good. Here is what she wrote about a boy named Stephen Dowling Bots who fell down a well and drowned:

Ode To Stephen Dowling Bots, Deceased

And did young Stephen become ill,
And did young Stephen die?
And did the sad hearts grow heavy,
And did the mourners cry?

No; such was not the destiny of
Young Stephen Dowling Bots;
Though sad hearts around him grew heavy,
It was not from illness's blows.

No whooping cough did torment his body,
Nor measles dreadful with spots;
Not these damaged the sacred name
Of Stephen Dowling Bots.

Rejected love did not strike with sorrow
That head of curly hair,
Nor stomach ailments brought him down,
Young Stephen Dowling Bots.

Oh no. Then listen with tearful eye,
While I tell his fate.
His soul did from this cold world depart
By falling down a well.

They pulled him out and drained him;
Alas it was too late;
His spirit had gone to play above
In the realms of the good and great.

If Emmeline Grangerford could write poetry like that before she turned fourteen, there's no telling what she might have accomplished later in life. Buck said she could compose poetry effortlessly. She never had to pause to think. He explained that she would write down a line, and if she couldn't find anything to rhyme with it, she would simply cross it out and write another one, then continue. She wasn't picky; she could write about any subject you gave her as long as it was sorrowful. Every time a man died, or a woman died, or a child died, she would be ready with her "tribute" before the body was even cold. She called them tributes. The neighbors said the order was always the doctor first, then Emmeline, then the undertaker—the undertaker never beat Emmeline except once, and that time she got stuck trying to find a rhyme for the dead person's name, which was Whistler. She was never the same after that incident; she never complained, but she sort of wasted away and didn't live much longer. Poor girl, many times I forced myself to go up to the little room that used to be hers and take out her old scrapbook and read it when her pictures had been irritating me and I had grown a bit tired of her. I liked that whole family, the dead ones and all, and I wasn't going to let anything drive a wedge between us. Poor Emmeline wrote poetry about all the dead people when she was alive, and it didn't seem right that there wasn't anyone to write some about her now that she was gone; so I tried to work out a verse or two myself, but I couldn't seem to make it work somehow. They kept Emmeline's room neat and tidy, with everything arranged just the way she liked it when she was alive, and no one ever slept there. The old lady maintained the room herself, even though there were plenty of servants, and she did her sewing there often and read her Bible there most of the time.

Well, as I was talking about the parlor, there were beautiful curtains hanging on the windows: white ones, with pictures painted on them showing castles with vines growing all down the walls, and cattle coming down to drink. There was also a little old piano that had tin pans inside it, I think, and nothing was ever as lovely as hearing the young ladies sing "The Last Link is Broken" and play "The Battle of Prague" on it. The walls of all the rooms were plastered, and most had carpets on the floors, and the entire house was whitewashed on the outside.

It was a double house, and the large open space between them had a roof and floor, and sometimes the table was set there in the middle of the day, making it a cool, comfortable place. Nothing could be better. And wasn't the cooking delicious, with plenty of it too!

Chapter XVIII.

Colonel Grangerford was a gentleman, you see. He was a gentleman through and through, and so was his family. He was well born, as the saying goes, and that's worth as much in a man as it is in a horse, so the Widow Douglas said, and nobody ever denied that she was part of the first aristocracy in our town; and my father always said it too, though he wasn't any more quality than a mudcat himself. Colonel Grangerford was very tall and very slim, and had a darkish-pale complexion, not a sign of red in it anywhere; he was clean shaved every morning all over his thin face, and he had the thinnest kind of lips, and the thinnest kind of nostrils, and a high nose, and heavy eyebrows, and the blackest kind of eyes, sunk so deep back that they seemed like they were looking out of caverns at you, as you might say. His forehead was high, and his hair was black and straight and hung to his shoulders. His hands were long and thin, and every day of his life he put on a clean shirt and a full suit from head to foot made out of linen so white it hurt your eyes to look at it; and on Sundays he wore a blue tail-coat with brass buttons on it. He carried a mahogany cane with a silver head to it. There wasn't any frivolousness about him, not a bit, and he was never loud. He was as kind as he could be—you could feel that, you know, and so you had confidence. Sometimes he smiled, and it was good to see; but when he straightened himself up like a liberty-pole, and the lightning began to flicker out from under his eyebrows, you wanted to climb a tree first, and find out what the matter was afterwards. He didn't ever have to tell anybody to mind their manners—everybody was always well-mannered where he was. Everybody loved to have him around, too; he was sunshine most of the time—I mean he made it seem like good weather. When he turned into a cloudbank it was awfully dark for half a minute, and that was enough; there wouldn't be anything going wrong again for a week.

When he and the old lady came down in the morning, all the family stood up from their chairs and greeted them good morning, and didn't sit back down until they had taken their seats. Then Tom and Bob went to the sideboard where the decanter was kept, and mixed a glass of bitters and handed it to him, and he held it in his hand and waited until Tom's and Bob's drinks were mixed, and then they bowed and said, "Our respects to you, sir, and madam;" and they bowed just slightly and said thank you, and so all three of them drank, and Bob and Tom poured a spoonful of water on the sugar and the small amount of whiskey or apple brandy in the bottom of their glasses, and gave it to me and Buck, and we drank to the old people as well.

Bob was the eldest, followed by Tom—both tall, handsome men with very broad shoulders and tanned faces, along with long black hair and dark eyes. They wore white linen clothing from head to toe, just like the old gentleman, and had on wide Panama hats.

Then there was Miss Charlotte; she was twenty-five, tall, proud, and grand, but as good as she could be when she wasn't upset; however, when she was angry, she had a look that would make you shrink back immediately, just like her father. She was beautiful.

So was her sister, Miss Sophia, but hers was a different type of beauty. She was gentle and sweet like a dove, and she was only twenty years old.

Each person had their own enslaved servant to wait on them—Buck too. My servant had an incredibly easy time, because I wasn't used to having anybody do anything for me, but Buck's was busy most of the time.

This was all that remained of the family now, but there had once been more—three sons who were killed, and Emmeline who had died.

The old gentleman owned many farms and over a hundred slaves. Sometimes a large group of people would come there on horseback from ten or fifteen miles around, and stay five or six days, and have such festivities in the surrounding area and on the river, with dances and picnics in the woods during the day, and formal balls at the house in the evenings. These people were mostly relatives of the family. The men brought their guns with them. It was an impressive gathering of high-society folks, I can tell you.

There was another aristocratic clan in the area—five or six families—mostly bearing the name Shepherdson. They were just as refined, well-bred, wealthy, and distinguished as the Grangerford family. The Shepherdsons and Grangerfords shared the same steamboat landing, which was located about two miles upstream from our house; so occasionally when I traveled there with several of our people, I would often see many of the Shepherdsons there with their magnificent horses.

One day Buck and I were out in the woods hunting, and we heard a horse approaching. We were crossing the road. Buck said:

"Quick! Run for the woods!"

We did it, and then peered down through the woods between the leaves. Soon a handsome young man came galloping down the road, sitting easily on his horse and looking like a soldier. He carried his gun across his saddle. I had seen him before. It was young Harney Shepherdson. I heard Buck's gun fire right next to my ear, and Harney's hat fell off his head. He grabbed his gun and rode straight toward the place where we were hidden. But we didn't wait. We took off running through the woods. The woods weren't thick, so I looked over my shoulder to avoid the bullet, and twice I saw Harney aim his gun at Buck; then he rode away in the direction he had come from—to get his hat, I suppose, but I couldn't tell for sure. We never stopped running until we got home. The old gentleman's eyes flashed for a moment—it was mostly pleasure, I thought—then his face kind of relaxed, and he said, rather gently:

"I don't like that shooting from behind a bush. Why didn't you step into the road, my boy?"

"The Shepherdsons don't, father. They always take advantage."

Miss Charlotte held her head high like a queen while Buck told his story, and her nostrils flared while her eyes flashed with anger. The two young men looked grim, but they didn't say anything. Miss Sophia turned pale, but her color returned when she discovered the man wasn't hurt.

As soon as I could get Buck alone by the corn storage buildings under the trees, I said:

"Did you want to kill him, Buck?"

"Well, I bet I did."

"What did he do to you?"

"Him? He never did anything to me."

"Well, then, what did you want to kill him for?"

"Why, nothing—it's just because of the feud."

"What's a feud?"

"Why, where were you raised? Don't you know what a feud is?"

"I've never heard of that before—tell me about it."

"Well," Buck says, "a feud works like this. A man gets into a fight with another man and kills him; then that other man's brother kills him; then the other brothers on both sides go after each other; then the cousins get involved—and eventually everybody gets killed off, and there's no more feud. But it's kind of slow and takes a long time."

"Has this one been going on for a long time, Buck?"

"Well, I should think so! It started thirty years ago, or somewhere around that time. There was trouble about something, and then a lawsuit to settle it; and the suit went against one of the men, and so he up and shot the man that won the suit—which he would naturally do, of course. Anybody would."

"What was the problem about, Buck—land?"

"I think maybe—I don't know."

"Well, who did the shooting? Was it a Grangerford or a Shepherdson?"

"Laws, how do I know? It was so long ago."

"Doesn't anyone know?"

"Oh, yes, dad knows, I think, and some of the other older folks; but they don't know now what the fight was about in the first place."

"Have many people been killed, Buck?"

"Yes, there's a pretty good chance of funerals. But they don't always kill people. Dad has some buckshot in him, but he doesn't mind it because he doesn't weigh much anyway. Bob has been cut up some with a bowie knife, and Tom has been hurt once or twice."

"Has anybody been killed this year, Buck?"

"Yes; we each got one. About three months ago my cousin Bud, who was fourteen years old, was riding through the woods on the other side of the river, and he didn't have any weapon with him, which was complete foolishness, and in a lonely place he heard a horse coming behind him, and saw old Baldy Shepherdson chasing after him with his gun in his hand and his white hair flying in the wind; and instead of jumping off and running into the brush, Bud thought he could outrun him; so they raced, neck and neck, for five miles or more, with the old man gaining ground the whole time; so finally Bud saw it was no use, so he stopped and turned

126

around so that the bullet holes would be in front, you know, and the old man rode up and shot him down. But he didn't get much chance to enjoy his luck, because within a week our people killed him."

"I think that old man was a coward, Buck."

"I believe he wasn't a coward. Not by a long shot. There isn't a coward among those Shepherdsons—not a single one. And there aren't any cowards among the Grangerfords either. Why, that old man held his own in a fight one day for half an hour against three Grangerfords, and came out the winner. They were all on horseback; he jumped off his horse and got behind a small woodpile, and kept his horse in front of him to block the bullets; but the Grangerfords stayed on their horses and danced around the old man, and shot at him repeatedly, and he shot back at them. He and his horse both went home pretty shot up and injured, but the Grangerfords had to be carried home—and one of them was dead, and another died the next day. No, sir; if someone's looking for cowards he doesn't want to waste any time among those Shepherdsons, because they don't produce that kind of person."

The following Sunday, we all went to church, which was about three miles away, with everyone riding on horseback. The men brought their guns with them, as did Buck, and they kept them between their knees or propped them within easy reach against the wall. The Shepherdsons did the same thing. The preaching was pretty mediocre—all about brotherly love and similar tedious topics; but everyone said it was a good sermon, and they all discussed it on the way home, having so much to say about faith and good works and free grace and predestination, and who knows what else, that it seemed to me like one of the most difficult Sundays I had experienced so far.

About an hour after dinner, everyone was dozing around, some in their chairs and some in their rooms, and it became pretty dull. Buck and a dog were stretched out on the grass in the sun, sound asleep. I went up to our room and figured I would take a nap myself. I found that sweet Miss Sophia standing in her doorway, which was next to ours, and she took me into her room and shut the door very softly, and asked me if I liked her, and I said I did; and she asked me if I would do something for her and not tell anybody, and I said I would. Then she said she had forgotten her Testament and left it in the pew at church between two other books, and would I slip out quietly and go there and fetch it for her, and not say anything to anybody. I said I would. So I slipped out and snuck off up the road, and there wasn't anybody at the church, except maybe a hog or two, because there wasn't any lock on the door, and hogs like a wooden plank floor in summertime because it's cool. If you notice, most people don't go to church except when they have to; but a hog is different.

I said to myself, something's going on; it's not normal for a girl to get so worked up about a Testament. So I shook it, and out fell a small piece of paper with "Half-past two" written on it in pencil. I searched through it thoroughly, but couldn't find anything else. I couldn't figure out what that meant, so I put the paper back in the book, and when I got home and went upstairs, Miss Sophia was standing in her doorway waiting for me. She pulled me inside and closed the door; then she looked through the Testament until she found the paper, and as soon as she read it, she looked happy; and before anyone could blink, she grabbed me and gave me a hug, and said I was the best boy in the world, and not to tell anyone. Her face turned bright red for a moment, and her eyes lit up, and it made her incredibly beautiful. I was quite surprised, but when I caught my breath I asked her what the paper was about, and she asked me if I had read it, and I said no, and she asked me if I could read handwriting, and I told her "no, only simple block letters," and then she said the paper was nothing but a bookmark to keep her place, and I could go and play now.

I walked down to the river, thinking about this situation, and soon I realized that the enslaved man was following behind me. When we were out of sight of the house, he looked back and around for a moment, then came running over and said:

"Good Lord, George, if you come down into the swamp I'll show you a whole pile of water moccasins."

I thought to myself, that's really strange; he said the same thing yesterday. He should know that nobody likes water moccasins enough to go out looking for them. What is he planning, anyway? So I said:

"All right; go ahead."

I followed him for half a mile; then he headed out across the swamp, wading through ankle-deep water for about another half mile. We reached a small flat area of dry land that was densely covered with trees, bushes, and vines, and he said:

"You just walk in there a few steps, Master George; that's where they are. I've seen them before; I don't care to see them anymore."

Then he walked carelessly along and disappeared, and soon the trees concealed him from view. I pushed my way into the area for a while and came upon a small clearing about the size of a bedroom, completely surrounded by hanging vines, and discovered a man lying there asleep—and, my goodness, it was my old Jim!

I woke him up, and I figured it would be a wonderful surprise for him to see me again, but it wasn't. He almost cried he was so happy, but he wasn't surprised. He said he had swum along behind me that night, and heard me yell every time, but didn't dare answer, because he didn't want anyone to pick him up and take him back into slavery. He says:

"I got hurt a little, and couldn't swim fast, so I was a considerable ways behind you towards the last; when you landed I reckoned I could catch up with you on the land without having to shout at you, but when I saw that house I began to go slow. I was off too far to hear what they said to you—I was afraid of the dogs; but when it was all quiet again, I knew you were in the house, so I struck out for the woods to wait for day. Early in the morning some of the slaves came along, going to the fields, and they took me and showed me this place, where the dogs can't track me on account of the water, and they bring me food to eat every night, and tell me how you're getting along."

"Why didn't you tell my Jack to bring me here sooner, Jim?"

"Well, it wasn't any use to disturb you, Huck, until we could do something—but we're all right now. I've been buying pots and pans and food, as I got a chance, and patching up the raft nights when—"

"What raft, Jim?"

"Our old raft."

"You mean to say our old raft wasn't smashed to pieces?"

"No, she wasn't. She was torn up quite a bit—one end of her was; but there wasn't any great harm done, only our belongings were mostly all lost. If we hadn't dived so deep and swum so far under water, and the night hadn't been so dark, and we weren't so scared, and been such blockheads, as the saying goes, we would have seen the raft. But it's just as well we didn't, because now she's all fixed up again almost as good as new, and we've got a new lot of stuff, in place of what was lost."

"Why, how did you get the raft back, Jim—did you catch it?"

"How was I going to catch her when I'm out in the woods? No; some of the men found her caught on a snag along here in the bend, and they hid her in a creek among the willows, and they were arguing so much about which one of them she belonged to the most that I came to hear about it pretty soon, so I got up and settled the trouble by telling them she didn't belong to any of them, but to you and me; and I asked them if they were going to grab a young white gentleman's property, and get a hiding for it? Then I gave them ten cents apiece, and they were mighty well satisfied, and wished some more rafts would come along and make them rich again. They're mighty good to me, these men are, and whatever I want them to do for me, I don't have to ask them twice, honey. That Jack's a good man, and pretty smart."

"Yes, he is. He never told me you were here; he told me to come, and he'd show me a lot of water moccasins. If anything happens, he isn't involved in it. He can say he never saw us together, and it'll be the truth."

I don't want to talk much about the next day. I think I'll keep it pretty short. I woke up around dawn and was about to turn over and go back to sleep when I noticed how quiet it was—there didn't seem to be anyone moving around. That wasn't normal. Then I noticed that Buck was up and gone. Well, I got up, wondering what was happening, and went downstairs—nobody around; everything as quiet as a mouse. It was the same outside. I thought to myself, what does this mean? Down by the woodpile I came across my Jack, and said:

"What's it all about?"

Says he:

"Don't you know, Master George?"

"No," I said, "I don't."

"Well, then, Miss Sophia has run off! Indeed she has. She ran off in the night sometime—nobody knows just when; ran off to get married to that young Harney Shepherdson, you know—at least, so they suspect. The family found it out about half an hour ago—maybe a little more—and I tell you they didn't waste any time. Such a hurrying up of guns and horses you never saw! The women folk have gone to stir up the relations, and old Master Saul and the boys took their guns and rode up the river road to try to catch that young man and kill him before he can get across the river with Miss Sophia. I reckon there's going to be mighty rough times."

131

"Buck left without waking me up."

"Well, I reckon he did! They weren't going to mix you up in it. Master Buck loaded up his gun and said he's going to bring home a Shepherdson or die trying. Well, there'll be plenty of them there, I reckon, and you can bet he'll get one if he gets a chance."

I took the river road as fast as I could go. After a while I began to hear gunshots from far away. When I came within sight of the log store and the woodpile where the steamboats dock, I worked my way along under the trees and brush until I reached a good spot, and then I climbed up into the fork of a cottonwood tree that was out of reach, and watched. There was a stack of wood about four feet high a short distance in front of the tree, and at first I was going to hide behind it; but maybe it was luckier that I didn't.

Four or five men were riding around on their horses in the open area in front of the log store, swearing and shouting, trying to get to a couple of young men who were hiding behind the stack of wood next to the steamboat landing, but they couldn't reach them. Every time one of the riders appeared on the river side of the woodpile, he was shot at. The two young men were crouched back to back behind the pile so they could keep watch in both directions.

Eventually the men stopped their wild dancing and shouting. They began riding toward the store; then one of the boys stood up, took careful aim over the pile of wood, and shot one of them right out of his saddle. All the men jumped down from their horses and grabbed the wounded man and started carrying him to the store; and at that very moment the two boys took off running. They made it halfway to the tree I was hiding in before the men spotted them. Then the men saw them, jumped back on their horses and chased after them. They started catching up to the boys, but it didn't matter because the boys had gotten too much of a head start; they reached the woodpile that sat in front of my tree

132

and ducked behind it, giving them the advantage over the men once again. One of the boys was Buck, and the other was a thin young man about nineteen years old.

The men rode around for a while, then left the area. As soon as they disappeared from view, I called out to Buck and told him what I had seen. At first, he couldn't figure out where my voice was coming from up in the tree. He was completely shocked. He told me to keep a sharp lookout and let him know when the men came back into sight; he said they were up to no good and wouldn't stay away long. I wanted to get out of that tree, but I didn't dare climb down. Buck started crying and cursing, and swore that he and his cousin Joe (who was the other young man) would get revenge for what happened that day. He said his father and his two brothers had been killed, along with two or three of the enemy. He said the Shepherdsons had set up an ambush and waited for them. Buck said his father and brothers should have waited for their relatives to help—the Shepherdsons were too powerful for them to face alone. I asked him what had happened to young Harney and Miss Sophia. He said they had made it across the river and were safe. I was relieved to hear that; but the way Buck carried on because he hadn't managed to kill Harney that day when he shot at him—I had never heard anything like it.

Suddenly, bang! bang! bang! Three or four guns fired—the men had slipped around through the woods and approached from behind without their horses! The boys jumped toward the river— both of them wounded—and as they swam down the current, the men ran along the bank shooting at them and shouting, "Kill them, kill them!" It made me so sick I nearly fell out of the tree. I'm not going to tell everything that happened—it would make me sick again if I were to do that. I wished I had never come ashore that night to see such things. I'll never be able to forget them—many times I dream about them.

I stayed in the tree until it began to get dark, afraid to come down. Sometimes I heard gunshots far off in the woods, and twice I saw small groups of men gallop past the log store with guns, so I figured the trouble was still going on. I was extremely discouraged, so I decided I would never go near that house again, because I thought I was to blame somehow. I concluded that the piece of paper meant Miss Sophia was supposed to meet Harney somewhere at half-past two and run away together, and I believed I should have told her father about that paper and the strange way she was acting, and then maybe he would have locked her up, and this terrible mess never would have happened.

When I climbed down from the tree, I crept along the riverbank for a while and discovered the two bodies lying at the water's edge, and I pulled at them until I managed to get them onto the shore; then I covered their faces and left as quickly as I could. I cried a little while I was covering Buck's face, because he had been very good to me.

It was just getting dark now. I never went near the house, but cut through the woods and headed for the swamp. Jim wasn't on his island, so I hurried off toward the creek, and pushed through the willows, desperate to jump aboard and get out of that terrible place. The raft was gone! My God, I was terrified! I couldn't catch my breath for almost a minute. Then I let out a yell. A voice not twenty-five feet from me said:

"Good Lord! Is that you, honey? Don't make any noise."

It was Jim's voice—nothing had ever sounded so wonderful before. I ran along the riverbank for a short distance and climbed aboard, and Jim grabbed me and hugged me, he was so happy to see me. He said:

"Good heavens, child, I was absolutely certain you were dead again. Jack has been here; he said he figured you'd been shot, because you didn't come home anymore; so I was just this minute starting the raft down toward the mouth of the creek, so as to be all ready to push off and leave as soon as Jack comes again and tells me for certain you are dead. Lord, I'm mighty glad to get you back again, honey."

I said:

"Alright—that's really good; they won't find me, and they'll think I've been killed and floated down the river—there's something up there that will help them think so—so don't waste any time, Jim, but just push off for the big water as fast as you can."

I never felt comfortable until the raft was two miles downstream from there and out in the middle of the Mississippi River. Then we hung up our signal lantern and figured that we were free and safe once more. I hadn't eaten anything since yesterday, so Jim brought out some corn cakes and buttermilk, along with pork and cabbage and greens—there's nothing in the world that tastes so good when it's prepared properly—and while I ate my supper we talked and had a wonderful time. I was extremely glad to escape from the feuds, and Jim was equally relieved to get away from the swamp. We agreed that there was no home quite like a raft, after all. Other places seem so confined and suffocating, but a raft doesn't. You feel incredibly free and relaxed and comfortable on a raft.

Chapter XIX.

Two or three days and nights passed by; I suppose I could say they floated by, they moved along so quietly and smoothly and beautifully. Here is how we spent our time. It was an enormous river down there—sometimes a mile and a half wide; we traveled at night, and stayed hidden during the day; as soon as night was nearly over we stopped traveling and tied up—almost always in the still water under a small island; and then we cut young cottonwoods and willows, and concealed the raft with them. Then we put out the fishing lines. Next we slipped into the river and took a swim, to refresh ourselves and cool off; then we sat down on the sandy bottom where the water was about knee deep, and watched the daylight arrive. Not a sound anywhere—perfectly quiet—just as if the whole world was asleep, except sometimes the bullfrogs croaking, perhaps. The first thing to see, looking out over the water, was a kind of dim line—that was the woods on the other side; you couldn't make out anything else; then a pale spot in the sky; then more paleness spreading around; then the river grew softer far off, and wasn't black anymore, but gray; you could see little dark spots drifting along very far away—trading boats, and such things; and long black streaks—rafts; sometimes you could hear an oar creaking; or mixed-up voices, it was so quiet, and sounds traveled so far; and gradually you could see a streak on the water which you knew by the look of the streak that there's a fallen tree there in a fast current which breaks on it and makes that streak look that way; and you see the mist rise up off the water, and the east turns red, and the river, and you make out a log cabin at the edge of the woods, far away on the bank on the other side of the river, being a lumber yard, probably, and stacked by those swindlers so carelessly you can throw a dog through it anywhere; then the pleasant breeze starts up, and comes blowing toward you from over there, so cool and fresh and sweet to smell because of the woods and the flowers; but sometimes not that way, because they've left dead fish lying around, gar and such, and they do get pretty foul; and then you've got the full day, and everything glowing in the sun, and the songbirds just singing away!

A little smoke wouldn't be noticed now, so we would take some fish from the lines and cook a hot breakfast. Afterward we would watch the loneliness of the river, and kind of drift along lazily, and eventually drift off to sleep. We'd wake up later and look around to see what had stirred us, and maybe spot a steamboat chugging along upstream, so far off toward the other side you couldn't tell anything about it except whether it was a stern-wheel or side-wheel; then for about an hour there wouldn't be anything to hear or anything to see—just complete loneliness. Next you'd see a raft sliding by, way off in the distance, and maybe some fellow on it chopping, because they're almost always doing that on a raft; you'd see the axe flash and come down—you don't hear anything; you see that axe go up again, and by the time it's above the man's head then you hear the thunk!—it had taken all that time to travel over the water. So we would spend the day, lounging around, listening to the silence. Once there was a thick fog, and the rafts and other vessels that went by were banging tin pans so the steamboats wouldn't run them over. A flat-bottomed boat or a raft went by so close we could hear them talking and swearing and laughing—heard them clearly; but we couldn't see any sign of them; it made you feel uneasy; it was like spirits carrying on that way in the air. Jim said he believed it was spirits; but I said:

"No; spirits wouldn't say, 'Damn the damn fog.'"

As soon as night fell, we pushed off; when we reached about the middle of the river, we left the raft alone and let it drift wherever the current took it; then we lit our pipes and hung our legs over the side into the water, talking about all sorts of things— we were always naked, day and night, whenever the mosquitoes allowed us to be—the new clothes Buck's family had made for me were too fine to be comfortable, and besides, I never cared much for clothes anyway.

Sometimes we'd have that entire river all to ourselves for the longest time. Over there were the banks and the islands, across the water; and maybe a spark—which was a candle in a cabin window; and sometimes on the water you could see a spark or two—on a raft or a small boat, you know; and maybe you could hear a fiddle or a song drifting over from one of those vessels. It's wonderful to live on a raft. We had the sky up there, all dotted with stars, and we used to lie on our backs and look up at them, and talk about whether they were created or just happened naturally. Jim believed they were made, but I thought they just happened; I figured it would have taken too long to make so many. Jim said the moon could have laid them; well, that seemed kind of reasonable, so I didn't argue against it, because I've seen a frog lay almost as many, so of course it could be done. We used to watch the stars that fell, too, and see them streak down. Jim thought they'd gotten spoiled and were thrown out of the nest.

Once or twice each night we would see a steamboat gliding along in the darkness, and occasionally it would shoot out a whole world of sparks from its smokestacks, and they would fall down into the river and look absolutely beautiful; then it would round a corner and its lights would disappear and its noise would stop and leave the river quiet again; and eventually its waves would reach us, long after it had passed, and rock the raft slightly, and after that you wouldn't hear anything for who knows how long, except perhaps frogs or something.

After midnight the people on shore went to bed, and then for two or three hours the shores were dark—no more lights in the cabin windows. These lights served as our clock—the first one that appeared again meant morning was approaching, so we immediately searched for a place to hide and tie up.

One morning around dawn, I found a canoe and crossed over a narrow channel to the main shore—it was only two hundred yards—and paddled about a mile up a creek through the cypress woods to see if I could find some berries. Just as I was passing a place where some kind of cattle path crossed the creek, two men came running up the path as fast as they could go. I thought I was done for, because whenever anyone was chasing someone, I figured it was me—or maybe Jim. I was about to get out of there quickly, but they were pretty close to me by then, and they called out and begged me to save their lives—said they hadn't been doing anything wrong, and were being chased anyway—said there were men and dogs coming after them. They wanted to jump right into the canoe, but I said:

"Don't do it. I can't hear the dogs and horses yet, so you still have time to push through the bushes and head up the creek a bit. Then get into the water and wade down to where I am and climb in—that will throw the dogs off your trail."

They did it, and as soon as they were aboard I took off for our sandbar, and in about five or ten minutes we heard the dogs and the men far away, shouting. We heard them coming along toward the creek, but couldn't see them; they seemed to stop and mess around for a while; then, as we got farther and farther away all the time, we could hardly hear them at all; by the time we had left a mile of woods behind us and reached the river, everything was quiet, and we paddled over to the sandbar and hid in the cottonwoods and were safe.

One of these men was around seventy years old or older, with a bald head and very gray whiskers. He wore an old beat-up slouch hat and a greasy blue wool shirt, along with worn-out old blue jeans tucked into his boot tops, and homemade suspenders—actually, he only had one suspender. He carried an old long-tailed blue jeans coat with shiny brass buttons draped over his arm, and both men had large, bulky, shabby-looking carpet bags.

The other man was around thirty years old and dressed just as shabbily. After breakfast we all relaxed and talked, and the first thing that became clear was that these two men didn't know each other.

"What got you into trouble?" the bald man asks the other fellow.

"Well, I had been selling a product to remove tartar from teeth—and it really does remove it, along with the tooth enamel most of the time—but I stayed in town one night longer than I should have, and was just about to leave when I met you on the path outside of town, and you told me they were coming after you, and asked me to help you escape. So I told you I was expecting trouble myself, and would leave town with you. That's my whole story—what's yours?"

"Well, I'd been running a little temperance revival there for about a week, and I was the favorite of the women folk, both big and little, because I was making it really tough for the drinkers, I tell you, and taking in as much as five or six dollars a night—ten cents per person, children and Black people free—and business was growing all the time, when somehow or another a little rumor got around last night that I had a habit of spending my time with a private jug in secret. A Black man woke me up this morning and told me the people were gathering quietly with their dogs and horses, and they'd be coming pretty soon and give me about half an hour's head start, and then hunt me down if they could; and if they caught me they'd tar and feather me and ride me on a rail, for sure. I didn't wait for any breakfast—I wasn't hungry."

"Old man," said the young one, "I think we could work together as a team; what do you think?"

"I'm not unwilling. What's your main line of work?"

"I'm a printer by trade; I dabble a bit in patent medicines; I'm a theater actor—tragedy, you know; I try my hand at mesmerism and phrenology when there's an opportunity; I teach singing-geography school for variety; I give a lecture sometimes—oh, I do lots of things—pretty much anything that comes along, as long as it isn't work. What's your line of business?"

"I've done considerable work in the medical field during my time. Laying on of hands is my specialty—for cancer and paralysis, and such conditions; and I can tell fortunes pretty well when I have someone with me to discover the facts for me. Preaching is my calling too, along with working at camp meetings and doing missionary work around the area."

Nobody said anything for a while; then the young man let out a sigh and said:

"Alas!"

"What are you worrying about?" says the bald man.

"To think that I would live to lead such a life and be brought down to such company." And he began to wipe the corner of his eye with a rag.

"Damn you, isn't our company good enough for you?" says the bald man, acting pretty bold and arrogant.

"Yes, it's good enough for me; it's as good as I deserve; for who brought me so low when I was so high? I did it myself. I don't blame you, gentlemen—not at all; I don't blame anyone. I deserve all of this. Let the cold world do its worst; one thing I know—there's a grave somewhere waiting for me. The world can keep going just as it always has, and take everything from me—loved ones, property, everything; but it can't take that away. Someday I'll lie down in it and forget it all, and my poor broken heart will finally be at rest." He continued wiping his eyes.

"Damn your poor broken heart," says the bald man; "what are you throwing your poor broken heart at us for? We haven't done anything."

"No, I know you haven't. I'm not blaming you, gentlemen. I brought myself down—yes, I did it myself. It's right that I should suffer—perfectly right—I'm not complaining."

"Brought you down from where? Where were you brought down from?"

"Ah, you wouldn't believe me; the world never believes—let it go—it doesn't matter. The secret of my birth—"

"The secret of your birth! Do you mean to say—"

"Gentlemen," the young man says with great seriousness, "I'm going to tell you the truth, because I believe I can trust you. I am rightfully a duke!"

Jim's eyes went wide when he heard that, and I think mine did too. Then the bald man said: "No! You can't be serious?"

"Yes. My great-grandfather, the eldest son of the Duke of Bridgewater, escaped to this country around the end of the last century to breathe the pure air of freedom; he married here and died, leaving behind a son, while his own father died around the same time. The second son of the late duke took control of the titles and estates—the infant who was the rightful duke was completely overlooked. I am the direct descendant of that infant—I am the legitimate Duke of Bridgewater; and here I am, abandoned, stripped of my noble position, pursued by men, scorned by the heartless world, dressed in rags, worn down, heartbroken, and reduced to keeping company with criminals on a raft!"

Jim felt deeply sorry for him, and so did I. We attempted to comfort him, but he explained it wouldn't help much since he couldn't really be consoled; he mentioned that if we were willing to acknowledge his status, that would benefit him more than almost anything else; therefore we agreed we would, provided he told us how. He explained we should bow whenever we addressed him, and say "Your Grace," or "My Lord," or "Your Lordship"—and he wouldn't object if we simply called him "Bridgewater," which, he noted, was actually a title rather than a name; and one of us should serve him during meals, and handle any small tasks he might need done.

Well, that was all easy, so we did it. All through dinner Jim stood around and waited on him, and said, "Will your Grace have some of this or some of that?" and so on, and anyone could see it was very pleasing to him.

But the old man became quite quiet after a while—he didn't have much to say and didn't seem very comfortable with all the attention and fawning that was happening around that duke. He appeared to have something weighing on his mind. So, later in the afternoon, he says:

"Listen here, Bilgewater," he says, "I'm really sorry for you, but you're not the only person who's had troubles like that."

"No?"

"No, you're not. You're not the only person who's been unfairly brought down from a position of power."

"Alas!"

"No, you're not the only person who's had a secret about his birth." And, by God, he starts to cry.

"Wait! What are you trying to say?"

"Nonsense, can I trust you?" says the old man, still somewhat sobbing.

"To the bitter death!" He grabbed the old man's hand and squeezed it tightly, then said, "That secret of your existence: tell me!"

"Nonsense, I am the late Dauphin!"

You can bet that Jim and I stared this time. Then the duke says: "What are you?"

"Yes, my friend, it is absolutely true—you are looking at this very moment upon the poor vanished Dauphin, Louis the Seventeenth, son of Louis the Sixteenth and Marie Antoinette."

"You! At your age! No! You mean you're the late Charlemagne; you must be six or seven hundred years old, at the very least."

"Hardship has caused this, Bilgewater, hardship has caused it; trouble has brought these gray hairs and this early baldness. Yes, gentlemen, you see before you, in blue jeans and misery, the wandering, exiled, trampled-on, and suffering rightful King of France."

Well, he cried and carried on so much that Jim and I hardly knew what to do, we felt so sorry for him—and so glad and proud we had him with us, too. So we got started, like we had done before with the duke, and tried to comfort him. But he said it was no use, nothing but being dead and finished with it all could do him any good; though he said it often made him feel easier and better for a while if people treated him according to his rights, and got down on one knee to speak to him, and always called him "Your Majesty," and waited on him first at meals, and didn't sit down in his presence until he asked them. So Jim and I started treating him like royalty, and doing this and that and everything else for him, and standing up until he told us we could sit down. This did him a lot of good, and so he became cheerful and comfortable. But the duke kind of turned sour on him, and didn't look a bit satisfied with the way things were going; still, the king acted really friendly toward him, and said the duke's great-grandfather and all the other Dukes of Bilgewater were thought very highly of by his father, and were allowed to come to the palace quite often; but the duke stayed irritated for a good while, until eventually the king says:

"We'll probably be stuck together on this raft for a long time, Bilgewater, so what's the point of being bitter? It'll just make everything uncomfortable. It's not my fault I wasn't born a duke, and it's not your fault you weren't born a king—so why worry about it? Make the best of things as you find them, I say—that's my motto. This situation we've found ourselves in isn't so bad—plenty of food and an easy life—come on, give me your hand, Duke, and let's all be friends."

The duke did it, and Jim and I were quite happy to see it happen. It removed all the tension and we felt really good about it, because it would have been a terrible situation to have any hostility on the raft; because what you want, above all else, on a raft, is for everyone to be content, and feel good and friendly toward each other.

It didn't take me long to decide that these liars weren't kings or dukes at all, but just low-down con artists and frauds. But I never said anything, never let on; I kept it to myself; it's the best way; then you don't have any quarrels, and don't get into any trouble. If they wanted us to call them kings and dukes, I didn't have any objections, as long as it would keep peace in the family; and it wasn't any use to tell Jim, so I didn't tell him. If I never learned anything else from my father, I learned that the best way to get along with his kind of people is to let them have their own way.

Chapter XX.

They asked us a lot of questions; they wanted to know why we covered up the raft like that, and why we stayed hidden during the day instead of traveling—was Jim a runaway slave? I said:

"Good heavens, would a runaway slave head south?"

No, they agreed he wouldn't. I had to explain things somehow, so I said:

"My family was living in Pike County, in Missouri, where I was born, and they all died except for me, my father, and my brother Ike. My father thought he'd pack up and go live with Uncle Ben, who owned a small farm by the river, forty-four miles below New Orleans. My father was quite poor and owed some money, so after he settled his debts, there was nothing left except sixteen dollars and our slave, Jim. That wasn't enough to get us fourteen hundred miles downriver, whether by deck passage or any other means. Well, when the river flooded, my father had a stroke of good fortune one day—he caught hold of this piece of a raft, so we figured we'd float down to New Orleans on it. My father's luck didn't last; a steamboat crashed into the front corner of the raft one night, and we all fell overboard and went under the paddle wheel. Jim and I surfaced safely, but my father was drunk, and Ike was only four years old, so they never came back up. Well, for the next day or two we had quite a bit of trouble, because people kept coming out in small boats trying to take Jim away from me, claiming they thought he was a runaway slave. We don't travel during the day anymore; at night they don't bother us."

The duke says:

"Leave me alone to figure out a way so we can travel during the day if we want to. I'll think this through—I'll come up with a plan that'll solve it. We'll leave it alone for today, because obviously we don't want to pass by that town over there in daylight—it might not be safe."

As evening approached, the sky began to darken and looked like rain was coming; heat lightning was flickering low across the horizon, and the leaves started to tremble—it was clear that bad weather was on the way. So the duke and the king went to examine our shelter to see what the sleeping arrangements were like. My bed was a straw mattress that was better than Jim's, which was stuffed with corn husks; there are always corncobs mixed in with a corn-husk mattress, and they poke into you and cause pain; and when you turn over, the dry husks make a sound like you're rolling around in a pile of dead leaves; the rustling is so loud that it wakes you up. Well, the duke decided he would take my bed; but the king said he wouldn't allow it. He says:

"I would have thought the difference in rank would have suggested to you that a corn-husk bed wasn't suitable for me to sleep on. Your Grace will take the husk bed yourself."

Jim and I were sweating nervously again for a minute, worried that there was going to be more trouble among them; so we were pretty relieved when the duke said:

"It's my destiny to always be crushed into the dirt under the iron boot of oppression. Bad luck has shattered my once proud spirit; I give in, I surrender; it's my fate. I am alone in the world—let me suffer; I can endure it."

We left as soon as it was completely dark. The king told us to stay well out toward the middle of the river, and not show a light until we got far below the town. We came in sight of the small

146

cluster of lights eventually—that was the town, you know—and slipped by, about half a mile out, without any problems. When we were three-quarters of a mile below, we raised our signal lantern; and around ten o'clock it started to rain and blow and thunder and lightning like crazy; so the king told us to both stay on watch until the weather got better; then he and the duke crawled into the shelter and went to sleep for the night. It was my watch until midnight, but I wouldn't have gone to sleep anyway even if I'd had a bed, because a person doesn't see such a storm as that every day of the week, not by a long shot. My goodness, how the wind did scream along! And every second or two there would come a flash that lit up the whitecaps for half a mile around, and you'd see the islands looking hazy through the rain, and the trees thrashing around in the wind; then comes a crash—boom! boom! rumble-rumble-rumble-boom-boom-boom-boom—and the thunder would go rolling and grumbling away, and stop—and then rip comes another flash and another tremendous crash. The waves almost washed me off the raft sometimes, but I didn't have any clothes on, and didn't mind. We didn't have any trouble with fallen trees; the lightning was flashing and flickering around so constantly that we could see them plenty soon enough to steer her this way or that and avoid them.

I was supposed to take the middle watch, but I was feeling pretty drowsy by then, so Jim offered to cover the first half for me; he was always incredibly kind like that. I crawled into the shelter, but the king and the duke had stretched their legs out everywhere, leaving no room for me; so I lay down outside—I didn't mind the rain since it was warm, and the waves weren't running as high anymore. Around two o'clock they started picking up again, and Jim was about to wake me; but he decided against it, figuring they weren't high enough yet to cause any trouble; however, he was wrong about that, because suddenly a massive wave came along and swept me overboard. Jim nearly died laughing. He was the most good-natured person you'd ever meet when it came to finding things funny.

I took the watch, and Jim lay down and snored away; eventually the storm stopped completely; and when the first cabin light appeared, I woke him up and we moved the raft into a hiding place for the day.

After breakfast, the king pulled out an old, worn deck of cards, and he and the duke played seven-up for a while, betting five cents per game. Eventually they grew tired of the card game and decided they would "plan a campaign," as they put it. The duke reached into his carpet bag and pulled out a collection of small printed flyers, which he read aloud. One flyer announced that "The celebrated Dr. Armand de Montalban, of Paris," would "lecture on the Science of Phrenology" at a certain location, on a specific date, for ten cents admission, and would "furnish charts of character at twenty-five cents apiece." The duke explained that this persona was him. Another flyer identified him as the "world-renowned Shakespearian tragedian, Garrick the Younger, of Drury Lane, London." On additional flyers he used various other names and claimed to perform other remarkable feats, such as locating water and gold using a "divining-rod," "dispelling witch spells," and similar activities. After a while he says:

"But the theatrical muse is the favorite. Have you ever acted on stage, Your Majesty?"

"No," says the king.

"You'll be performing within three days, Fallen Grandeur," the duke declares. "At the first decent town we reach, we'll rent a hall and put on the sword fight from Richard III and the balcony scene from Romeo and Juliet. What do you think of that?"

"I'm all in, completely committed to anything that will make us money, Bilgewater; but you see, I don't know anything about acting, and I've never really seen much of it. I was too young when my father used to put on shows at the palace. Do you think you can teach me?"

"Easy!"

"All right. I'm just freezing for something fresh, anyway. Let's start right away."

So the duke explained to him who Romeo was and who Juliet was, and mentioned that he was accustomed to playing Romeo, so the king could take on the role of Juliet.

"But if Juliet's such a young woman, duke, my bald head and my white whiskers are going to look uncommonly strange on her, maybe."

"No, don't worry about it; these small-town folks will never think of that. Besides, you know, you'll be wearing a costume, and that changes everything; Juliet's on a balcony, enjoying the moonlight before going to bed, and she's wearing her nightgown and her frilled nightcap. Here are the costumes for the roles."

He pulled out two or three suits made of curtain calico, which he claimed was medieval armor for Richard III and the other character, along with a long white cotton nightshirt and a matching ruffled nightcap. The king was pleased with this; so the duke took out his book and read through the parts in the most magnificent, bombastic style, strutting around and performing at the same time to demonstrate how it should be done; then he handed the book to the king and instructed him to memorize his part.

There was a small town with just one main street about three miles down the river bend, and after dinner the duke said he had figured out his plan for how to travel during daylight without it being dangerous for Jim; so he decided he would go down to the town and arrange that matter. The king decided he would go too, and see if he couldn't find some opportunity. We were out of coffee, so Jim said I should go along with them in the canoe and get some.

When we arrived, no one was moving around; the streets were empty and completely quiet and still, like Sunday. We found a sick

Black man sitting in the sun in a backyard, and he told us that everyone who wasn't too young or too sick or too old had gone to a camp meeting about two miles back in the woods. The king got the directions and said he would go and work that camp meeting for all it was worth, and I could come along too.

The duke explained that he was looking for a printing office. We located one; it was a small operation situated above a carpenter's workshop—both the carpenters and printers had all left for the meeting, leaving no doors locked. The place was messy and cluttered, with ink stains and handbills featuring pictures of horses and runaway slaves covering the walls. The duke removed his coat and announced he was all set now. So the king and I headed out for the camp meeting.

We arrived there in about half an hour, completely soaked with sweat, because it was an extremely hot day. There were at least a thousand people there from twenty miles around. The woods were full of teams and wagons, tied up everywhere, with horses feeding from the wagon troughs and stamping their feet to keep the flies away. There were shelters made from poles and covered with branches, where vendors sold lemonade and gingerbread, along with piles of watermelons and fresh corn and similar produce.

The preaching was taking place under the same types of shelters, except they were larger and accommodated crowds of people. The benches were constructed from outer slabs of logs, with holes drilled in the rounded side to insert sticks that served as legs. They had no backs. The preachers stood on elevated platforms positioned at one end of the shelters. The women wore sun bonnets; some had on linsey-woolsey dresses, others wore gingham ones, and a few of the younger women were dressed in calico. Some of the young men were barefoot, and some of the children wore nothing but a rough linen shirt. Some of the older women were knitting, and some of the young people were secretly flirting.

The first tent we reached had a preacher who was leading the congregation in a hymn. He would call out two lines, everyone would sing them back, and it sounded magnificent to hear because there were so many voices joining together in such an energetic way; then he would call out two more lines for them to sing—and this continued throughout. The crowd became increasingly animated and sang with growing volume; and near the end some people started to moan while others began to shout. Then the preacher started his sermon, and he began with real intensity; he moved back and forth from one side of the platform to the other, then leaned forward over the front edge, his arms and body in constant motion, bellowing his words with tremendous force; and repeatedly he would raise his Bible high and open it wide, waving it in all directions while shouting, "It's the bronze serpent in the wilderness! Look upon it and live!" And the congregation would cry out, "Glory!—Amen!" And he continued this way, with the people moaning and weeping and calling out amen:

"Oh, come to the mourners' bench! come, black with sin! (amen!) come, sick and sore! (amen!) come, lame and halt and blind! (amen!) come, poor and needy, sunk in shame! (a-a-men!) come, all that's worn and soiled and suffering!—come with a broken spirit! come with a contrite heart! come in your rags and sin and dirt! the waters that cleanse are free, the door of heaven stands open—oh, enter in and be at rest!" (a-a-men! glory, glory hallelujah!)

The noise continued like this. You could no longer hear what the preacher was saying because of all the shouting and crying. People stood up throughout the crowd and pushed their way through using sheer force to reach the mourners' bench, with tears streaming down their faces; and when all the mourners had gathered up there at the front benches in a group, they sang and shouted and threw themselves down on the straw, completely frenzied and wild.

151

Well, the first thing I knew, the king started talking, and you could hear him above everyone else; then he charged up onto the platform, and the preacher urged him to speak to the people, which he did. He told them he was a pirate—had been a pirate for thirty years out in the Indian Ocean—and his crew had been significantly reduced last spring in a fight, and he was home now to recruit some fresh men, and thank goodness he had been robbed last night and put ashore from a steamboat without a penny, and he was glad about it; it was the most blessed thing that ever happened to him, because he was a changed man now, and happy for the first time in his life; and, poor as he was, he was going to start right away and work his way back to the Indian Ocean, and spend the rest of his life trying to turn the pirates to the true path; for he could do it better than anyone else, being familiar with all the pirate crews in that ocean; and though it would take him a long time to get there without money, he would get there anyway, and every time he converted a pirate he would say to him, "Don't thank me, don't give me any credit; it all belongs to those dear people in Pokeville camp-meeting, natural brothers and benefactors of the human race, and that dear preacher there, the truest friend a pirate ever had!"

And then he broke down crying, and everyone else did too. Then someone called out, "Take up a collection for him, take up a collection!" Well, about six people jumped up to do it, but someone shouted, "Let him pass the hat around!" Then everyone agreed with that, including the preacher.

So the king moved through the entire crowd with his hat, wiping his eyes, and blessing the people while praising them and thanking them for being so kind to the poor pirates far away. Every so often, the most beautiful young women, with tears streaming down their faces, would come up and ask if they could kiss him to remember him by. He always allowed it, and he hugged and kissed some of them as many as five or six times. He was invited to stay for a week, and everyone wanted him to stay in their homes, saying they would consider it an honor. But he explained that since this was the final day of the camp meeting, he couldn't accomplish anything worthwhile, and besides, he was eager to get to the Indian Ocean immediately and begin working on converting the pirates.

When we returned to the raft and he began counting, he discovered he had collected eighty-seven dollars and seventy-five cents. He had also taken a three-gallon jug of whiskey that he found under a wagon while heading home through the woods. The king said that overall, it was better than any day he had ever spent doing missionary work. He said there was no point in arguing about it—heathens couldn't compare to pirates when it came to working a camp meeting.

The duke believed he had been performing quite well until the king appeared on the scene, but afterward he wasn't so confident about his success. He had prepared and printed two small jobs for local farmers at the printing office—advertising flyers for horses—and collected the payment of four dollars. He had also secured ten dollars' worth of advertisements for the newspaper, though he told customers he would include them for four dollars if they paid upfront—which they did. The newspaper's subscription price was two dollars per year, but he sold three subscriptions for fifty cents each with the requirement that customers pay in advance; while they typically would have paid with cordwood and onions as was customary, he explained that he had just purchased the business and reduced the price as much as he could manage, and planned to operate it on a cash-only basis. He composed a short poem entirely from his own imagination— three stanzas—that was somewhat sweet and melancholy—titled "Yes, crush, cold world, this breaking heart"—and he prepared it for publication in the newspaper without charging anything for it. In total, he earned nine dollars and fifty cents, and declared that he had accomplished a fairly honest day's work.

Then he showed us another small job he'd printed without charging for it, since it was for us. It featured a picture of a runaway slave with a bundle on a stick over his shoulder, and "$200 reward" printed beneath it. The text was all about Jim, describing him perfectly. It stated he had run away from St. Jacques' plantation, forty miles below New Orleans, the previous winter, and had likely headed north, and whoever caught him and sent him back could claim the reward and expenses.

"Now," the duke says, "after tonight we can travel during the day if we want to. Whenever we spot someone approaching, we can tie Jim's hands and feet with rope, put him in the wigwam, and show this poster while claiming we caught him upriver. We were too broke to afford steamboat passage, so we borrowed this small raft from friends and are heading downstream to collect the reward. Handcuffs and chains would look even more convincing on Jim, but they wouldn't fit with our story about being poor. That would be too much like expensive accessories. Ropes are the right choice—we need to maintain consistency in our story, as we say in the theater."

We all agreed the duke was quite clever, and there wouldn't be any trouble traveling during the day. We figured we could cover enough miles that night to get beyond the reach of the commotion we expected the duke's activities in the printing office would cause in that small town; then we could move along quickly if we wanted to.

We stayed hidden and remained quiet, and we didn't venture out until almost ten o'clock; then we slipped past, keeping a good distance from the town, and we didn't raise our lantern until we were completely out of sight.

When Jim woke me up to take my turn on watch at four in the morning, he said:

"Huck, do you think we're going to run across any more kings on this trip?"

"No," I said, "I don't think so."

"Well," he says, "that's all right, then. I don't mind one or two kings, but that's enough. This one's powerfully drunk, and the duke isn't much better."

I discovered that Jim had been attempting to persuade him to speak French so he could listen to how it sounded, but the man explained that he had lived in this country for such a long time and experienced so many hardships that he had forgotten the language.

Chapter XXI.

It was after sunrise now, but we kept going and didn't stop to tie up. The king and the duke eventually came out looking pretty rough; but after they had jumped overboard and taken a swim, it cheered them up considerably. After breakfast, the king took a seat on the corner of the raft, pulled off his boots and rolled up his pants, and let his legs hang in the water to be comfortable, lit his pipe, and started memorizing his Romeo and Juliet. When he had learned it fairly well, he and the duke began to practice it together. The duke had to teach him over and over again how to deliver every speech; and he made him sigh, and put his hand on his heart, and after a while he said he was doing it pretty well; "only," he says, "you mustn't shout out Romeo! that way, like a bull—you must say it soft and sick and lovesick, like this—R o o mco! that's the idea; because Juliet's a dear sweet young girl, you know, and she doesn't bray like a donkey."

Well, next they pulled out a couple of long swords that the duke had made from oak strips, and started practicing their sword fight—the duke called himself Richard III.; and the way they attacked and danced around the raft was magnificent to watch. But eventually the king stumbled and fell overboard, and after that they took a break, and talked about all sorts of adventures they'd experienced at other times along the river.

After dinner the duke says:

"Well, Capet, we'll want to make this a first-class show, you know, so I guess we'll add a little more to it. We want a little something to answer encores with, anyway."

"What's onkores, Bilgewater?"

The duke told him, and then said:

"I'll respond by performing the Highland fling or the sailor's hornpipe; and you—well, let me think—oh, I have it—you can perform Hamlet's soliloquy."

"Hamlet's which?"

"You know Hamlet's soliloquy—the most famous passage in all of Shakespeare. Oh, it's absolutely magnificent! It never fails to captivate an audience. I don't have it in my book—I only own one volume—but I think I can put it together from memory. Let me pace back and forth for a moment and see if I can retrieve it from the depths of my recollection."

So he started pacing back and forth, deep in thought, scowling terribly from time to time; then he would raise his eyebrows high; next he would press his hand against his forehead and stumble backward while groaning; then he would sigh, and after that he'd pretend to shed a tear. It was magnificent to watch him. Eventually he figured it out. He told us to pay attention. Then he struck a truly noble pose, with one leg thrust forward, his arms stretched high above, and his head tilted back, gazing up at the sky; and then he began to rant and rave and grind his teeth; and throughout his entire speech, he bellowed, gestured wildly, puffed out his chest, and completely outdid any acting I had ever seen before. This is the speech—I memorized it easily enough while he was teaching it to the king:

To be, or not to be; that is the dagger
That makes disaster of such a long life;
For who would carry burdens,
until Birnam Wood comes to Dunsinane,
Except that the fear of something after death
Kills peaceful sleep,
Nature's great second gift,
And makes us instead endure the arrows of cruel fortune
Rather than escape to others we don't know.

There's the consideration that must make us hesitate:
Wake Duncan with your knocking! I wish you could;
For who would endure the beatings and mockery of time,
The oppressor's injustice, the arrogant man's insults,
The law's delays, and the final rest that his suffering might bring.

In the dead emptiness and middle of the night,
when graveyards open wide
In their usual clothes of serious black,
But that the unexplored country from whose boundary no
traveler returns,
Spreads disease upon the world,
And thus the natural color of determination,
like the poor cat in the saying,
Is made pale with worry.
And all the clouds that hung threateningly over our rooftops,
With this thought their streams turn off course,
And lose the identity of action.

It is a completion earnestly to be desired.
But wait, the beautiful Ophelia:
Do not open your heavy and stone jaws.
But go to a convent—leave!

Well, the old man really enjoyed that speech, and he quickly became excellent at delivering it. It seemed like he was naturally

157

gifted for it; and when he got into the rhythm and became enthusiastic, it was absolutely wonderful the way he would become passionate and animated when he was performing it.

At the first opportunity, the duke had some show posters printed, and for the next two or three days as we drifted along the river, the raft became an extraordinarily lively place, with nothing but sword-fighting and rehearsing—as the duke called it— happening constantly. One morning, when we were well into Arkansas, we spotted a small, modest town situated in a large river bend, so we moored about three-quarters of a mile upstream at the mouth of a creek that was enclosed like a tunnel by cypress trees, and everyone except Jim took the canoe and headed down there to see if that place offered any opportunities for our show.

We got incredibly lucky; there was going to be a circus there that afternoon, and the country folks were already starting to arrive in all sorts of rickety old wagons and on horseback. The circus would be gone before nightfall, so our show would have a really good opportunity. The duke rented the courthouse, and we went around putting up our posters. They read like this:

Shakespearean Revival!!!
Wonderful Attraction!
For One Night Only!
The world renowned tragedians,
David Garrick the younger,
of Drury Lane Theatre, London, and
Edmund Kean the elder, of the Royal Haymarket Theatre,
Whitechapel, Pudding Lane, Piccadilly, London,
and the Royal Continental Theatres, in their sublime
Shakespearean Spectacle entitled
The Balcony Scene In
Romeo and Juliet!!!
Romeo   Mr. Garrick.
Juliet   Mr. Kean.

Assisted by the whole strength of the company!
New costumes, new scenery, new appointments!
Also:
The thrilling, masterly, and blood-curdling
Broad-sword conflict
In Richard III.!!!
Richard III   Mr. Garrick.
Richmond   Mr. Kean.
also:
(by special request,)
Hamlet's Immortal Soliloquy!!
By the Illustrious Kean!
Done by him 300 consecutive nights in Paris!
For One Night Only,
On account of imperative European engagements!
Admission 25 cents; children and servants, 10 cents.

Then we wandered around the town. The stores and houses were mostly old, rickety, dried-up wooden structures that had never been painted; they were built three or four feet above the ground on stilts, so they would stay above the water when the river flooded. The houses had small gardens around them, but they didn't seem to grow much of anything except jimsonweed and sunflowers, along with ash piles, old worn-out boots and shoes, broken bottle pieces, rags, and discarded tin items. The fences were made from different types of boards, nailed up at various times; they tilted in every direction and had gates that usually only had one hinge—a leather one. Some of the fences had been whitewashed at some point, but the duke said it was probably back in Columbus's time. There were usually pigs in the gardens, with people chasing them out.

All the stores were located along one street. They had white canvas awnings out front, and the country folks tied their horses to the awning posts. There were empty dry goods boxes sitting under the awnings, and lazy men perched on them all day long, whittling them with their pocket knives and chewing tobacco, gaping and yawning and stretching—a really worthless bunch. They usually wore yellow straw hats almost as wide as umbrellas, but didn't wear any coats or vests. They called each other Bill, and Buck, and Hank, and Joe, and Andy, and spoke in slow, drawn-out voices, using quite a few curse words. There was at least one loafer leaning against every awning post, and he almost always had his hands in his pants pockets, except when he pulled them out to share some chewing tobacco or scratch himself. What you could hear among them all the time was:

"Give me some chewing tobacco, Hank."

"Can't; I only have one chew left. Ask Bill."

Perhaps Bill gives him some chewing tobacco; perhaps he lies and says he doesn't have any. Some of these types of loafers never have a cent to their name, nor any chewing tobacco of their own. They get all their tobacco by borrowing; they say to someone, "I wish you'd lend me some chewing tobacco, Jack, I just this minute gave Ben Thompson the last bit I had"—which is a lie almost every time; it doesn't fool anyone except a stranger; but Jack isn't a stranger, so he says:

"You gave him some chewing tobacco, did you? Well, so did your sister's cat's grandmother. You pay me back the chewing tobacco you've already borrowed from me, Lafe Buckner, then I'll lend you a ton or two of it, and won't charge you any back interest, either."

"Well, I did pay you back some of it once."

"Yes, you did—about six chews. You borrowed store tobacco and paid back cheap tobacco."

Store-bought tobacco comes in flat black plugs, but these men usually chew the natural leaf that's been twisted. When they borrow a chew, they don't typically cut it off with a knife, but instead place the plug between their teeth and gnaw at it while pulling with their hands until they break it in two; then sometimes the person who owns the tobacco looks sadly at it when it's returned, and says sarcastically:

"Here, give me the chewing tobacco, and you take the plug."

All the streets and lanes were nothing but mud—they weren't anything else except mud—mud as black as tar and nearly a foot deep in some places, and two or three inches deep everywhere else. The pigs lounged and grunted around everywhere. You'd see a muddy sow and a litter of pigs come strolling along the street and plop herself right down in the middle of the path, where people had to walk around her, and she'd stretch out and close her eyes and flap her ears while the piglets were nursing, and look as content as if she was getting paid for it. And soon enough you'd hear some idler shout out, "Hey! Go get her, Tiger!" and off the sow would go, squealing terribly, with a dog or two hanging onto each ear, and three or four dozen more coming after them; and then you would see all the loafers stand up and watch the whole thing until it disappeared from sight, and laugh at the entertainment and look thankful for the commotion. Then they'd settle back down again until there was a dog fight. Nothing could wake them up completely, and make them completely happy, like a dog fight—unless it might be putting turpentine on a stray dog and lighting him on fire, or tying a tin pan to his tail and watching him run himself to death.

Along the riverfront, some of the houses were jutting out over the bank, and they were warped and twisted, almost ready to collapse into the water. The residents had already moved out of these homes. The bank had eroded away beneath one corner of several other houses, leaving that corner suspended in midair. People still lived in those buildings, but it was dangerous, since sometimes a strip of land as wide as an entire house would cave in all at once. Occasionally, a section of land a quarter-mile deep would begin to collapse and keep caving in until the whole area

161

tumbled into the river during a single summer. A town like this one had to keep moving backward, farther and farther back, because the river was constantly eating away at it.

The closer it got to noon that day, the more crowded the streets became with wagons and horses, and more kept arriving all the time. Families brought their meals with them from the countryside and ate them in their wagons. There was quite a bit of whiskey drinking happening, and I saw three fights break out. Before long, somebody shouted:

"Here comes old Boggs!—in from the country for his little old monthly drunk; here he comes, boys!"

All the idle men looked pleased; I figured they were accustomed to getting entertainment from Boggs. One of them says:

"Wonder who he's going to chew up this time. If he had chewed up all the men he's been going to chew up in the last twenty years, he'd have quite a reputation by now."

Another one says, "I wish old Boggs would threaten me, because then I'd know I wasn't going to die for a thousand years."

Boggs came racing along on his horse, shouting and yelling like a Native American, and calling out:

"Clear the track there. I'm on the warpath, and the price of coffins is going to rise."

He was drunk and swaying unsteadily in his saddle; he was over fifty years old and had a very red face. Everyone shouted at him and laughed at him and gave him sass, and he talked back, saying he'd deal with them and knock them out one by one in due time, but he couldn't wait around now because he'd come to town to kill old Colonel Sherburn, and his motto was, "Meat first, and spoon food to finish off with."

He saw me and rode up and said:

"Where did you come from, boy? Are you prepared to die?"

Then he continued riding. I felt frightened, but a man said:

"He doesn't mean anything by it; he's always acting like that when he's drunk. He's the most good-natured old fool in Arkansas—never hurt anybody, drunk or sober."

Boggs rode up in front of the largest store in town, leaned his head down so he could see beneath the awning's curtain, and shouted:

"Come out here, Sherburn! Come out and meet the man you've swindled. You're the hound I'm after, and I'm going to have you, too!"

And so he continued, calling Sherburn every name he could think of, while the entire street filled with people listening and laughing and carrying on. Eventually a proud-looking man about fifty-five—and he was by far the best dressed man in that town, too—stepped out of the store, and the crowd moved back on both sides to let him through. He spoke to Boggs, very calm and slow—he said:

"I'm fed up with this, but I'll put up with it until one o'clock. Until one o'clock, understand—not a minute longer. If you say one word against me after that time, there's nowhere you can go that I won't track you down."

Then he turns and goes inside. The crowd looked extremely serious; nobody moved, and there was no more laughing. Boggs rode off cursing Sherburn as loudly as he could shout, all the way down the street; and soon he comes back and stops in front of the store, still keeping it up. Some men gathered around him and tried to get him to be quiet, but he wouldn't; they told him it would be one o'clock in about fifteen minutes, and so he had to go home—he had to leave right away. But it didn't do any good. He swore with all his strength, and threw his hat down in the mud and rode over it, and soon he went raging down the street again, with his gray hair flying. Everyone who could get a chance at him tried their best to persuade him off his horse so they could lock him up and get him sober; but it was no use—up the street he would charge again, and give Sherburn another round of cursing. Eventually somebody says:

"Go get his daughter!—hurry, go get his daughter; sometimes he'll listen to her. If anyone can convince him, she can."

So someone took off running. I walked down the street a bit and stopped. After about five or ten minutes, here comes Boggs again, but he wasn't on his horse. He was staggering across the street toward me, without his hat, with a friend on each side of him holding his arms and rushing him along. He was quiet and looked nervous; he wasn't resisting at all, but was doing some of the hurrying himself. Someone calls out:

"Boggs!"

I glanced over to see who had spoken, and there stood Colonel Sherburn. He remained completely motionless in the street, holding a pistol in his right hand—not pointing it at anyone, but gripping it with the barrel angled upward toward the sky. At that exact moment, I spotted a young woman running toward us, accompanied by two men. Boggs and his companions spun around to identify who had called out to him, and when they noticed the pistol, the men quickly stepped aside as the weapon's barrel slowly and deliberately lowered to aim straight ahead—both hammers pulled back and ready to fire. Boggs raised both hands above his head and pleaded, "Oh Lord, please don't shoot!" The first shot rang out with a loud bang, causing him to stumble backward while frantically grasping at the air—then came the second shot with another bang, and he collapsed backward onto the ground with a heavy thud, his arms stretched wide. The young woman let out a piercing scream and came running forward, throwing herself down on top of her father while weeping and crying out, "Oh, he's killed him, he's killed him!" The crowd pressed in tightly around them, pushing and shoving against each other with their necks craned forward, all trying to get a better view, while those closest to the scene attempted to push the others back, yelling, "Move back, move back! Let him breathe, let him breathe!"

Colonel Sherburn threw his pistol to the ground, spun around on his heels, and walked away.

They brought Boggs to a small pharmacy, with the crowd pressing around them just as before, and the entire town following behind. I hurried ahead and secured a good spot at the window, where I was close enough to him and could see inside clearly. They placed him on the floor and positioned one large Bible beneath his head, then opened another Bible and laid it across his chest. However, they first ripped open his shirt, and I could see where one of the bullets had entered his body. He took about twelve long, labored breaths, his chest raising the Bible upward as he inhaled, then lowering it back down as he exhaled—and after that he lay motionless; he was dead. Then they pulled his daughter away from him as she screamed and wept, and led her away. She appeared to be around sixteen years old, and had a very sweet and gentle appearance, but looked terribly pale and frightened.

Before long, the entire town had gathered there, squirming and squeezing and pushing and shoving to get to the window for a look, but the people who had secured the good spots wouldn't give them up, and the folks behind them kept saying, "Listen, you've looked long enough, you guys; it isn't right and it isn't fair for you to stay there the whole time and never give anyone else a chance; other people have their rights just as much as you do."

There was a lot of arguing going back and forth, so I slipped away, thinking there might be trouble brewing. The streets were crowded, and everyone was worked up. Every person who had witnessed the shooting was describing how it all went down, and large groups of people gathered around each witness, craning their necks and listening intently. One tall, thin man with long hair and a big white fur top hat tilted back on his head, carrying a crooked-handled walking stick, marked out the spots on the ground where Boggs had stood and where Sherburn had stood. People followed him from one location to the other, watching his every move and nodding their heads to show they understood, bending forward slightly and placing their hands on their knees as they watched him mark the positions on the ground with his cane. Then he straightened up and stood rigid where Sherburn had been positioned, scowling and pulling his hat brim down over his eyes, and called out, "Boggs!" He then slowly lowered his cane to a horizontal position and shouted "Bang!" He staggered backward, yelled "Bang!" once more, and collapsed flat on his back. The people who had actually witnessed the incident said his reenactment was perfect; they said it was exactly how everything had happened. Then at least a dozen people pulled out their bottles and bought him drinks.

Well, before long somebody said Sherburn should be lynched. Within about a minute everybody was saying it; so off they went, furious and shouting, and grabbing down every clothesline they came across to use for the hanging.

Chapter XXII.

They swarmed up towards Sherburn's house, whooping and raging like wild people, and everything had to clear the way or get run over and trampled to pieces, and it was awful to see. Children were running ahead of the mob, screaming and trying to get out of the way; and every window along the road was full of women's heads, and there were young people in every tree, and men and women looking over every fence; and as soon as the mob would get nearly to them they would break and scatter back out of reach. Lots of the women and girls were crying and carrying on, scared most to death.

The crowd packed together as tightly as possible in front of Sherburn's fence, and the noise was so loud you couldn't think straight. It was a small yard, only about twenty feet across. Some people shouted "Tear down the fence! tear down the fence!" Then came the sound of ripping and tearing and smashing, and down it went, with the front of the crowd starting to surge forward like a wave.

Just then Sherburn stepped out onto the roof of his small front porch, holding a double-barreled gun in his hand, and took his position, completely calm and deliberate, without saying a word. The noise stopped, and the crowd pulled back.

Sherburn didn't say anything—he just stood there, looking down. The silence was terribly eerie and uncomfortable. Sherburn slowly moved his gaze across the crowd; and wherever his eyes landed, people tried briefly to stare back at him, but they couldn't manage it; they lowered their eyes and looked guilty. Then after a moment Sherburn kind of laughed; not the pleasant type, but the kind that makes you feel like you're eating bread with sand in it.

Then he speaks, slowly and with contempt:

"The thought of you lynching anyone! It's ridiculous. The notion that you believe you have the courage to lynch a man! Just because you're bold enough to tar and feather poor helpless outcast women who wander through here, did that convince you that you possess the nerve to attack a man? Listen, a man is perfectly safe among ten thousand of your type—provided it's daylight and you're not sneaking up behind him."

"Do I know you? I know you completely. I was born and raised in the South, and I've lived in the North, so I understand the average person everywhere. The average person is a coward. In the North, people let anyone who wants to walk all over them, then go home and pray for the humility to endure it. In the South, one man acting alone has stopped a stagecoach full of passengers in broad daylight and robbed them all. Your newspapers tell you so often that you're brave people that you actually believe you're braver than everyone else—when really you're just as brave as anyone else, and no braver. Why don't your juries convict murderers? Because they're scared the killer's friends will shoot them in the back under cover of darkness—and that's exactly what those friends would do.

"So they always find the person not guilty; and then someone goes out at night, with a hundred masked cowards behind him and kills the criminal by hanging. Your mistake is that you didn't bring a real man with you; that's one mistake, and the other is that you didn't come in the darkness wearing your masks. You brought only part of a man—Buck Harkness, over there—and if you hadn't had him to get you started, you would have just talked big and done nothing.

"You didn't want to come. The ordinary person doesn't like trouble and danger. You don't like trouble and danger. But when just half a man—like Buck Harkness over there—shouts 'Lynch him! lynch him!' you're scared to back down—afraid you'll be exposed for what you really are—cowards—so you start yelling, and latch onto that half-man's coattails, and come charging up here, bragging about all the big things you're going to do. The most pathetic thing in the world is a mob; that's what an army is— a mob; they don't fight with courage that comes from within them, but with courage they borrow from their numbers and from their officers. But a mob without any leader is beyond pathetic. What you need to do now is tuck your tails between your legs and go home and hide in a hole. If any real lynching is going to happen, it will happen in the dark, Southern style; and when they come they'll bring their masks and bring a real man with them. Now get out—and take your half-man with you"—raising his gun across his left arm and cocking it as he says this.

The crowd suddenly surged backward, then completely scattered, rushing off in every direction, and Buck Harkness hurried after them, looking quite foolish. I could have stayed if I had wanted to, but I didn't want to.

I went to the circus and hung around the back until the security guard passed by, then slipped under the tent. I had my twenty-dollar gold coin and some other cash, but I figured I should save it, since you never know how quickly you might need money when you're far from home and surrounded by strangers like that. You can never be too cautious. I'm not against spending money on circuses when there's no other option, but there's no point in wasting it on them.

It was an absolutely magnificent circus. It was the most spectacular sight I had ever witnessed when they all came riding in, two by two, a gentleman and lady side by side, the men wearing only their underwear and undershirts, with no shoes or stirrups, resting their hands casually and comfortably on their thighs—there must have been twenty of them—and every lady had a beautiful complexion and was perfectly gorgeous, looking just like a group of real queens, dressed in clothing that cost millions of dollars and covered with diamonds. It was an incredibly wonderful sight; I had never seen anything so beautiful. And then one by one they stood up and began weaving around the ring so smoothly and gracefully, the men looking so tall and light and upright, with their heads bobbing and gliding along up there beneath the tent ceiling, and every lady's delicate dress flowing softly and silkily around her hips, making her look like the most beautiful parasol.

And then they moved faster and faster, all of them dancing, first putting one foot out in the air and then the other, with the horses leaning more and more, and the ringmaster going around and around the center pole, cracking his whip and shouting "Hi!—hi!" while the clown cracked jokes behind him; and gradually all the riders dropped their reins, and every lady put her hands on her hips and every gentleman folded his arms, and then how those horses did lean over and arch themselves! And so one after another they all jumped off into the ring, and made the most graceful bow I ever saw, and then rushed out, and everybody clapped their hands and went absolutely wild.

Throughout the entire circus performance, they did the most amazing things, and the whole time that clown kept everyone entertained so much it nearly killed the audience with laughter. The ringmaster couldn't say a single word to him without the clown firing back instantly with the funniest responses anyone had ever heard, and how he could think of so many clever comebacks so quickly and perfectly was something I couldn't understand at all. I couldn't have thought of those responses in a whole year. Eventually, a drunk man tried to get into the ring—he said he wanted to ride and claimed he could ride as well as anyone who ever lived. They argued and tried to keep him out, but he wouldn't listen, and the entire show came to a complete stop. Then the audience started yelling at him and making fun of him, which made him angry, and he started getting violent and destructive, which stirred up the crowd, and many men started climbing down from the benches and moving toward the ring, shouting, "Knock him down! Throw him out!" and a couple of women started screaming. So then the ringmaster gave a short speech, saying he hoped there wouldn't be any trouble, and if the man promised he wouldn't cause any more problems, he would let him ride if he thought he could stay on the horse. So everyone laughed and agreed, and the man got on. The moment he mounted, the horse started bucking and rearing and jumping and thrashing around, with two circus workers holding onto his bridle trying to control him, and the drunk man clinging to the horse's neck, with his feet flying through the air with every jump, and the entire crowd standing up shouting and laughing until tears streamed down their faces. And finally, despite everything the circus workers could do, the horse broke free and took off like lightning, racing around and around the ring, with that drunk man lying flat against him and holding onto his neck, with first one leg dangling almost to the ground on one side, then the other leg on the other side, and the people going absolutely wild. It wasn't funny to me, though; I was trembling with fear for his safety. But soon he managed to pull himself upright in the saddle and grabbed the bridle, swaying back and forth, and the next moment he jumped up and let go of the bridle and stood up while the horse was still racing like a house on fire. He just stood there, gliding around as easily and comfortably as if he had never been drunk in his life—and then he started removing his clothes and throwing them around. He shed them so rapidly they seemed to fill the air, and altogether he removed seventeen different outfits. And then, there he was, lean and handsome, dressed in the most colorful and beautiful costume you ever saw, and he started whipping that horse and made it really fly—and finally jumped off, took his bow, and danced away to the dressing room, while everyone roared with delight and amazement.

Then the ringmaster realized how he had been tricked, and he was the most embarrassed ringmaster you could ever imagine, I suppose. The whole thing was actually one of his own performers! The man had come up with that entire prank by himself and hadn't told anyone about it. Well, I felt foolish enough for being deceived like that, but I wouldn't have wanted to be in that ringmaster's position for a thousand dollars. I don't know if there might be better circuses than that one, but I've never encountered any. In any case, it was more than good enough for me, and whenever I come across it again, it will have my business every single time.

Well, that night we had our show, but there were only about twelve people there—just enough to cover expenses. And they laughed the entire time, which made the duke angry; and everyone left before the show was over anyway, except for one boy who had fallen asleep. So the duke said these Arkansas blockheads couldn't appreciate Shakespeare; what they wanted was lowbrow comedy—and maybe something even worse than lowbrow comedy, he figured. He said he could understand their taste. So the next morning he got some large sheets of wrapping paper and some black paint, and drew up some advertisements, and posted them all over the village. The flyers said:

AT THE COURT HOUSE!
FOR 3 NIGHTS ONLY!
The World-Renowned Tragedians
DAVID GARRICK THE YOUNGER!
AND
EDMUND KEAN THE ELDER!
Of the London and Continental Theatres,
In their Thrilling Tragedy of
THE KING'S CAMELOPARD
OR
THE ROYAL NONESUCH!!!
Admission 50 cents.

Then at the bottom was the biggest line of all—which said:
WOMEN AND CHILDREN NOT ALLOWED.

"There," he says, "if that line doesn't get them,
I don't know Arkansas!"

Chapter XXIII.

Well, all day long he and the king worked hard at it, setting up a stage and a curtain and a row of candles for footlights; and that night the house was packed full of men in no time. When the place couldn't hold any more, the duke stopped tending the door and went around the back way and came onto the stage and stood up before the curtain and made a little speech, and praised this tragedy, and said it was the most thrilling one that ever was; and so he went on bragging about the tragedy, and about Edmund Kean the Elder, who was to play the main principal part in it; and at last when he'd gotten everybody's expectations up high enough, he rolled up the curtain, and the next minute the king came prancing out on all fours, naked; and he was painted all over, ring-streaked-and-striped, all sorts of colors, as splendid as a rainbow. And—but never mind the rest of his outfit; it was just wild, but it was awfully funny. The people nearly killed themselves laughing; and when the king finished capering and capered off behind the scenes, they roared and clapped and cheered and laughed till he came back and did it over again, and after that they made him do it another time. Well, it would make a cow laugh to see the antics that old fool performed.

Then the duke lowered the curtain, bowed to the audience, and announced that the great tragedy would be performed for only two more nights due to urgent London commitments, where all the seats had already been sold at Drury Lane; then he bowed again and said that if he had managed to please and educate them, he would be deeply grateful if they would tell their friends about it and encourage them to come see the show.

Twenty people sing out:

"What, is it over? Is that all?"

The duke agrees. Then all hell breaks loose. Everyone yells "We've been tricked!" and jumps up furious, ready to storm the stage and go after those actors. But a big, impressive-looking man leaps up on a bench and shouts:

"Wait! Just one moment, gentlemen." They paused to hear him out. "We've been tricked—completely fooled. But I don't think we want to become the laughingstock of this entire town and never live this down for as long as we're alive. No. What we should do is leave here quietly, promote this show, and trick the rest of the town! Then we'll all be in the same situation. Doesn't that make sense?" ("Absolutely it does!—the judge is right!" everyone calls out.) "All right, then—not a single word about being fooled. Go on home, and tell everyone they should come see the tragedy."

The next day, all you could hear around that town was talk about how magnificent the show had been. The theater was packed again that night, and we fooled this audience the same way. When the king, the duke, and I returned to the raft, we all ate supper together; and later, around midnight, they had Jim and me push off and float down the middle of the river, then bring her in and hide her about two miles below town.

The third night the house was packed again—and these weren't newcomers this time, but people who had been at the show the other two nights. I stood beside the duke at the door, and I could see that every man who went in had his pockets bulging, or something wrapped up under his coat—and I could tell it wasn't perfume, not by a long shot. I smelled rotten eggs by the barrel, and spoiled cabbages, and things like that; and if I know the signs of a dead cat being around, and I'm sure I do, there were sixty-four of them that went in. I pushed in there for a minute, but it was too much for me; I couldn't stand it. Well, when the place couldn't hold any more people, the duke gave a fellow a quarter and told him to watch the door for him for a minute, and then he headed around toward the stage door, with me following him; but the moment we turned the corner and were in the dark, he says:

"Walk quickly now until you get away from the houses, and then run for the raft as fast as you can, like the devil himself is chasing you!"

I did it, and he did the same. We reached the raft at the same time, and in less than two seconds we were gliding downstream, everything dark and quiet, drifting toward the middle of the river with nobody saying a word. I figured the poor king was going to have a terrible time with the audience, but that wasn't the case at all; soon enough he crawled out from under the shelter and said:

"Well, how did the old thing work out this time, duke?"

He hadn't been to the city center at all.

We didn't show any light until we were about ten miles below the village. Then we lit up and had supper, and the king and the duke laughed so hard they nearly fell apart over how they had fooled those people. The duke says:

"Newcomers, fools! I knew the first audience would stay quiet and let the rest of the town get tricked; and I knew they'd wait for us on the third night, thinking it was their turn now. Well, it is their turn, and I'd give something to know how much they'd pay for it. I would just like to know how they're using their opportunity. They can turn it into a picnic if they want to—they brought plenty of food."

Those troublemakers made four hundred and sixty-five dollars during those three nights. I had never seen money brought in by the wagon-load like that before. Later, when they were asleep and snoring, Jim says:

"Doesn't it surprise you the way those kings carry on, Huck?"

"No," I said, "it doesn't."

"Why doesn't it, Huck?"

"Well, it doesn't, because it's in their nature. I think they're all the same."

"But, Huck, these kings of ours are complete scoundrels; that's exactly what they are; they're complete scoundrels."

"Well, that's what I'm saying; all kings are mostly scoundrels, as far as I can tell."

"Is that so?"

"You read about them once—you'll see. Look at Henry the Eighth; this one's a Sunday-school Superintendent compared to him. And look at Charles the Second, and Louis the Fourteenth, and Louis the Fifteenth, and James the Second, and Edward the Second, and Richard the Third, and forty more; besides all those Saxon kingdoms that used to rampage around so in old times and raise hell. My, you should have seen old Henry the Eighth when he was in his prime. He was something else. He used to marry a new wife every day, and chop off her head the next morning. And he would do it just as casually as if he was ordering up eggs. 'Bring up Nell Gwynn,' he says. They bring her up. Next morning, 'Chop off her head!' And they chop it off. 'Bring up Jane Shore,' he says; and up she comes. Next morning, 'Chop off her head'—and they chop it off. 'Call up Fair Rosamund.' Fair Rosamund answers the call. Next morning, 'Chop off her head.' And he made every one of them tell him a story every night; and he kept that up until he had collected a thousand and one tales that way, and then he put them all in a book, and called it Domesday Book—which was a good name and described the situation perfectly. You don't know kings, Jim, but I know them; and this old scoundrel of ours is one of the most decent I've encountered in history. Well, Henry gets the idea he wants to stir up some trouble with this country. How does he go about it—give notice?—give the country a fair chance? No. All of a sudden he throws all the tea in Boston Harbor overboard, and puts out a declaration of independence, and dares them to come fight. That was his style—he never gave anybody a chance. He had suspicions about his father, the Duke of Wellington. Well, what did he do? Ask him to explain? No—drowned him in a barrel of wine, like a cat. Suppose people left money lying around where he was—what did he do? He grabbed it. Suppose he agreed to do something, and you paid him, and didn't sit there and make sure he did it—what did he do? He always did the opposite. Suppose he opened his mouth—what then? If he didn't shut it up real quick he'd let out a lie every time. That's the kind of character Henry was; and if we'd had him along instead of our kings he would have fooled that town a lot worse than ours did. I don't say that ours are saints, because they aren't, when you get right down to the hard facts; but they're nothing compared to that old devil, anyway. All I'm saying is, kings are kings, and you have to make allowances. Take them all together, they're a pretty worthless bunch. It's the way they're brought up."

"But this one smells so much like the real thing, Huck."

"Well, they all do, Jim. We can't help the way a king smells; history doesn't tell us otherwise."

"Now the duke, he's a reasonably promising man in some ways."

"Yes, a duke is different. But not very different. This one's a moderately tough character for a duke. When he's drunk, no nearsighted person could mistake him for anything other than a king."

"Well, anyway, I don't want any more of them, Huck. These are all I can stand."

"That's exactly how I feel too, Jim. But we're stuck dealing with them, and we have to keep in mind what they're like and make excuses for their behavior. Sometimes I wish we could find a country that doesn't have any kings."

What was the point of telling Jim that these weren't real kings and dukes? It wouldn't have done any good; and besides, it was just like I said: you couldn't tell them apart from the genuine ones.

I went to sleep, and Jim didn't call me when it was my turn. He often did that. When I woke up just at daybreak, he was sitting there with his head down between his knees, moaning and mourning to himself. I didn't take notice or let on. I knew what it was about. He was thinking about his wife and his children, away up there, and he was low and homesick; because he had never been away from home before in his life; and I do believe he cared just as much for his people as white folks do for theirs. It doesn't seem natural, but I reckon it's so. He was often moaning and mourning that way at night, when he thought I was asleep, and saying, "Poor little Elizabeth! Poor little Johnny! It's mighty hard; I expect I'm never going to see you anymore, no more!" He was a mighty good man, Jim was.

But this time I somehow ended up talking with him about his wife and children; and eventually he says:

"What makes me feel so terrible this time is because I heard something over there on the bank like a whack, or a slam, a while ago, and it reminded me of the time I treated my little Elizabeth so badly. She was only about four years old, and she caught scarlet fever, and had a very rough time; but she got well, and one day she was standing around, and I said to her, I said:

"'Shut the door.'"

"She never did it; just stood there, kind of smiling up at me. It made me mad; and I said again, very loud, I said:

"'Don't you hear me?—shut the door!'"

"She just stood there the same way, kind of smiling up. I was boiling mad! I said:

"'I swear I will make you mine!'"

"And with that I gave her a slap on the side of her head that sent her sprawling. Then I went into the other room and was gone about ten minutes; and when I came back there was that door standing open still, and that child standing almost right in it, looking down and mourning, and the tears running down. My, but I was mad! I was going for the child, but just then—it was a door that opened inward—just then, along came the wind and slammed it shut, behind the child, ker-blam!—and my Lord, the child never moved! My breath almost jumped out of me; and I felt so—so— I don't know how I felt. I crept out, all trembling, and crept around and opened the door easy and slow, and poked my head in behind the child, soft and still, and all of a sudden I said pow! just as loud as I could yell. She never budged! Oh, Huck, I burst out crying and grabbed her up in my arms, and said, 'Oh, the poor little thing! The Lord God Almighty forgive poor old Jim, because he's never going to forgive himself as long as he lives!' Oh, she was completely deaf and mute, Huck, completely deaf and mute—and I'd been treating her so!"

Chapter XXIV.

The next day, as evening approached, we anchored beneath a small willow sandbar in the middle of the river, with a village on each side, and the duke and the king began planning how to work those towns. Jim spoke to the duke and said he hoped it wouldn't take more than a few hours, because it became extremely uncomfortable and exhausting for him to lie in the wigwam all day tied up with rope. You see, whenever we left him alone, we had to tie him up, because if anyone came across him by himself and untied, it wouldn't look like he was a runaway slave, you understand. So the duke said it was rather harsh to have to lie there bound all day, and he would figure out some way to solve the problem.

The duke was exceptionally clever, and he quickly came up with an idea. He dressed Jim in King Lear's costume—a long curtain-calico gown with a white horsehair wig and whiskers. Then he used his theater makeup to paint Jim's face, hands, ears, and neck completely blue—a dead, dull, solid blue color, like someone who had drowned nine days ago. I swear he was the most horrible-looking sight I had ever seen. After that, the duke wrote out a sign on a wooden shingle that read:

Sick Arab—but harmless when not out of his mind.

He attached the shingle to a wooden strip and positioned it four or five feet in front of the shelter. Jim felt pleased with the arrangement. He mentioned it was much better than being tied up for hours each day and shaking with fear whenever he heard any noise. The duke advised him to relax and feel comfortable, and if anyone came around causing trouble, he should jump out of the shelter, put on a show, and let out a howl or two like a wild animal, figuring that would scare them off and make them leave him alone.

This seemed like reasonable thinking; however, most people wouldn't even wait around long enough to hear him howl. The truth was, he didn't just appear dead—he looked far worse than that.

These troublemakers wanted to try the Nonesuch show again because there was so much money to be made from it, but they figured it wouldn't be safe since the news might have spread by now. They couldn't come up with any scheme that seemed just right, so finally the duke said he thought he'd take a break and think for an hour or two to see if he could come up with something for the Arkansas village. The king said he would head over to the other village without any plan, just trusting Providence to guide him toward profit—though I suspect he meant the devil. We had all bought regular clothes at our last stop, and now the king put his on and told me to put mine on. I did it, naturally. The king's outfit was all black, and he looked really elegant and formal. I had never realized how much clothes could transform a person before. Why, earlier he had looked like the most worthless old scoundrel that ever lived, but now, when he would tip his new white hat and bow and smile, he looked so dignified and virtuous and holy that you'd think he had walked straight out of the ark, and might even be old Leviticus himself. Jim cleaned up the canoe, and I got my paddle ready. There was a large steamboat docked at the shore way up past the point, about three miles above the town—it had been there for a couple of hours, loading cargo. The king says:

"Given how I'm dressed, I think it would be better if I arrived from St. Louis or Cincinnati, or some other major city. Head to the steamboat, Huckleberry; we'll ride it down to the village."

I didn't need to be told twice to go take a steamboat ride. I reached the shore about half a mile upstream from the village, then cruised along the steep riverbank in the calm water. Before long we came across a harmless-looking young country fellow sitting on a log wiping the sweat from his face, since it was extremely hot weather; and he had a couple of large travel bags beside him.

"Steer her nose toward shore," says the king. I did it. "Where are you headed, young man?"

"For the steamboat; going to Orleans."

"Get on board," the king says. "Wait just a moment, my servant will help you with those bags. Jump out and help the gentleman, Adolphus"—he was referring to me, I could see.

I did so, and then all three of us started walking again. The young man was extremely grateful and said it was hard work carrying his luggage in such weather. He asked the king where he was headed, and the king told him he had come down the river and arrived at the other village that morning, and now he was traveling up a few miles to visit an old friend on a farm up there. The young fellow says:

"When I first saw you, I said to myself, 'That's Mr. Wilks for sure, and he almost made it here on time.' But then I thought again, 'No, I don't think it's him, or else he wouldn't be rowing up the river.' You're not him, are you?"

"No, my name is Blodgett—Alexander Blodgett—Reverend Alexander Blodgett, I suppose I should say, since I'm one of the Lord's humble servants. But I'm still just as capable of feeling sorry for Mr. Wilks for not arriving on time, all the same, if he's missed anything because of it—which I hope he hasn't."

"Well, he doesn't lose any property because of it, since he'll get all of that anyway; but he missed seeing his brother Peter die—which might not bother him, nobody can say for sure about that—but his brother would have given anything in this world to see him before he passed away; never talked about anything else for these past three weeks; hadn't seen him since they were boys together—and had never seen his brother William at all—that's the deaf and mute one—William isn't more than thirty or thirty-five years old. Peter and George were the only ones who came out here; George was the married brother; he and his wife both died last year. Harvey and William are the only ones left now; and, as I was saying, they didn't get here in time."

"Did anyone tell them?"

"Oh, yes; a month or two ago, when Peter first got sick; because Peter said then that he sort of felt like he wasn't going to get well this time. You see, he was pretty old, and George's girls were too young to be much company for him, except Mary Jane, the red-headed one; and so he was kind of lonely after George and his wife died, and didn't seem to care much about living. He desperately wanted to see Harvey—and William, too, for that matter—because he was one of those people who can't bear to make a will. He left a letter behind for Harvey, and said he'd explained in it where his money was hidden, and how he wanted the rest of the property divided up so George's girls would be all right—because George didn't leave anything. And that letter was all they could get him to put a pen to."

"Why do you think Harvey isn't coming? Where does he live?"

"Oh, he lives in England—Sheffield—preaches there—has never been to this country. He hasn't had much time—and besides, he might not have received the letter at all, you know."

"It's such a shame he couldn't live to see his brothers, poor soul. You said you're going to Orleans?"

"Yes, but that's only part of it. I'm sailing on a ship next Wednesday to Rio de Janeiro, where my uncle lives."

"It's quite a long trip. But it will be wonderful; I wish I were going. Is Mary Jane the oldest? How old are the others?"

"Mary Jane is nineteen, Susan is fifteen, and Joanna is about fourteen—she's the one who devotes herself to charitable work and has a cleft lip."

"Poor things! To be left all alone in such a cold world."

"Well, they could be in a worse situation. Old Peter had friends, and they're not going to let them come to any harm. There's

Hobson, the Baptist preacher; and Deacon Lot Hovey, and Ben Rucker, and Abner Shackleford, and Levi Bell, the lawyer; and Dr. Robinson, and their wives, and the widow Bartley, and—well, there are many of them; but these are the ones that Peter was closest with, and used to write about sometimes, when he wrote home; so Harvey will know where to look for friends when he arrives."

Well, the old man kept asking questions until he had completely drained that young fellow of information. I'll be damned if he didn't ask about every single person and everything in that entire town, and all about the Wilks family; and about Peter's work—which was tanning leather; and about George's job—which was carpentry; and about Harvey's profession—which was being a dissenting minister; and so on, and so on. Then he says:

"Why did you want to walk all the way up to the steamboat?"

"Because she's a large Orleans steamboat, and I was worried she might not stop there. When they're riding deep in the water they won't stop when you call out to them. A Cincinnati boat will stop, but this one's from St. Louis."

"Was Peter Wilks wealthy?"

"Oh, yes, he was quite well off. He owned houses and land, and people estimate he left three or four thousand dollars in cash hidden somewhere."

"When did you say he died?"

"I didn't say, but it was last night."

"Funeral tomorrow, probably?"

"Yes, around the middle of the day."

"Well, it's all terribly sad; but we all have to go at some point. So what we need to do is be prepared; then we'll be fine."

"Yes, sir, it's the best way. Mom always used to say that."

When we reached the boat, it was nearly finished loading, and before long it departed. The king didn't say anything about getting on board, so I ended up losing my ride after all. After the boat left, the king had me paddle upstream for another mile to an isolated spot, and then he stepped ashore and said:

"Now hurry back immediately and bring the duke up here, along with the new carpet bags. And if he's gone over to the other side, go over there and get him. And tell him to get himself up here no matter what. Get moving now."

I could see what he was planning, but I didn't say anything, naturally. When I returned with the duke, we hid the canoe, and then they sat down on a log, and the king told him everything, exactly like the young man had described it—every single word of it. And the entire time he was doing this, he tried to speak like an Englishman, and he did it quite well, too, for someone so careless. I can't imitate him, and so I'm not going to try, but he really did it pretty well. Then he says:

"How are you at playing deaf and mute, Bilgewater?"

The duke said to leave him alone for that; he mentioned that he had played a deaf and mute person on the theatrical stage. So then they waited for a steamboat.

Around the middle of the afternoon, a couple of small boats came by, but they hadn't come from far enough up the river; finally, though, there was a large one, and they called out to her. She sent out her small boat, and we went aboard, and she was from Cincinnati; when they discovered we only wanted to go four or five miles, they were extremely angry and cursed at us, saying they wouldn't let us off at our destination. But the king remained calm. He says:

"If gentlemen can afford to pay a dollar per mile each to be picked up and dropped off by a small boat, then a steamboat can afford to carry them, can't it?"

So they calmed down and said everything was fine; and when we reached the village they rowed us to shore. About two dozen men gathered around when they saw the small boat approaching, and when the king said:

"Can any of you gentlemen tell me where Mr. Peter Wilks lives?" They exchanged glances with one another and nodded their heads, as if to say, "What did I tell you?" Then one of them spoke in a soft and gentle voice:

"I'm sorry sir, but the best we can do is tell you where he was living yesterday evening."

Suddenly, as quick as a blink, the stubborn old creature completely broke down and collapsed against the man, resting his chin on his shoulder and crying down his back, saying:

"Oh no, oh no, our poor brother is gone, and we never had the chance to see him; this is just too, too painful!"

Then he turns around, sobbing, and makes a bunch of ridiculous gestures to the duke with his hands, and I'll be damned if he didn't drop a carpet bag and burst out crying. If they weren't the most pathetic pair, those two con artists, that I'd ever encountered.

Well, the men gathered around and showed sympathy for them, saying all kinds of compassionate things to them, and carried their travel bags up the hill for them, and let them lean on them and weep, and told the king all about his brother's final moments, and the king repeated it all over again using hand gestures to the duke, and both of them grieved over that dead leather worker as if they had lost the twelve apostles. Well, if I ever encountered anything like it, I'll be damned. It was enough to make a person ashamed of the human race.

Chapter XXV.

The news spread throughout the entire town within two minutes, and you could see people rushing down the streets from every direction, some of them still putting on their coats as they ran.

Before long we found ourselves in the middle of a crowd, and the sound of all the footsteps was like soldiers marching. The windows and front yards were packed with people; and every minute someone would call out over a fence:

"Is it them?"

And someone jogging along with the group would respond and say:

"You bet it is."

When we reached the house, the street in front of it was crowded, and the three girls were standing in the doorway. Mary Jane had red hair, but that didn't matter because she was absolutely beautiful, and her face and eyes were glowing with joy since she was so happy that her uncles had arrived. The king spread his arms wide, and Mary Jane jumped into them, while the girl with the cleft lip jumped toward the duke, and there they embraced! Almost everyone, especially the women, cried tears of joy to see them reunited at last and sharing such wonderful moments together.

Then the king nudged the duke privately—I saw him do it—and then he looked around and spotted the coffin over in the corner resting on two chairs. So then he and the duke, with one hand across each other's shoulder and the other hand covering their eyes, walked slowly and solemnly over there. Everyone stepped back to give them space, and all the talking and noise stopped, with people whispering "Shh!" and all the men removing their hats and bowing their heads, so quiet you could have heard a pin drop. When they reached the coffin, they bent over and looked inside, took one look, and then burst into such loud crying that you could have heard them all the way to New Orleans. Then they wrapped their arms around each other's necks and rested their chins on each other's shoulders. For three or maybe four minutes, I had never seen two men cry the way they did. And keep in mind, everyone else was doing the same thing, and the place was so damp with tears I had never seen anything like it. Then one of them positioned himself on one side of the coffin and the other on the opposite side, and they knelt down and rested their foreheads on the coffin, pretending to pray silently to themselves. Well, when it came to that, it affected the crowd like nothing I had ever seen, and everyone broke down and started sobbing out loud—including the poor girls. Nearly every woman went up to the girls without saying a word and kissed them solemnly on the forehead, then placed their hand on their heads and looked up toward the sky with tears streaming down their faces, then burst out crying and walked away sobbing and wiping their eyes, making room for the next woman. I had never seen anything so disgusting.

Eventually, the king stands up and steps forward a bit, working himself into an emotional state and delivering a tearful speech filled with nonsense about how difficult it is for him and his poor brother to lose the deceased, and how heartbreaking it is to miss seeing the deceased alive after their long journey of four thousand miles, but it's a hardship that's made sweeter and more meaningful by this precious sympathy and these sacred tears, and so he thanks them from his heart and from his brother's heart, because they can't express it with their mouths, words being too inadequate and emotionless, and all that kind of garbage and sentimentality, until it was absolutely nauseating; and then he sobs out a sanctimonious, overly pious Amen, and lets himself go completely and starts crying uncontrollably.

As soon as he finished speaking, someone in the crowd started singing the doxology, and everyone joined in with tremendous enthusiasm, which warmed your heart and made you feel as wonderful as leaving church on Sunday. Music truly is a beautiful thing; after all that smooth talk and nonsense, I had never seen anything refresh the atmosphere so completely or sound so genuine and uplifting.

Then the king starts working his jaw again and says that he and his nieces would be happy if some of the main close friends of the family would have supper here with them this evening and help keep watch over the remains of the deceased. He says that if his poor brother lying over there could speak, he knows who he would choose, because these were names that meant a lot to him and were mentioned frequently in his letters. So he will name the same people, which are as follows: Reverend Mr. Hobson, and Deacon Lot Hovey, and Mr. Ben Rucker, and Abner Shackleford, and Levi Bell, and Dr. Robinson, and their wives, and the widow Bartley.

Reverend Hobson and Doctor Robinson were down at the end of town hunting together—that is, I mean the doctor was helping a sick man pass to the other world, and the preacher was guiding him properly. Lawyer Bell was away up in Louisville on business. But the rest were present, and so they all came and shook hands with the king and thanked him and spoke with him; and then they shook hands with the duke and said nothing, but just kept smiling and nodding their heads like a bunch of fools while he made all kinds of gestures with his hands and said "Goo-goo—goo-goo-goo" the whole time, like a baby who can't speak.

So the king kept talking and managed to ask about practically everyone and their dog in town by name, and he brought up all kinds of small incidents that had happened at one time or another in the town, or to George's family, or to Peter. And he always pretended that Peter had written him about these things; but that was a lie: he had gotten every single one of them from that young fool we had paddled up to the steamboat with.

Then Mary Jane brought out the letter her father had left behind, and the king read it aloud while crying over it. The letter gave the house and three thousand dollars in gold to the girls, and it gave the tannery (which was running a profitable business), along with some other houses and land (worth about seven thousand dollars), and three thousand dollars in gold to Harvey and William. It also explained where the six thousand dollars in cash was hidden down in the cellar. So these two con men said they would go and bring it up, and make everything honest and transparent; they told me to come along with a candle. We closed the cellar door behind us, and when they found the bag they dumped it out on the floor, and it was a beautiful sight, all those gold coins. My goodness, how the king's eyes lit up! He slapped the duke on the shoulder and said:

"Oh, this isn't great or anything! Oh, no, I don't think so! Why, Billy, it's better than the Nonesuch, isn't it?"

The duke agreed that it did. They handled the gold coins, running them through their fingers and letting them jingle as they fell to the floor; and the king says:

"There's no point in arguing; being brothers to a wealthy dead man and representatives of foreign heirs who have been left behind is the path for you and me, Bilge. This here comes from trusting in Providence. It's the best approach in the long run. I've tried them all, and there isn't a better way."

Most everyone would have been satisfied with the pile of money and taken it on trust, but no, they had to count it. So they counted it, and it came out four hundred and fifteen dollars short. The king said:

"Damn him, I wonder what he did with that four hundred and fifteen dollars?"

They spent some time worrying about that and searched everywhere for it. Then the duke said:

"Well, he was quite ill, and he probably made an error—I think that's what happened. The best approach is to let it go and stay quiet about it. We can afford to overlook it."

"Oh, sure, yes, we can spare it. I don't care anything about that—it's the count I'm thinking about. We want to be completely honest and open and above-board here, you know. We want to carry this money upstairs and count it in front of everybody—then there isn't anything suspicious. But when the dead man says there's six thousand dollars, you know, we don't want to—"

"Wait," the duke says. "Let's make up the difference," and he started pulling gold coins out of his pocket.

"That's an absolutely brilliant idea, duke—you've got a really sharp mind," says the king. "I'll be damned if the old Royal Nonesuch isn't helping us out again," and he started pulling out gold coins and stacking them up.

They nearly went broke doing it, but they managed to come up with the full six thousand dollars, completely paid and accounted for.

"Listen," the duke says, "I have another idea. Let's go upstairs and count this money, then take it and give it to the girls."

"Good heavens, duke, let me hug you! It's the most brilliant idea that any man ever came up with. You certainly have the most amazing mind I've ever seen. Oh, this is the perfect scheme, there's no doubt about it. Let them bring their suspicions now if they want to—this will put them to rest."

When we went upstairs, everyone gathered around the table, and the king counted the money and stacked it up—three hundred dollars in a pile, making twenty elegant little piles. Everyone stared at it hungrily and licked their lips. Then they raked it back into the bag, and I saw the king start to puff himself up for another speech. He said:

"Friends, my poor brother lying over there was generous to those he left behind in this valley of sorrows. He was generous to these poor little children that he loved and cared for, who are now left without father or mother. Yes, and those of us who knew him understand that he would have been even more generous to them if he hadn't been afraid of hurting his dear William and me. Wouldn't he have? There's no question about it in my mind. Well then, what kind of brothers would we be to stand in his way at such a time? And what kind of uncles would we be to rob—yes, rob—such poor sweet children that he loved so much at such a time? If I know William—and I think I do—he—well, I'll just ask him." He turns around and begins making many hand gestures to the duke, and the duke looks at him confused and bewildered for a while; then suddenly he seems to understand what he means, and jumps toward the king, making excited sounds with all his energy out of joy, and hugs him about fifteen times before he stops. Then the king says, "I knew it; I think that will convince anyone how he feels about it. Here, Mary Jane, Susan, Joanna, take the money— take it all. It's the gift from him who lies over there, cold but at peace."

Mary Jane rushed to him, while Susan and the girl with the cleft lip hurried to the duke, and then I witnessed such embracing and kissing as I had never seen before. Everyone gathered around with tears streaming down their faces, and nearly shook the hands clean off those con artists, saying the whole time:

"You wonderful, kind people! How beautiful! How could you possibly do this!"

Well, then, pretty soon everyone started talking about the deceased again, discussing how good he was, what a loss he was, and all that; and before long a big iron-jawed man pushed his way in there from outside, and stood listening and looking, without saying anything; and nobody said anything to him either, because the king was talking and they were all busy listening. The king was saying—in the middle of something he had started discussing—

"—they being particular friends of the deceased. That's why they're invited here this evening; but tomorrow we want everyone to come—everybody; for he respected everybody, he liked everybody, and so it's fitting that his funeral ceremonies should be public."

And so he continued rambling on and on, enjoying the sound of his own voice, and every now and then he brought up his funeral orgies again, until the duke couldn't tolerate it anymore; so he writes on a small piece of paper, "obsequies, you old fool," and folds it up, and starts making gestures and reaching it over people's heads to him. The king reads it and puts it in his pocket, and says:

"Poor William, troubled as he is, his heart is always in the right place. He asks me to invite everyone to come to the funeral—he wants me to make them all feel welcome. But he didn't need to worry about that—it was exactly what I was planning to do."

Then he weaves along again, perfectly calm, and goes back to dropping in his funeral orgies every now and then, just like he had done before. And when he did it the third time he says:

"I say orgies, not because it's the common term, because it isn't—obsequies being the common term—but because orgies is the right term. Obsequies aren't used in England anymore now—it's gone out. We say orgies now in England. Orgies is better, because it means the thing you're after more exactly. It's a word that's made up out of the Greek orgo, outside, open, abroad; and the Hebrew jeesum, to plant, cover up; hence inter. So, you see, funeral orgies is an open or public funeral."

He was the worst person I had ever encountered. Well, that iron-jawed man just laughed right in his face. Everyone was shocked. Everyone said, "Why, doctor!" and Abner Shackleford said:

"Why, Robinson, haven't you heard the news? This is Harvey Wilks."

The king smiled eagerly, extended his hand, and said:

"Is it my poor brother's dear good friend and physician? I—"

"Keep your hands off me!" the doctor says. "You talk like an Englishman, don't you? That's the worst imitation I've ever heard. You claim to be Peter Wilks's brother! You're a fraud, that's what you are!"

Well, what a commotion they all made! They gathered around the doctor and tried to calm him down, attempting to explain to him how Harvey had proven in forty different ways that he was indeed Harvey, and knew everyone by name, including the names of their dogs, and they pleaded with him not to hurt Harvey's feelings or the poor girl's feelings, and all of that. But it was no use; he continued his angry tirade, declaring that any man who claimed to be an Englishman but couldn't imitate the accent any better than he did was a fraud and a liar. The poor girls were clinging to the king and crying; and suddenly the doctor turned on them. He says:

"I was your father's friend, and I'm your friend too. As someone who cares about you and wants to keep you safe from harm and trouble, I'm warning you to turn your back on that scoundrel and stay away from him—that ignorant drifter with his ridiculous Greek and Hebrew, as he pretends it to be. He's nothing but a fraud of the worst kind—he's shown up here with a bunch of meaningless names and facts that he picked up somewhere, and you're treating them as proof, fooling yourselves with help from these misguided friends here who should know better. Mary Jane Wilks, you know I'm your friend, and that I care about you without any selfish motives. Now listen to me carefully—throw this pathetic con man out. I'm begging you to do it. Will you?"

Mary Jane stood up straight, and wow, she was beautiful! She said:

"Here is my answer." She lifted up the bag of money and placed it in the king's hands, saying, "Take this six thousand dollars, and invest it for me and my sisters however you want to, and don't give us any receipt for it."

Then she wrapped her arm around the king on one side, while Susan and the girl with the cleft lip did the same on the other side. Everyone clapped their hands and stomped on the floor like a thunderous storm, while the king held his head high and smiled with pride. The doctor said:

"All right; I wash my hands of the matter. But I warn you all that a time is coming when you're going to feel sick whenever you think of this day." And away he went.

"All right, doctor," the king said, somewhat mockingly, "we'll try to get them to send for you," which made everyone laugh, and they said it was an excellent joke.

***

Chapter XXVI.

Well, when they had all left, the king asked Mary Jane about their available spare rooms, and she said she had one spare room that would work for Uncle William, and she would give her own room to Uncle Harvey since it was a little larger, and she would move in with her sisters and sleep on a cot; and upstairs in the attic was a small room with a bed in it. The king said the small room would work for his servant—meaning me.

So Mary Jane led us upstairs and showed them their rooms, which were simple but pleasant. She offered to remove her dresses and various other belongings from her room if they would be in Uncle Harvey's way, but he assured her they wouldn't be a problem. The dresses hung along the wall, with a calico curtain in front of them that reached down to the floor. An old hair-covered trunk sat in one corner, a guitar case in another, and all kinds of small decorative items and trinkets were scattered around, the way girls brighten up a room. The king said all these personal touches made the room feel more homelike and welcoming, so she shouldn't move anything. The duke's room was quite small, but perfectly adequate, and my little space was fine too.

That night they had a large dinner, and all the men and women were there, and I stood behind the king and the duke's chairs and served them, and the servants waited on the rest. Mary Jane sat at the head of the table, with Susan beside her, and complained about how terrible the biscuits were, and how awful the preserves were, and how nasty and tough the fried chicken was—and all that kind of nonsense, the way women always do to fish for compliments;

and everyone knew everything was excellent, and said so—said "How do you get biscuits to brown so beautifully?" and "Where on earth did you get these amazing pickles?" and all that kind of fake small talk, just the way people always do at a dinner, you know.

And when everything was finished, the girl with the cleft lip and I had supper in the kitchen, eating the leftovers while the others were helping the servants clean up. The girl with the cleft lip started questioning me about England, and I'll be damned if I didn't think I was on thin ice sometimes. She says:

"Did you ever see the king?"

"Who? William Fourth? Well, I'm sure I have—he attends our church." I knew he had been dead for years, but I didn't let on. So when I said he goes to our church, she said:

"What—regular?"

"Yes—regular. His pew is right across from ours—on the other side of the pulpit."

"I thought he lived in London?"

"Well, he does. Where would he live?"

"But I thought you lived in Sheffield?"

I could see I was completely stuck. I had to pretend to choke on a chicken bone to buy myself some time to figure out how to get out of this situation. Then I said:

"I mean he attends our church regularly when he's in Sheffield. That's only during the summer, when he comes there to take the sea baths."

"Why, what are you talking about—Sheffield isn't on the sea."

"Well, who said it was?"

"Why, you did."

"I didn't either."

"You did!"

"I didn't."

"You did."

"I never said anything like that."

"Well, what did you say, then?"

"He said he came to take the sea baths—that's what I said."

"Well, then, how is he going to take the sea baths if it's not on the sea?"

"Look here," I said, "have you ever seen any Congress-water?"

"Yes."

"Well, did you have to go to Congress to get it?"

"Why, no."

"Well, King William IV doesn't need to travel to the ocean just to take a sea bath either."

"How does he get it, then?"

"Gets it the same way people down here get mineral water—delivered in barrels. There in the palace at Sheffield they have furnaces, and he wants his water heated. They can't boil that much water way out there by the sea. They don't have the right equipment for it."

"Oh, I understand now. You could have said that from the beginning and saved us some time."

When she said that, I could see I was out of trouble again, and I felt comfortable and relieved. Then she said:

"Do you go to church, too?"

"Yes—regular."

"Where do you set?"

"Why, in our pew."

"Whose pew?"

"Why, ours—your Uncle Harvey's."

"His? What does he want with a pew?"

"Wants it to take hold. What do you think he wanted with it?"

"Why, I thought he'd be in the pulpit."

"Darn it, I forgot he was a preacher. I could see I was stuck again, so I stalled for time and tried to think of something. Then I said:"

"Darn it, do you think there's only one preacher per church?"

"Why, what do they want with more?"

"What! Preach in front of a king? I've never seen a girl like you. They have no fewer than seventeen."

"Seventeen! Good heavens! I would never attempt such an elaborate display, not even if my life depended on it. It must take them an entire week to set up."

"Well, they don't all preach on the same day—only one of them."

"Well, then, what does the rest of them do?"

"Oh, nothing much. Hang around, pass the collection plate—and this and that. But mostly they don't do anything."

"Well, then, what are they for?"

"Why, they're for style. Don't you know anything?"

"Well, I don't want to hear any such nonsense as that. How are servants treated in England? Do they treat them better than we treat our slaves?"

"No! A servant is nobody there. They treat them worse than dogs."

"Don't they give them holidays like we do—Christmas, New Year's week, and the Fourth of July?"

"Oh, just listen! Anyone could tell you've never been to England by saying that. Why, Hare-l—why, Joanna, they never see a holiday from one year's end to the next; they never go to the circus, or the theater, or minstrel shows, or anywhere."

"Nor church?"

"Nor church."

"But you always went to church."

Well, I was back to my old ways again. I forgot I was supposed to be the old man's servant. But the next minute I jumped into some kind of explanation about how a valet was different from a regular servant and had to go to church whether he wanted to or not, and sit with the family, because that was the law. But I didn't

197

do it very well, and when I finished I could see she wasn't satisfied. She says:

"I swear, haven't you been telling me a bunch of lies?"

"I swear it's true," I said.

"None of it at all?"

"None of it at all. Not a lie in it," I said.

"Place your hand on this book and say it."

I saw it was nothing but a dictionary, so I placed my hand on it and said it. Then she looked a little more satisfied, and said:

"Well, then, I'll believe some of it; but I hope to gracious if I'll believe the rest."

"What is it you won't believe, Joe?" Mary Jane asks, walking in with Susan right behind her. "It's not right or kind for you to speak to him like that, especially when he's a stranger and so far away from his family. How would you feel if someone treated you that way?"

"That's always how you are, Ma'am—always rushing in to help someone before they're even hurt. I haven't done anything to him. He's told some lies, I think, and I said I wouldn't believe all of it; and that's absolutely everything I said. I think he can handle a little thing like that, can't he?"

"I don't care whether it was little or whether it was big; he's here in our house and a stranger, and it wasn't good of you to say it. If you were in his place it would make you feel ashamed; and so you shouldn't say a thing to another person that will make them feel ashamed."

"Why, Mom, he said—"

"It doesn't matter what he said—that's not the point. The point is for you to treat him kindly, and not say things that remind him he's not in his own country among his own people."

I said to myself, this is a girl whose money I'm letting that old snake steal from her!

Then Susan waltzed right in, and believe me, she really gave Hare-lip a serious scolding!

"I tell myself, here's another situation where I'm allowing him to steal her money!"

Then Mary Jane took another turn and spoke sweetly and lovingly again—which was her usual way; but when she finished, there was hardly anything left of poor Hare-lip. So she cried out.

"All right, then," the other girls say; "you just ask for his forgiveness."

She did it, too; and she did it beautifully. She did it so beautifully that it was wonderful to hear; and I wished I could tell her a thousand lies, so she could do it again.

I told myself, this is another situation where I'm letting him steal her money. And when she finished, they all went out of their way to make me feel at home and let me know I was among friends. I felt so guilty and low-down and terrible that I said to myself, my mind's made up; I'll get that money back for them or die trying.

So then I headed off—to bed, I said, meaning sometime or other. When I was alone I started thinking the whole thing through. I said to myself, should I go to that doctor privately and expose these con artists? No—that wouldn't work. He might reveal who told him; then the king and the duke would make things difficult for me. Should I go privately and tell Mary Jane? No—I wouldn't dare do it. Her expression would tip them off for sure; they have the money, and they'd slip away immediately and escape with it. If she brought in help I'd get tangled up in the mess before it was over, I figured. No; there's no good approach except one. I have to steal that money somehow; and I have to steal it in a way that they won't suspect I did it. They have a profitable scheme here, and they're not going to leave until they've swindled this family and this town for everything they're worth, so I'll find an opportunity soon enough. I'll steal it and hide it; and later, when I'm far down the river, I'll write a letter and tell Mary Jane where it's hidden. But I'd better grab it tonight if I can, because the doctor might not have backed down as much as he pretends he has; he might still frighten them away from here.

So, I thought to myself, I'll go and search those rooms. Upstairs the hallway was dark, but I found the duke's room and started feeling around it with my hands; but I remembered it wouldn't be much like the king to let anyone else take care of that money except himself; so then I went to his room and began feeling around there. But I could see I couldn't do anything without a candle, and I didn't dare light one, of course. So I figured I'd have to do the other thing—wait for them and listen in. About that time I heard their footsteps coming, and was going to slip under the bed; I reached for it, but it wasn't where I thought it would be; but I touched the curtain that hid Mary Jane's dresses, so I jumped in behind that and nestled in among the gowns, and stood there perfectly still.

They walked in and closed the door behind them, and the first thing the duke did was get down on his hands and knees to look under the bed. I was relieved then that I hadn't found the bed when I was looking for a hiding spot earlier. Still, you know how it is—it's only natural to think about hiding under the bed when you're doing something you don't want others to see. After that, they both sat down, and the king said:

"Well, what is it? And keep it fairly short, because it's better for us to be down there stirring up the mourning than up here giving them a chance to talk about us."

"Well, this is it, Capet. I'm not at ease; I'm not comfortable. That doctor weighs on my mind. I wanted to know your plans. I have an idea, and I think it's a good one."

"What is it, duke?"

"We should slip away from here before three in the morning and head down the river with what we have. Especially since we got it so easily—handed back to us, practically thrown at us, you could say, when we naturally expected we'd have to steal it back. I'm in favor of calling it quits and getting out of here."

That made me feel really terrible. Just an hour or two earlier, it would have affected me differently, but now it left me feeling awful and let down. The king burst out and said:

"What! And not sell the rest of the property? March off like a bunch of fools and leave eight or nine thousand dollars' worth of property lying around just waiting to be scooped up?—and all good, sellable stuff, too."

The duke grumbled, saying the bag of gold was enough, and he didn't want to go any deeper—he didn't want to rob a bunch of orphans of everything they had.

"Why, how you talk!" says the king. "We won't rob them of anything at all except just this money. The people who buy the property are the ones who will suffer; because as soon as it's discovered that we didn't own it—which won't be long after we've left—the sale won't be valid, and it'll all go back to the estate. These orphans will get their house back again, and that's enough for them; they're young and energetic, and can easily earn a living. They aren't going to suffer. Why, just think—there are thousands and thousands who aren't nearly so well off. Bless you, they don't have anything to complain about."

Well, the king kept talking and talking until he wore him down completely; so finally he gave in and said all right, but he still thought it was complete foolishness to stay around with that doctor watching over them suspiciously. But the king says:

"Damn the doctor! What do we care about him? Don't we have all the fools in town on our side? And isn't that a big enough majority in any town?"

So they prepared to head downstairs once more. The duke said:

"I don't think we put that money in a good place."

That cheered me up. I had started to think I wasn't going to get any kind of hint to help me. The king says:

"Why?"

"Because Mary Jane will be in mourning from now on, and before you know it, the servant who cleans the rooms will get orders to pack up these clothes and put them away. Do you think a servant could come across money and not take some of it?"

"Your head's level again, duke," says the king, and he comes fumbling under the curtain two or three feet from where I was. I pressed tight against the wall and kept very still, though trembling; and I wondered what those fellows would say to me if they caught me; and I tried to think what I'd better do if they did catch me. But the king got the bag before I could think more than about half a thought, and he never suspected I was around. They took and shoved the bag through a tear in the straw mattress that was under the feather bed, and crammed it in a foot or two among the straw and said it was all right now, because a servant only makes up the feather bed, and doesn't turn over the straw mattress only about twice a year, and so it wasn't in any danger of getting stolen now.

But I knew better. I had gotten it out of there before they were halfway down the stairs. I felt my way up to my small room and hid it there until I could find a chance to do something better with it. I figured I should hide it somewhere outside the house, because if they discovered it was missing they would search the house thoroughly: I knew that for certain. Then I went to bed with all my clothes still on; but I couldn't have fallen asleep even if I had wanted to, I was so anxious to get this whole matter finished. After a while I heard the king and the duke coming upstairs; so I rolled off my bed and lay there with my chin at the top of my ladder, waiting to see if anything was going to happen. But nothing did.

So I waited until all the nighttime sounds had stopped and the morning sounds hadn't started yet; then I quietly climbed down the ladder.

———————————————

Chapter XXVII.

I crept to their doors and listened; they were snoring. So I tiptoed along and got downstairs all right. There wasn't a sound anywhere. I peeked through a crack of the dining-room door and saw the men who were watching the corpse all sound asleep on their chairs. The door was open into the parlor, where the corpse was lying, and there was a candle in both rooms. I passed along, and the parlor door was open; but I saw there wasn't nobody in there but the remains of Peter; so I moved on by; but the front door was locked, and the key wasn't there. Just then I heard somebody coming down the stairs, back behind me. I ran into the parlor and took a quick look around, and the only place I could see to hide the bag was in the coffin. The lid was pushed along about a foot, showing the dead man's face down in there, with a wet cloth over it, and his shroud on. I tucked the money bag in under the lid, just down beyond where his hands were crossed, which made me shudder, they were so cold, and then I ran back across the room and in behind the door.

The person approaching was Mary Jane. She walked to the coffin very quietly and knelt down to look inside; then she raised her handkerchief, and I could see she had started to cry, though I couldn't hear her, and her back was turned toward me. I slipped out, and as I went past the dining room I thought I should make certain those watchers hadn't seen me; so I peered through the crack, and everything was fine. They hadn't moved.

I went up to bed feeling rather dejected, because of how things had turned out after I had gone to so much trouble and taken so many risks. I thought to myself, if the money could stay where it is, that would be fine; because when we get a hundred or two miles down the river I could write back to Mary Jane, and she could dig it up again and retrieve it; but that's not what's going to happen; what's going to happen is, the money will be discovered when they come to screw on the coffin lid. Then the king will get it back, and it will be a long time before he gives anyone another opportunity to steal it from him. Of course I wanted to sneak down and get it out of there, but I didn't dare try it. Every minute it was getting later now, and pretty soon some of those watchers would begin to stir, and I might get caught—caught with six thousand dollars in my hands that nobody had hired me to take care of. I don't want to be involved in that kind of business, I said to myself.

When I came downstairs in the morning, the parlor was closed off, and the people who had been keeping watch were gone. Nobody was around except the family, the widow Bartley, and our group. I studied their faces to see if anything had happened, but I couldn't tell.

Toward the middle of the day, the undertaker arrived with his assistant, and they placed the coffin in the center of the room on a pair of chairs, then arranged all our chairs in rows, borrowing additional ones from the neighbors until the hall, parlor, and dining room were completely filled. I noticed the coffin lid remained as it had been before, but I didn't dare look underneath it with people around.

Then people began to gather, and the relatives and the young women took seats in the front row near the head of the coffin, and for half an hour people filed around slowly, in single file, and looked down at the dead man's face for a minute, and some shed a tear, and everything was very quiet and solemn, with only the young women and relatives holding handkerchiefs to their eyes and keeping their heads bowed, and crying softly. There was no other sound except the scraping of feet on the floor and the blowing of noses—because people always blow their noses more at a funeral than they do in other places except church.

When the place was completely packed, the undertaker glided around in his black gloves with his gentle, soothing manner, adding the final touches and arranging people and things to be orderly and comfortable, making no more noise than a cat. He never said a word; he moved people around, squeezed in latecomers, opened up walkways, and accomplished it all with nods and hand gestures. Then he positioned himself against the wall. He was the quietest, most graceful, most silent man I had ever seen; and he had no more expression on his face than a piece of ham.

They had borrowed a melodeon—a broken one; and when everything was ready a young woman sat down and played it, and it was pretty squeaky and wheezy, and everybody joined in and sang, and Peter was the only one that had a good thing, in my opinion. Then Reverend Hobson opened up, slow and solemn, and began to talk; and right away the most outrageous noise burst out in the cellar anyone ever heard; it was only one dog, but he made a tremendously loud racket, and he kept it up continuously; the minister had to stand there, over the coffin, and wait—you couldn't hear yourself think. It was really awkward, and nobody seemed to know what to do. But pretty soon they saw that tall undertaker make a sign to the preacher as if to say, "Don't worry—just rely on me." Then he bent down and began to glide along the wall, with just his shoulders showing above people's heads. So he glided along, and the commotion and racket getting more and more outrageous all the time; and finally, when he had gone around two sides of the room, he disappeared down into the cellar. Then in about two seconds we heard a whack, and the dog finished up with one or two amazing howls, and then everything was completely quiet, and the minister began his solemn talk where he had left off. In a minute or two here came this undertaker's back and shoulders gliding along the wall again; and so he glided and glided around three sides of the room, and then stood up, and cupped his mouth with his hands, and stretched his neck out toward the preacher, over people's heads, and said, in a kind of rough whisper, "He had a rat!" Then he crouched down and glided along the wall again to his place. You could see it was a great satisfaction to the people, because naturally they wanted to know. A little thing like that doesn't cost anything, and it's just the little things that make a man respected and liked. There wasn't a more popular man in town than that undertaker was.

Well, the funeral sermon was very good, but extremely long and tiresome; and then the king pushed forward and delivered some of his usual nonsense, and at last the ceremony was finished, and the undertaker began to quietly approach the coffin with his screwdriver. I was sweating then, and watched him very carefully. But he never interfered at all; just slid the lid along as gently as possible, and screwed it down tight and secure. So there I was! I didn't know whether the money was in there or not. So, I thought to myself, suppose somebody has stolen that bag secretly?—now how do I know whether to write to Mary Jane or not? Suppose she dug him up and didn't find anything, what would she think of me? Darn it, I said, I might get tracked down and imprisoned; I'd better stay hidden and keep quiet, and not write at all; the situation's terribly complicated now; trying to improve it, I've made it a hundred times worse, and I wish I had just left it alone, curse the whole business!

They buried him, and we returned home, where I found myself watching faces again—I couldn't help myself, and I couldn't find peace. But nothing came of it; the faces revealed nothing to me.

The king made his rounds that evening, charming everyone and acting incredibly friendly. He spread the word that his congregation back in England would be worried about him, so he needed to quickly settle the estate and head home. He expressed regret about being in such a hurry, and everyone else felt sorry about it too. They all wished he could stay longer, but they understood it wasn't possible. He mentioned that naturally, he and William would take the girls back home with them. This pleased everyone because it meant the girls would be well taken care of and among their own family. The girls were delighted too—so thrilled that they completely forgot all their troubles. They told him to sell everything as quickly as he wanted because they'd be ready to go. Those poor girls were so happy and excited that it broke my heart to watch them being deceived and lied to like that, but I couldn't see any safe way to step in and change what was happening.

Well, I'll be damned if the king didn't put the house and the slaves and all the property up for auction right away—sale scheduled for two days after the funeral; but anyone could make a private purchase beforehand if they wanted to.

So the next day after the funeral, around noon, the girls received their first devastating blow. A couple of slave traders arrived, and the king sold the enslaved people to them at a reasonable price, accepting what they called three-day drafts as payment, and off they went—the two sons were taken upriver to Memphis, while their mother was sent downriver to New Orleans. I thought those poor girls and the enslaved family members would break their hearts from grief; they cried together and carried on so much that it nearly made me sick to watch. The girls said they had never imagined seeing the family separated or sold away from the town. I can never erase from my memory the sight of those poor, miserable girls and the enslaved people clinging to each other's necks and weeping; and I believe I couldn't have endured it all and would have had to speak up and expose our gang, if I hadn't known the sale wasn't legitimate and that the enslaved people would be back home within a week or two.

The incident caused quite a commotion in the town as well, and many people spoke out directly, saying it was outrageous to separate the mother and her children like that. This hurt the con artists' reputation somewhat, but the old fool pressed forward stubbornly, despite everything the duke could say or do, and I can tell you the duke was extremely worried.

The next day was auction day. Around dawn, the king and the duke came up to the attic and woke me up, and I could tell by their expressions that there was trouble. The king says:

"Were you in my room the night before last?"

"No, your majesty"—which was how I always addressed him when it was just our group around.

"Were you in there yesterday or last night?"

"No, your majesty."

"I'm being completely honest with you—no lies."

"I swear on my honor, your majesty, I'm telling you the truth. I haven't been anywhere near your room since Miss Mary Jane took you and the duke and showed it to you."

The duke says:

"Have you seen anyone else go in there?"

"No, your grace, not as I remember, I believe."

"Stop and think."

I studied for a while and saw my opportunity; then I said:

"Well, I see Black people go in there several times."

Both of them jumped slightly and looked as though they had never expected it, and then as if they had. Then the duke said:

"What, all of them?"

"No—at least, not all at the same time—I mean, I don't think I've ever seen them all come out at once except for just one time."

"Hello! When was that?"

"It was the day we held the funeral. In the morning. It wasn't early, because I had overslept. I was just starting down the ladder, and I saw them."

"Well, go on, go on! What did they do? How did they act?"

"They didn't do anything. And they didn't really act much, as far as I could see. They tiptoed away; so I could see, easily enough, that they had gone in there to clean up your majesty's room, or something, assuming you were awake; and found you weren't up, and so they were hoping to slip away from trouble without waking you up, if they hadn't already woken you up."

"Good heavens, this is really happening!" says the king; and both of them looked quite sick and reasonably foolish. They stood there thinking and scratching their heads for a minute, and the duke burst into a kind of little harsh chuckle, and says:

"It's absolutely amazing how skillfully those slaves performed their act. They pretended to be sorry they were leaving this area! And I believed they were genuinely sorry, and so did you, and so did everyone else. Don't ever tell me again that a slave doesn't have any acting talent. The way they performed that scene would have fooled anyone. In my opinion, there's a fortune to be made with them. If I had the money and a theater, I couldn't ask for a better setup than that—and here we've gone and sold them for practically nothing. Yes, and we're not even allowed to collect that pittance yet. Say, where is that money—that bank draft?"

"In the bank to be collected. Where would it be?"

"Well, that's all right then, thank goodness."

I said, somewhat hesitantly:

"Is something wrong?"

The king spins around to face me and shouts:

"None of your business! You keep your mouth shut, and mind your own affairs—if you have any. As long as you're in this town don't you forget that—you hear?" Then he says to the duke, "We have to just swallow it and say nothing: silence is the word for us."

As they were starting down the ladder, the duke chuckled again and said:

"Quick sales and small profits! It's a good business—yes."

The king whirls around toward him and says:

"I was trying to do what was best by selling them out so quickly. If the profits turned out to be nothing, lacking considerably, with nothing left to carry forward, is it my fault any more than it's yours?"

"Well, they would still be in this house and we wouldn't be if I could have gotten my advice listened to."

The king talked back as much as he dared, and then turned around and attacked me again. He scolded me harshly for not coming to tell him I had seen the slaves coming out of his room acting that way—said any fool would have known something was wrong. And then he went ahead and cursed himself for a while, and said it all happened because he hadn't stayed in bed late and gotten his proper rest that morning, and he'd be damned if he'd ever do it again. So they went off arguing; and I felt terribly relieved that I'd managed to put all the blame on the slaves, and yet hadn't actually caused the slaves any harm by doing it.

Chapter XXVIII.

Soon it was time to get up. So I climbed down the ladder and headed downstairs; but when I reached the girls' room, the door was open, and I saw Mary Jane sitting by her old trunk, which was open and she had been packing things in it—getting ready to go to England. But she had stopped now with a folded dress in her lap, and had her face in her hands, crying. I felt terrible seeing it; of course anyone would. I went in there and said:

"Miss Mary Jane, you can't stand to see people in trouble, and neither can I—almost always. Tell me about it."

So she did it. And it was the enslaved people—I had expected as much. She said the beautiful trip to England was nearly ruined for her; she didn't know how she could ever be happy there, knowing the mother and children would never see each other again—and then she broke down more bitterly than ever, threw up her hands, and said:

"Oh, how heartbreaking to think they will never see each other again!"

"But they will—and within two weeks—and I know it!" I said.

Laws, the words escaped before I could even think! And before I could move, she threw her arms around my neck and begged me to say it again, say it again, say it again!

I could see I had spoken too quickly and revealed too much, and now I was trapped in a difficult situation. I asked her to give me a moment to think; and she sat there, very impatient and excited and beautiful, but appearing somewhat happy and relieved, like someone who just had a tooth extracted. So I began working through the problem in my mind. I told myself that I figured anyone who decides to tell the truth when they're in a tough spot is taking quite a few risks, though I didn't have any experience with it and couldn't say for sure; but that's how it seemed to me, anyway; and yet here was a situation where I'd be damned if it didn't seem like the truth would be better and actually safer than a lie. I needed to file this away in my memory and consider it more carefully sometime, because it was so unusual and irregular. I had never seen anything like it. Well, I finally told myself, I'm going to take the chance; I'll go ahead and tell the truth this time, even though it feels like sitting on a barrel of gunpowder and lighting it just to see where you'll end up. Then I said:

"Miss Mary Jane, is there somewhere outside of town where you could go and stay for three or four days?"

"Yes; Mr. Lothrop's. Why?"

"Don't worry about why just yet. If I tell you how I know those men will see each other again within two weeks—right here in this house—and prove how I know it—will you go to Mr. Lothrop's and stay for four days?"

"Four days!" she says; "I'll stay a year!"

"All right," I said, "I don't want anything more from you than just your word—I'd rather have it than another man's sworn oath on the Bible." She smiled and blushed very sweetly, and I said, "If you don't mind, I'll close the door—and lock it."

Then I returned and sat down again, and said:

"Don't shout. Just sit quietly and handle this like an adult. I have to tell you the truth, and you need to prepare yourself, Miss Mary, because it's bad news that's going to be difficult to hear, but there's no way around it. These uncles of yours aren't really your uncles at all; they're a pair of con artists—complete frauds. There, now we've gotten through the worst part, so you can handle the rest fairly easily."

It shocked her completely, naturally; but I had passed the dangerous part now, so I continued on, her eyes burning brighter and brighter the whole time, and told her every single thing, from where we first encountered that young fool heading up to the steamboat, all the way through to where she threw herself onto the king's chest at the front door and he kissed her sixteen or seventeen times—and then she leaps up, with her face glowing like a sunset, and says:

"That monster! Come on, don't waste a minute—not a second—we'll have them covered in tar and feathers, and thrown in the river!"

Says I:

"Certainly. But do you mean before you go to Mr. Lothrop's, or—"

"Oh," she said, "what was I thinking!" she exclaimed, and sat right back down. "Don't pay attention to what I said—please don't—you won't, will you?" She placed her soft hand on mine in such a gentle way that I said I would rather die first. "I wasn't thinking clearly, I was so upset," she said; "now continue, and I won't act like that again. Tell me what to do, and I'll do whatever you say."

"Well," I said, "those two con artists are a dangerous bunch, and I'm stuck having to travel with them for a while longer, whether I like it or not—I'd rather not explain why; and if you were to expose them, this town would free me from their grip, and

I'd be fine; but there's another person you don't know about who would be in serious trouble. Well, we have to save him, don't we? Of course. Well, then, we won't expose them."

Speaking those words gave me a good idea. I could see how I might get Jim and myself free of these con men by having them arrested here, then we could leave. But I didn't want to navigate the raft during daylight with no one else aboard to answer questions except me, so I didn't want the plan to start working until fairly late tonight. I said:

"Miss Mary Jane, I'll tell you what we'll do, and you won't have to stay at Mr. Lothrop's for so long, either. How far is it?"

"Just under four miles—way out in the countryside, back this way."

"Alright, that will work. Now go out there and stay hidden until nine or nine-thirty tonight, then have them bring you back home—tell them you remembered something. If you arrive here before eleven, put a candle in this window, and if I don't show up, wait until eleven. If I still haven't appeared by then, it means I've escaped and gotten away safely. Then you can come out and spread the word around, and get these criminals arrested."

"Good," she says, "I'll do it."

"And if it turns out that I don't escape, but get caught along with them, you have to speak up and say I told you everything ahead of time, and you must support me as much as you can."

"I'll stand by you! I absolutely will. They won't touch a single hair on your head!" she says, and I can see her nostrils flare and her eyes flash with determination when she speaks.

"If I escape, I won't be here," I said, "to prove these scoundrels aren't your uncles, and I couldn't do it even if I stayed. I could testify that they're frauds and con men, that's all, though that counts for something. Well, there are others who can do that better than I can, and they're people who won't be doubted as quickly as I would be. I'll tell you how to find them. Give me a pencil and a piece of paper. There—'Royal Nonesuch, Bricksville.' Put it away, and don't lose it. When the court wants to find out something about these two, have them send word to Bricksville and say they've got the men who performed the Royal Nonesuch, and ask for some witnesses—why, you'll have that entire town down here before you can blink, Miss Mary. And they'll come rushing down here, too."

I figured we had everything set up just right at this point. So I said:

"Just let the auction continue as planned, and don't worry about it. Nobody has to pay for the things they buy until a full day after the auction because of the short notice, and they won't be leaving here until they get that money; and the way we've arranged it, the sale won't be valid, and they won't receive any money. It's just like what happened with the slaves—it wasn't a real sale, and the slaves will be back before long. Why, they can't collect the money for the slaves yet—they're in the worst kind of trouble, Miss Mary."

"Well," she says, "I'll go down to breakfast now, and then I'll head straight to Mr. Lothrop's."

"'No, that's not the right approach, Miss Mary Jane," I said, "not at all; go before breakfast."

"Why?"

"What did you think I wanted you to leave for, Miss Mary?"

"Well, I never thought about it—and now that I think about it, I don't know. What was it?"

"Why, it's because you're not one of those people with a poker face. I don't need any better book than your face. Anyone can sit down and read it like large print. Do you think you can go and face your uncles when they come to kiss you good morning, and never—"

"There, there, don't! Yes, I'll go before breakfast—I'll be glad to. And leave my sisters with them?"

"Yes; don't worry about them. They have to endure it for a little while longer. They might become suspicious if all of you were to leave. I don't want you to see them, or your sisters, or anyone in this town; if a neighbor were to ask how your uncles are doing this morning, your face would give something away. No, you go ahead, Miss Mary Jane, and I'll handle everything with all of them. I'll tell Miss Susan to give your love to your uncles and say you've gone away for a few hours to get a little rest and a change of scenery, or to see a friend, and you'll be back tonight or early in the morning."

"It's fine to go visit a friend, but I won't allow my affection to be given to them."

"Well, then, it won't be." It was fine to tell her that—no harm in it. It was just a small thing to do, and no trouble; and it's the small things that smooth people's paths the most, down here below; it would make Mary Jane comfortable, and it wouldn't cost anything. Then I said: "There's one more thing—that bag of money."

"Well, they have that; and it makes me feel quite foolish to think about how they obtained it."

"No, you're wrong about that. They don't have it."

"Why, who's got it?"

"I wish I knew, but I don't. I had it because I stole it from them, and I stole it to give to you. I know where I hid it, but I'm afraid it's not there anymore. I'm terribly sorry, Miss Mary Jane, I'm as sorry as I can be. But I did the best I could—I did, honestly. I almost got caught, and I had to shove it into the first place I came to and run—and it wasn't a good place."

"Oh, stop blaming yourself—it's terrible to do that, and I won't let you—you couldn't help it; it wasn't your fault. Where did you hide it?"

I didn't want to get her thinking about her troubles again, and I couldn't bring myself to tell her what would help her picture that

215

dead body lying in the coffin with that bag of money on his chest. So for a moment I said nothing; then I said:

"I'd rather not tell you where I put it, Miss Mary Jane, if you don't mind letting me off the hook; but I'll write it down for you on a piece of paper, and you can read it on your way to Mr. Lothrop's, if you want to. Do you think that will work?"

"Oh, yes."

"So I wrote: 'I put it in the coffin. It was in there when you were crying there, away in the night. I was behind the door, and I felt really sorry for you, Miss Mary Jane.'"

It brought tears to my eyes to think of her crying there all alone in the darkness, with those terrible men lying right beneath her own roof, bringing shame upon her and stealing from her; and when I folded it up and handed it to her, I saw tears well up in her eyes as well; and she gripped my hand tightly and said:

"Goodbye. I'm going to do everything exactly as you've told me; and if I never see you again, I'll never forget you and I'll think of you many, many times, and I'll pray for you, too!"—and she was gone.

Pray for me! I figured if she knew me she'd take on a job that was more suited to her abilities. But I bet she did it anyway—that was just the kind of person she was. She had the courage to pray for Judas if she set her mind to it—there was no backing down in her, I believe. You can say whatever you want, but in my opinion she had more grit than any girl I've ever seen; in my opinion she was completely full of courage. It sounds like flattery, but it's not flattery at all. And when it comes to beauty—and goodness, too— she surpasses them all. I haven't seen her since that time when I watched her walk out that door; no, I haven't seen her since then, but I think I've thought about her many, many millions of times, and about her promise that she would pray for me; and if I had ever thought it would do any good for me to pray for her, I'll be damned if I wouldn't have done it or died trying.

Well, Mary Jane must have left through the back door, I figure, because nobody saw her go. When I found Susan and the girl with the cleft lip, I said:

"What's the name of those people on the other side of the river that you all go to see sometimes?"

They say:

"There are several, but it's mainly the Proctors."

"That's the name," I said; "I almost forgot it. Well, Miss Mary Jane told me to tell you she's gone over there in a terrible hurry—one of them is sick."

"Which one?"

"I don't know; at least, I kind of forget; but I think it's—"

"Good heavens, I hope it's not Hannah?"

"I hate to say it," I said, "but Hannah's the one."

"My goodness, and she was so well just last week! Has she taken ill?"

"There's no name for it. They stayed up with her all night, Miss Mary Jane said, and they don't think she'll survive many more hours."

"Just think about that! What's wrong with her?"

I couldn't come up with anything sensible right away, so I said:

"Mumps."

"Mumps your granny! They don't associate with people who have the mumps."

"They don't, do they? You can bet they certainly do with these mumps. These mumps are different. It's a new kind, Miss Mary Jane said."

"How is it a new kind?"

"Because it's mixed up with other things."

"What other things?"

"Well, measles, and whooping cough, and erysipelas, and tuberculosis, and yellow jaundice, and meningitis, and I don't know what else."

"My goodness! And they call it the mumps?"

"That's what Miss Mary Jane said."

"Well, what on earth do they call it the mumps for?"

"Why, because it is the mumps. That's what it starts with."

"Well, there's no sense in it. A person might stub his toe, and take poison, and fall down the well, and break his neck, and smash his brains out, and somebody come along and ask what killed him, and some fool up and say, 'Why, he stubbed his toe.' Would there be any sense in that? No. And there's no sense in this, either. Is it contagious?"

"Is it contagious? What are you talking about? Is a harrow catching—in the dark? If you don't catch on one tooth, you're sure to catch on another, aren't you? And you can't get away with that tooth without bringing the whole harrow along, can you? Well, this kind of mumps is like a harrow, you might say—and it's no ordinary harrow either, when you get properly caught on it."

"Well, I think it's terrible," says the hare-lip. "I'll go to Uncle Harvey and—"

"Oh, yes," I said, "I would. Of course I would. I wouldn't waste any time."

"Well, why wouldn't you?"

"Just take a look at this for a moment, and maybe you'll understand. Don't your uncles have to get back home to England as quickly as possible? And do you think they'd be cruel enough to leave and make you travel all that way by yourselves? You know they'll wait for you. So far, so good. Your uncle Harvey's a preacher, isn't he? Very well, then; would a preacher lie to a steamboat clerk? Would he lie to a ship clerk just to get them to let Miss Mary Jane board? Now you know he wouldn't. What will he do, then? Well, he'll say, 'It's a terrible shame, but my church business will have to manage the best way it can; my niece has been exposed to the awful pluribus-unum mumps, and so it's my sacred duty to stay here and wait the three months it takes to see

218

if she's caught it.' But never mind, if you think it's best to tell your uncle Harvey—"

"Darn, and stay fooling around here when we could all be having a good time in England while we were waiting to find out whether Mary Jane's got it or not? Why, you talk like an idiot."

"Well, anyway, maybe you should tell some of the neighbors."

"Listen to that. You really are incredibly stupid by nature. Can't you see that they would go and tell everyone? There's no other way except to simply not tell anybody at all."

"Well, maybe you're right—yes, I think you are right."

"But I think we should tell Uncle Harvey that she's stepped out for a bit, at least, so he won't worry about her?"

"Yes, Miss Mary Jane wanted you to do that. She says, 'Tell them to give Uncle Harvey and William my love and a kiss, and say I've gone across the river to see Mr.'—Mr.—what's the name of that wealthy family your uncle Peter used to think so highly of?—I mean the one that—"

"Why, you must be talking about the Apthorps, right?"

"Of course; those kinds of names are hard to remember—a person can't seem to keep them straight half the time. Yes, she said to tell you that she's gone over to ask the Apthorps to make sure they come to the auction and buy this house, because she thinks her uncle Peter would rather have them own it than anyone else. She's planning to stay with them until they agree to come, and then, if she's not too tired, she'll come home tonight. If she is tired, she'll be home in the morning for sure. She said not to mention anything about the Proctors, but only talk about the Apthorps— which will be completely true, because she really is going there to discuss them buying the house. I know this because she told me so herself."

"All right," they said, and left to wait for their uncles, give them their love and kisses, and deliver the message.

Everything was fine now. The girls wouldn't say anything because they wanted to go to England; and the king and the duke would rather have Mary Jane working away from the auction than nearby where Doctor Robinson could reach her. I felt really good; I thought I had handled it quite cleverly—I figured Tom Sawyer couldn't have done it any more skillfully himself. Of course he would have added more flair to it, but I can't do that very easily, not being raised that way.

Well, they held the auction in the public square, toward the end of the afternoon, and it dragged on and on, with the old man standing right there looking his most pious, up alongside the auctioneer, throwing in a little Scripture now and then, or some kind of sanctimonious saying, and the duke was going around making sympathetic sounds as much as he could, just putting on a show in general.

But eventually the whole thing dragged on, and everything was sold—everything except a small, worthless plot in the graveyard. So they had to get rid of that too—I never saw anyone as greedy as the king was for wanting to take everything. Well, while they were working on it, a steamboat arrived, and in about two minutes up came a crowd whooping and yelling and laughing and making a commotion, and shouting out:

"Here's your opposing side! Here are your two sets of heirs to old Peter Wilks—and you pay your money and you make your choice!"

Chapter XXIX.

They were bringing along a very distinguished-looking elderly gentleman and an attractive younger man with his right arm in a sling. And goodness, how the crowd shouted and laughed, keeping it going without pause. But I couldn't see anything funny about it, and I figured it would be difficult for the duke and the king to find any humor in it either. I expected they would turn pale. But no, they didn't turn pale at all. The duke never let on that he suspected what was happening, but just went around making cheerful sounds, happy and content, like a jug gurgling out buttermilk; and as for the king, he just stared and stared down sadly at those newcomers as if it broke his heart to think there could be such fraudsters and scoundrels in the world. Oh, he performed it wonderfully. Many of the important people gathered around the king to show him they were on his side. That elderly gentleman who had just arrived looked completely bewildered. Soon he began to speak, and I could tell right away that he spoke with an English accent—not like the king's way of speaking, though the king's imitation was pretty convincing. I can't repeat the old gentleman's exact words, and I can't mimic his accent; but he turned to the crowd and said something like this:

"This comes as a surprise that I wasn't expecting, and I'll admit honestly and openly that I'm not well prepared to handle this situation or respond to it properly. My brother and I have encountered some unfortunate circumstances—he has broken his arm, and our luggage was mistakenly unloaded at a town upstream from here last night. I am Harvey, Peter Wilks' brother, and this is his brother William, who cannot hear or speak and can barely communicate through gestures now that he only has one functioning hand to make them with. We are exactly who we claim to be, and in a day or two, once I retrieve our luggage, I can provide proof. But until then, I won't say anything more except that we'll go to the hotel and wait."

So he and the new dummy set off together; and the king laughed and rambled on:

"Broke his arm—very likely, isn't it?—and very convenient, too, for a fraud who has to make signs and hasn't learned how. Lost their baggage! That's really good!—and really clever—under the circumstances!"

So he laughed again, and everyone else did too, except for three or four people, or maybe half a dozen. One of them was that doctor; another was a sharp-looking gentleman carrying an old-fashioned carpet bag made from carpet material, who had just gotten off the steamboat and was speaking quietly with the doctor, occasionally glancing toward the king and nodding—this was Levi Bell, the lawyer who had gone to Louisville; and another was a big, rough, burly man who had come over and listened to everything the old gentleman had said, and was now listening to the king. When the king finished speaking, this burly man stepped forward and said:

"Listen here; if you're really Harvey Wilks, when did you arrive in this town?"

"The day before the funeral, friend," the king says.

"But what time of day?"

"In the evening—about an hour or two before sundown."

"How did you come?"

"I arrived on the Susan Powell from Cincinnati."

"Well, then, how did you end up at the Point in the morning—in a canoe?"

"I wasn't up at the Point in the morning."

"It's a lie."

Several of them rushed toward him and pleaded with him not to speak that way to an elderly man and a minister.

"Forget the preacher—he's nothing but a fraud and a liar. He was at the Pint that morning. I live up there, don't I? Well, I was there, and so was he. I saw him with my own eyes. He arrived in a canoe with Tim Collins and some boy."

The doctor stood up and said:

"Would you recognize the boy again if you saw him, Hines?"

"I think I would, but I'm not sure. Look, there he is right now. I can recognize him easily."

It was me he pointed at. The doctor says:

"Neighbors, I don't know whether the new couple is fraudulent or not; but if these two aren't frauds, then I'm an idiot, that's all. I think it's our responsibility to make sure they don't get away from here until we've investigated this matter. Come along, Hines; come along, the rest of you. We'll take these fellows to the tavern and confront them with the other couple, and I believe we'll discover something before we're finished."

It was exciting for the crowd, though perhaps not for the king's supporters; so we all began. It was around sunset. The doctor led me along by the hand, and was kind enough, but he never released my hand.

We all gathered in a large room at the hotel, lit some candles, and brought in the newlyweds. First, the doctor said:

"I don't want to be too harsh on these two men, but I believe they're frauds, and they may have accomplices that we don't know anything about. If they do, won't the accomplices escape with that bag of gold Peter Wilks left behind? It's quite possible. If these men aren't frauds, they won't object to sending for that money and letting us hold onto it until they prove they're legitimate—isn't that right?"

Everyone agreed to that. So I figured they had our group in a really tough spot right from the beginning. But the king just looked sad, and said:

"Gentlemen, I wish the money was there, because I have no intention of interfering with a fair, open, and thorough investigation of this terrible situation; but unfortunately, the money isn't there; you can go and check for yourselves, if you want to."

"Where is it, then?"

"Well, when my niece gave it to me to keep for her, I took it and hid it inside the straw mattress of my bed, not wanting to put it in the bank for the few days we'd be here, and thinking the bed was a safe place. We weren't used to having Black servants around, and I assumed they were honest, like servants back in England. The Black servants stole it the very next morning after I had gone downstairs, and when I sold them I hadn't noticed the money was missing yet, so they got completely away with it. My servant here can tell you about it, gentlemen."

The doctor and several others said "Nonsense!" and I could see that nobody completely believed him. One man asked me if I had seen the slaves steal it. I said no, but I had seen them sneaking out of the room and hurrying away, and I hadn't thought anything of it, except I figured they were afraid they had woken up my master and were trying to get away before he caused trouble for them. That was all they asked me. Then the doctor turned on me and said:

"Are you English, too?"

I said yes, and he and some others laughed and said, "Nonsense!"

Well, then they launched into a full investigation, and there we were, going back and forth, hour after hour, and nobody ever mentioned supper or seemed to think about it—so they just kept going and going; it was the most confusing mess you've ever seen. They made the king tell his story, and they made the old gentleman tell his; and anyone except a bunch of biased blockheads would have seen that the old gentleman was telling the truth and the other one was lying. Eventually they called me up to tell what I knew. The king shot me a suspicious look from the corner of his eye, so I knew enough to say the right things. I started telling them about Sheffield, and how we had lived there, and all about the English Wilks family, and so on; but I hadn't gotten very far when the doctor started laughing; and Levi Bell, the lawyer, said:

"Sit down, my boy; I wouldn't push myself if I were you. I figure you're not used to lying—it doesn't seem to come naturally to you. What you need is practice. You do it pretty clumsily."

I didn't care at all about the compliment, but I was glad to be let off the hook anyway.

The doctor began to say something, then turned and said:

"If you had been in town from the beginning, Levi Bell—" The king interrupted and extended his hand, saying:

"Wait, is this my poor dead brother's old friend that he wrote about so often?"

The lawyer and he shook hands, and the lawyer smiled and appeared pleased, and they talked continuously for a while, and then moved to one side and spoke quietly; and finally the lawyer spoke up and said:

"That will solve the problem. I'll take the order and send it along with your brother's, and then they'll know everything is fine."

So they brought some paper and a pen, and the king sat down and tilted his head to one side, and chewed his tongue, and scribbled something; and then they handed the pen to the duke—and then for the first time the duke looked sick. But he took the pen and wrote. So then the lawyer turned to the new old gentleman and said:

"Please write a line or two and sign your names, both you and your brother."

The elderly gentleman wrote something down, but no one could read it. The lawyer appeared extremely surprised and said:

"Well, this has me completely stumped"—and he pulled a bunch of old letters from his pocket, examined them carefully, then studied the old man's handwriting, and looked at the letters again. Then he said: "These old letters are from Harvey Wilks; and here we have these two different handwriting samples, and anyone can see they didn't write them" (the king and the duke looked completely fooled and embarrassed, I can tell you, seeing how the lawyer had caught them), "and here's this old gentleman's handwriting, and anyone can tell easily enough that he didn't write them either—the truth is, the marks he makes aren't really proper writing at all. Now, here are some letters from—"

The new old gentleman says:

"If you don't mind, let me clarify. No one can read my handwriting except my brother over there—so he writes things down for me. What you have there is his handwriting, not mine."

"Well!" the lawyer said, "this is quite a situation. I have some of William's letters as well, so if you can get him to write a line or two, we can compare—"

"He can't write with his left hand," the old gentleman says. "If he could use his right hand, you would see that he wrote his own letters and mine as well. Please look at both—they're written by the same person."

The lawyer did it, and said:

"I believe that's true—and if it isn't true, there's a much stronger resemblance than I had noticed before, anyway. Well, well, well! I thought we were right on the track of a solution, but it's fallen apart, partially. But anyway, one thing is proven—these two aren't either of them Wilkses"—and he nodded his head towards the king and the duke.

Well, what do you think? That stubborn old fool wouldn't give in at that point! He certainly wouldn't. He said it wasn't a fair test. He claimed his brother William was the most mischievous prankster in the world, and hadn't actually tried to write—he could see William was going to pull one of his tricks the moment he picked up the pen. And so he got worked up and kept talking and talking until he was actually starting to believe what he was saying himself; but soon the new gentleman interrupted, and said:

"I just thought of something. Is there anyone here who helped prepare my br—who helped prepare the late Peter Wilks for burial?"

"Yes," someone says, "Ab Turner and I did it. We're both here."

Then the old man turns toward the king and says:

"Perhaps this gentleman can tell me what was tattooed on his chest?"

The king had to pull himself together incredibly fast, or he would have collapsed like a riverbank that's been eroded and caves in—the question hit him so suddenly. Keep in mind, this was the kind of thing that would make almost anyone crumble when they got hit with such a direct blow without any warning, because how could he possibly know what was tattooed on the man? His face went pale; he couldn't prevent it; and the room became dead silent, with everyone leaning forward slightly and staring at him. I thought to myself, "Now he'll give up—there's no point in continuing." Well, did he? You can hardly believe it, but he didn't. I think he figured he'd keep up the act until he wore those people down, so they'd start leaving, and he and the duke could escape and get away. In any case, he sat there, and before long he started to smile, and said:

"My goodness! That's a really difficult question, isn't it! Yes, sir, I can tell you what's tattooed on his chest. It's just a small, thin, blue arrow—that's what it is; and if you don't look closely, you can't see it. Now what do you say—hey?"

Well, I've never seen anything like that old fool for pure, shameless nerve.

The newcomer quickly turned toward Ab Turner and his partner, his eyes lighting up as if he believed he had finally caught the king red-handed, and said:

"There—you heard what he said! Was there any mark like that on Peter Wilks' chest?"

Both of them spoke up and said:

"We didn't see any such mark."

"Excellent!" the elderly man exclaimed. "What you actually observed on his chest was a faint, small P, along with a B (an initial he had abandoned in his youth), and a W, with dashes separating them like this: P—B—W"—and he drew them in that manner on a sheet of paper. "Now then, isn't that exactly what you witnessed?"

Both of them spoke up again and said:

"No, we didn't. We never saw any marks at all."

Well, everyone was upset now, and they shouted out:

"The whole bunch of them are frauds! Let's duck them! Let's drown them! Let's ride them on a rail!" and everybody was shouting at once, and there was a thunderous uproar. But the lawyer jumps on the table and yells, and says:

"Gentlemen—gentlemen! Listen to me for just a moment—just one word—please! There's still one option left—let's go dig up the body and take a look."

That got to them.

"Hooray!" they all shouted, and were about to start immediately; but the lawyer and the doctor called out:

"Wait, wait! Arrest all four of these men and the boy, and bring them along as well!"

"We'll do it!" they all shouted; "and if we don't find those marks we'll lynch the entire gang!"

I was terrified now, I'm telling you. But there was no way to escape, you understand. They grabbed all of us and forced us to march straight ahead, directly toward the graveyard, which was about a mile and a half down the river, with the entire town following behind us, because we were making enough noise, and it was only nine o'clock in the evening.

As we passed by our house, I wished I hadn't sent Mary Jane away from town; because now if I could give her a signal, she would leave quickly and rescue me, and expose our fraudsters.

We rushed along the river road, acting wild and reckless; and to make things even more frightening, the sky was growing dark, lightning was starting to flash and flicker, and the wind was rustling through the leaves. This was the most terrible trouble and most dangerous situation I had ever found myself in; and I was somewhat stunned; everything was happening so differently from what I had expected; instead of being in a position where I could take my time if I wanted to, and watch all the excitement, and have Mary Jane behind me to rescue me and set me free when things got tight, there was nothing in the world between me and sudden death except those tattoo marks. If they didn't find them—

I couldn't stand thinking about it, yet somehow I couldn't focus on anything else. The darkness was growing deeper, creating the perfect opportunity to escape from the crowd, but that large, powerful man had a firm grip on my wrist—Hines—and trying to slip away from him would be like attempting to escape from Goliath. He pulled me along with him, his excitement driving him forward, and I had to run just to keep pace with him.

When they arrived, they swarmed into the graveyard and flooded over it like water overflowing its banks. Upon reaching the grave, they discovered they had brought roughly a hundred times more shovels than they needed, but no one had remembered to bring a lantern. Nevertheless, they began digging by the flickering light of the lightning and sent someone to the nearest house, half a mile away, to borrow one.

So they dug and dug with everything they had; and it became terribly dark, and the rain began, and the wind whistled and whooshed around, and the lightning came faster and faster, and the thunder roared; but those people never paid any attention to it, they were so absorbed in this task; and one moment you could see everything and every face in that large crowd, and the shovelfuls of dirt flying up out of the grave, and the next second the darkness erased it all, and you couldn't see anything at all.

Finally they brought out the coffin and started to unscrew the lid, and then there was such crowding and pushing and shoving as everyone tried to squeeze in and get a look that you've never seen anything like it; and in the darkness like that, it was terrible. Hines hurt my wrist something awful with all his pulling and tugging, and

I think he completely forgot I even existed, he was so excited and out of breath.

All of a sudden the lightning released a perfect flood of white light, and somebody shouted:

"By God, there's the bag of gold on his chest!"

Hines let out a shout, just like everyone else, and released my wrist and made a big push to force his way in and get a look, and the way I took off and ran for the road in the darkness is something nobody can describe.

I had the entire road to myself, and I practically flew down it—at least, I had it completely to myself except for the thick darkness, the occasional flashes of lightning, the drumming of the rain, the whipping of the wind, and the cracking of the thunder; and I'm telling you, I really raced along that road!

When I reached the town, I saw that nobody was out in the storm, so I didn't bother looking for any back streets, but headed straight through the main one; and when I started to get close to our house I focused my eyes and looked at it. No light there; the house was completely dark—which made me feel sorry and disappointed, though I didn't know why. But finally, just as I was passing by, a light suddenly appeared in Mary Jane's window! and my heart swelled up suddenly, ready to burst; and at that same moment the house and everything was behind me in the darkness, and would never be in front of me again in this world. She was the best girl I had ever seen, and had the most courage.

As soon as I was high enough above the town to see that I could reach the sandbar, I started looking carefully for a boat to borrow, and the first time the lightning revealed one that wasn't chained up, I grabbed it and pushed off. It was a canoe, and it wasn't secured with anything but a rope. The sandbar was an incredibly long distance away, far out there in the middle of the river, but I didn't waste any time; and when I finally reached the raft I was so exhausted I would have just laid down to rest and catch my breath if I could have afforded to. But I didn't. As I jumped aboard I called out:

"Get out there, Jim, and set her free! Thank God, we're finally rid of them!"

Jim rushed toward me with both arms outstretched, overflowing with joy; but when I caught sight of him in the lightning flash, my heart jumped into my throat and I tumbled backward into the water; I had forgotten he was disguised as old King Lear and a drowned Arab all at once, and it nearly frightened me to death. But Jim pulled me out of the water, and was about to hug me and shower me with blessings, and so forth, he was so happy I had returned and that we were finally free of the king and the duke, but I said:

"Not now; save it for breakfast, save it for breakfast! Break free and let her go!"

In just two seconds we were sliding down the river, and it felt so wonderful to be free again and completely alone on the great river, with no one to disturb us. I had to dance around a little and jump up and click my heels several times—I couldn't stop myself; but around the third click I heard a sound that I recognized very well, so I held my breath and listened and waited; and sure enough, when the next lightning flash burst out over the water, there they came!—rowing hard and making their small boat fly through the water! It was the king and the duke.

So I collapsed right down onto the wooden planks then, and gave up; and it was all I could do to keep myself from crying.

Chapter XXX.

When they climbed aboard, the king came after me, grabbed me by the collar, and said:

"Trying to give us the slip, were you, you pup! Tired of our company, hey?"

I said:

"No, your majesty, we weren't—please don't, your majesty!"

"Hurry up and tell us what you were thinking, or I'll shake your guts out!"

"Honestly, I'll tell you everything exactly as it happened, your majesty. The man who was holding onto me treated me very well, and he kept saying he had a boy about my size who died last year, and he felt sorry to see a boy in such a dangerous situation; and when they were all caught off guard by discovering the gold, and rushed toward the coffin, he released me and whispered, 'Run for it now, or they'll hang you for sure!' and I took off. It didn't seem like any good would come from me staying—I couldn't do anything, and I didn't want to be hanged if I could escape. So I never stopped running until I found the canoe; and when I arrived here I told Jim to hurry, or they'd catch me and hang me still, and said I was afraid you and the duke weren't alive anymore, and I was terribly sorry, and so was Jim, and we were incredibly relieved when we saw you coming; you can ask Jim if I'm not telling the truth."

Jim confirmed this was true, and the king told him to be quiet, saying, "Oh yes, that's very likely!" He shook me again and said he thought he would drown me. But the duke said:

"Let go of the boy, you old fool! Would you have done anything different? Did you ask around for him when you got free? I don't recall that happening."

So the king released me and started cursing that town and everyone in it. But the duke says:

"You better give yourself a good scolding, because you're the one who deserves it most. You haven't done a single thing from the beginning that made any sense, except for coming out so calm and bold with that made-up blue-arrow mark. That was clever—it was absolutely brilliant; and it was the thing that saved us. Because if it hadn't been for that, they would have thrown us in jail until those Englishmen's luggage arrived—and then—the penitentiary, you can bet on it! But that trick led them to the graveyard, and the gold did us an even bigger favor; because if those excited fools hadn't let go of everything and made that rush to get a look, we would have slept in our nooses tonight—nooses guaranteed to last, too—longer than we'd need them."

They remained quiet for a moment, lost in thought; then the king spoke, somewhat distracted:

"Man! And we thought the slaves stole it!"

That made me squirm!

"Yes," says the duke, speaking slowly and deliberately with a sarcastic tone, "We did."

After about thirty seconds, the king slowly drawls:

"At least, I did."

The duke says, in the same manner:

"On the contrary, I did."

The king became somewhat agitated and said:

"Look here, Bilgewater, what are you referring to?"

The duke speaks up, quite energetically:

"When it comes to that, maybe you'll let me ask, what were you referring to?"

"Darn!" says the king, very sarcastically; "but I don't know—maybe you were asleep, and didn't know what you were doing."

The duke gets angry now and says:

"Oh, cut it out with this ridiculous nonsense; do you think I'm a complete idiot? Don't you think I know who hid that money in that coffin?"

"Yes, sir! I know you do know, because you did it yourself!"

"It's a lie!"—and the duke went for him. The king cried out:

"Take your hands off!—let go of my throat!—I take it all back!"

The duke says:

"Well, you need to admit, first of all, that you did hide that money there, planning to run away from me someday, then come back and dig it up, and keep it all for yourself."

"Wait just a minute, duke—answer me this one question, honest and fair; if you didn't put the money there, say it, and I'll believe you, and take back everything I said."

"You old scoundrel, I didn't, and you know I didn't. There, now!"

"Well, then, I believe you. But answer me just this one more thing—now don't get mad; didn't you have it in your mind to steal the money and hide it?"

The duke remained silent for a moment; then he said:

"Well, I don't care if I did, I didn't do it, anyway. But you not only had it in mind to do it, but you done it."

"I swear I'll never die if I actually did it, duke, and that's the honest truth. I won't claim I wasn't planning to do it, because I was; but you—I mean someone—beat me to it."

"It's a lie! You did it, and you have to admit that you did it, or—"

The king started to make gurgling sounds, and then he gasped out:

"Enough!—I admit it!"

I was really happy to hear him say that; it made me feel much more at ease than I had been feeling before. So the duke took his hands off and said:

"If you ever deny it again I'll drown you. It's good for you to sit there and cry like a baby—it suits you, after the way you've behaved. I never saw such an old fool for wanting to grab everything—and me trusting you all the time, like you were my own father. You should have been ashamed of yourself to stand by and hear it blamed on a bunch of poor black people, and you never said a word for them. It makes me feel ridiculous to think I was foolish enough to believe that nonsense. Damn you, I can see now why you were so eager to make up the shortage—you wanted to get whatever money I had from the Royal Nonesuch and other things, and take it all!"

The king speaks timidly, still sniffling:

"Why, duke, it was you who said to make up the deficit; it wasn't me."

"Shut up! I don't want to hear another word from you!" says the duke. "And now you see what you've accomplished. They've gotten all their own money back, and all of ours except for a dollar or two. Go to bed, and don't you dare defy me with any more defiance, as long as you live!"

So the king slipped into the tent and turned to his bottle for comfort, and before long the duke grabbed his bottle too; and within about half an hour they were as close as thieves again, and the drunker they became, the more affectionate they grew, and they went off snoring in each other's arms. They both became very drunk, but I noticed the king didn't get drunk enough to forget to remember not to deny hiding the money bag again. That made me feel relieved and satisfied. Of course when they started snoring we had a long conversation, and I told Jim everything.

Chapter XXXI.

We couldn't stop at any town for days and days; we kept moving straight down the river. We were now down south in the warm weather, and we were a very long way from home. We began to see trees with Spanish moss hanging from their branches like long, gray beards. It was the first time I had ever seen it growing, and it made the woods look solemn and gloomy. So now the con men figured they were out of danger, and they started working the villages again.

First they gave a lecture on temperance, but they didn't make enough money for both of them to get drunk on. Then in another village they started a dancing school, but they didn't know any more about how to dance than a kangaroo does, so the first move they made, the general public jumped in and ran them out of town. Another time they tried their hand at elocution, but they didn't speak long before the audience got up and gave them a thorough scolding, and made them leave quickly. They tried missionary work, and mesmerizing, and doctoring, and telling fortunes, and a little of everything, but they couldn't seem to have any luck. So finally they were completely broke, and lay around the raft as it floated along, thinking and thinking, and never saying anything, for half a day at a time, feeling terribly dejected and desperate.

Eventually, they changed their behavior and started huddling together in the wigwam, speaking in hushed, secretive tones for hours at a stretch. Jim and I grew worried. We didn't like how this looked. We suspected they were planning some kind of scheme worse than anything they'd done before. We discussed it endlessly, and finally concluded they were either planning to break into someone's house or store, or getting into counterfeiting money, or something along those lines. This made us quite frightened, so we agreed that we wanted absolutely nothing to do with such activities, and if we ever got the slightest opportunity, we would abandon them completely and get away. Early one morning, we concealed the raft in a secure hiding spot about two miles downstream from a small, run-down village called Pikesville, and the king went ashore and instructed us to remain hidden while he headed into town to investigate whether anyone had heard about the Royal Nonesuch performance yet. ("You mean a house to rob," I thought to myself, "and after you finish robbing it, you'll return here wondering what happened to Jim, the raft, and me—and you'll just have to keep wondering.") He told us that if he wasn't back by noon, the duke and I should assume everything was fine and follow him into town.

So we remained where we were. The duke grew restless and agitated, becoming extremely irritable. He criticized us for everything, and we couldn't seem to do anything right; he complained about every small detail. Something was definitely brewing. I felt relieved when noon arrived and the king still hadn't returned; we could at least have some relief—and perhaps an opportunity for escape on top of that. So the duke and I went up to the village and searched around for the king, and eventually we discovered him in the back room of a small, run-down tavern, completely drunk, with a bunch of idle troublemakers harassing him for entertainment, while he cursed and made threats with all his strength, so intoxicated he couldn't walk and was powerless against them. The duke began berating him as an old fool, and the king started talking back defiantly, and the moment they were fully engaged in their argument I took off and ran as fast as my legs could carry me, racing down the river road like a deer, because I saw our opportunity; and I decided it would be a very long time before they would see Jim and me again. I arrived there completely out of breath but filled with excitement, and called out:

"Let her go, Jim! We're safe now!"

But there was no answer, and nobody came out of the wigwam. Jim was gone! I let out a shout—and then another—and then another one; and ran this way and that in the woods, whooping and screeching; but it was no use—old Jim was gone. Then I sat down and cried; I couldn't help it. But I couldn't sit still long. Pretty soon I went out on the road, trying to think what I should do, and I ran across a boy walking, and asked him if he'd seen a strange Black man dressed so and so, and he says:

"Yes."

"Where?" I asked.

"Down to Silas Phelps' place, two miles below here. He's a runaway slave, and they've got him. Were you looking for him?"

"You bet I'm not! I ran into him in the woods about an hour or two ago, and he said if I yelled he'd cut my liver out—and told me to lie down and stay where I was; and I did it. I've been there ever since, afraid to come out."

"Well," he says, "you don't need to be afraid anymore, because they've caught him. He ran away from somewhere down South."

"It's a good thing they caught him."

"Well, I suppose! There's a two hundred dollar reward on him. It's like picking up money from the road."

"Yes, it is—and I could have had it if I'd been big enough; I saw him first. Who nailed him?"

"It was an old man—a stranger—and he sold his share in him for forty dollars, because he had to go up the river and couldn't wait. Think about that! You can bet I'd wait, even if it took seven years."

"That's me, every time," I said. "But maybe his opportunity isn't worth any more than that, if he's willing to sell it so cheap. Maybe there's something not right about it."

"But it is, though—straight as a string. I saw the poster myself. It describes everything about him perfectly—paints him like a picture, and tells which plantation he's from, below New Orleans. No sir, there's no doubt about that investment, you can bet on it. Say, give me some chewing tobacco, won't you?"

I didn't have any, so he left. I went to the raft and sat down in the shelter to think. But I couldn't come up with anything. I thought until my head ached, but I couldn't see any way out of the trouble. After this entire long journey, and after everything we'd done for those scoundrels, here it had all come to nothing, everything completely broken up and ruined, because they could have the heart to play such a cruel trick on Jim, and make him a slave again for his whole life, and among strangers too, for forty dirty dollars.

Once I told myself it would be a thousand times better for Jim to be a slave at home where his family was, as long as he had to be a slave, and so I'd better write a letter to Tom Sawyer and tell him to tell Miss Watson where he was. But I soon gave up that idea for two reasons: she'd be angry and disgusted at his bad behavior and ingratitude for leaving her, and so she'd sell him straight down the river again; and if she didn't, everybody naturally despises an ungrateful slave, and they'd make Jim feel it all the time, and so he'd feel mean and disgraced. And then think of me! It would get all around that Huck Finn helped a slave to get his freedom; and if I was ever to see anybody from that town again I'd be ready to get down and lick his boots for shame. That's just the way: a person does a low-down thing, and then he doesn't want to take any consequences of it. Thinks as long as he can hide it, it isn't any disgrace. That was my situation exactly. The more I thought about this, the more my conscience went to grinding me, and the more wicked and low-down and mean I got to feeling. And at last, when it hit me all of a sudden that here was the plain hand of Providence slapping me in the face and letting me know my wickedness was being watched all the time from up there in heaven, while I was stealing a poor old woman's slave that hadn't ever done me any harm, and now was showing me there's One that's always on the lookout, and isn't going to allow no such miserable doings to go only just so far and no further, I most dropped in my tracks I was so scared. Well, I tried the best I could to kind of soften it up somehow for myself by saying I was brought up wicked, and so I wasn't so much to blame; but something inside of me kept saying, "There was the Sunday-school, you could have gone to it; and if you'd have done it they'd have learned you there that people that acts as I'd been acting about that slave goes to everlasting fire."

It made me shiver. And I almost decided to pray and see if I couldn't try to stop being the kind of boy I was and become better. So I knelt down. But the words wouldn't come. Why wouldn't they? It wasn't any use trying to hide it from Him. Not from me, either. I knew very well why they wouldn't come. It was because my heart wasn't right; it was because I wasn't honest; it was because I was being two-faced. I was pretending to give up sin, but deep inside me I was holding on to the biggest one of all. I was trying to make my mouth say I would do the right thing and the proper thing, and go and write to that slave's owner and tell where he was; but deep down in me I knew it was a lie, and He knew it. You can't pray a lie—I discovered that.

I was completely overwhelmed with worry, as troubled as anyone could possibly be, and had no idea what I should do. Finally, a thought came to me, and I said to myself, I'll go ahead and write the letter—and then see if I'm able to pray. It was remarkable how immediately I felt weightless as a feather, and all my worries simply disappeared. So I found a piece of paper and a pencil, feeling happy and eager, and sat down to write:

> Miss Watson, your runaway slave Jim is located two miles south of Pikesville, and Mr. Phelps has captured him and will turn him over for the reward if you contact him.
>
> HUCK FINN.

I felt good and completely cleansed of sin for the first time I had ever felt that way in my life, and I knew I could pray now. But I didn't do it right away, instead I put the paper down and sat there thinking—thinking about how good it was that all this had happened this way, and how close I had come to being lost and going to hell. And I kept on thinking. And I started thinking about our trip down the river; and I could see Jim in front of me all the time: during the day and at night, sometimes in moonlight, sometimes in storms, and we were floating along, talking and singing and laughing. But somehow I couldn't seem to find any moments that would harden me against him, but only the opposite kind. I would see him standing watch on top of his own shift, instead of calling me, so I could keep sleeping; and I could see how glad he was when I came back out of the fog; and when I returned to him in the swamp, up there where the feud was taking place; and times like that; and he would always call me honey, and treat me kindly and do everything he could think of for me, and how good he always was; and finally I remembered the time I saved him by telling the men we had smallpox on board, and he was so grateful, and said I was the best friend old Jim ever had in the world, and the only one he had now; and then I happened to look around and see that paper.

It was a tight spot. I picked it up and held it in my hand. I was trembling, because I had to decide, forever, between two things, and I knew it. I thought for a minute, sort of holding my breath, and then said to myself:

"All right, then, I'll go to hell"—and tore it up.

It was terrible thoughts and terrible words, but they were said. And I let them remain said; and never thought any more about reforming. I pushed the whole thing out of my head, and said I would take up wickedness again, which was in my nature, being brought up to it, and the other wasn't. And for a starter I would go to work and steal Jim out of slavery again; and if I could think up anything worse, I would do that, too; because as long as I was in, and in for good, I might as well go all the way.

Then I started thinking about how to approach this, and I considered quite a few different options; eventually I settled on a plan that worked for me. I took note of the location of a wooded island that was further down the river, and once it got completely dark I quietly slipped out with my raft and headed toward it, where I hid it, and then settled in for the night. I slept through the entire night, and woke up before dawn, ate my breakfast, and put on my good clothes, and bundled up some other clothes and various items, and took the canoe and headed for the shore. I came ashore below what I believed was Phelps's property, and concealed my bundle in the woods, and then filled the canoe with water, and loaded it with rocks and sank it where I could locate it again when I needed it, roughly a quarter mile downstream from a small steam-powered sawmill that sat on the riverbank.

Then I started walking down the road, and when I passed the mill I saw a sign on it that read "Phelps's Sawmill." When I reached the farmhouses a couple hundred yards further down, I kept my eyes open but didn't see anyone around, even though it was broad daylight by now. That didn't bother me though, since I didn't want to run into anybody just yet—I only wanted to get a feel for the area. According to my plan, I was supposed to approach from the village direction, not from down below. So I just took a quick look around and kept moving, heading straight for town. Well, the very first person I saw when I got there was the duke. He was putting up a poster for the Royal Nonesuch—a three-night show—just like that other time. Those con artists had some nerve! I was right up on him before I could get away. He looked shocked and said:

"Hello! Where did you come from?" Then he said, sounding both pleased and excited, "Where's the raft? Did you get it to a safe spot?"

I said:

"Why, that's exactly what I was about to ask you, your grace."

Then he didn't look so happy, and he said:

"What was your idea for asking me?" he says.

"Well," I said, "when I saw the king in that tavern yesterday, I told myself we couldn't get him home for hours until he sobered up, so I went wandering around town to pass the time and wait. A man approached me and offered ten cents to help him pull a boat across the river and back to fetch a sheep, so I went along. But when we were dragging the sheep to the boat, and the man left me holding the rope while he went behind the animal to push it forward, the sheep was too strong for me and broke free and ran off, with us chasing after it. We didn't have a dog, so we had to chase the sheep all over the countryside until we wore it out. We didn't catch it until dark, then we brought it across the river, and I headed down to the raft. When I arrived there and saw it was gone, I said to myself, 'they've gotten into trouble and had to leave, and they've taken my slave, who is the only slave I have in the world, and now I'm in a strange place with no property left, nothing at all, and no way to earn a living.' So I sat down and cried. I spent the night sleeping in the woods. But what happened to the raft then? And Jim—poor Jim!"

"I have no idea what happened to the raft. That old fool made some kind of deal and earned forty dollars, but when we found him at the tavern, the drifters had been flipping coins with him for money and taken every cent except what he'd already spent on whiskey. When I brought him home late last night and discovered the raft was missing, we figured, 'That little troublemaker stole our raft, ditched us, and escaped down the river.'"

"I wouldn't betray my slave, would I?—the only slave I had in the world, and the only property."

"We never thought of that. The truth is, I think we had come to consider him our responsibility; yes, we did think of him that way—heaven knows we had enough trouble because of him. So when we saw the raft was gone and we were completely broke, there wasn't anything else to do but try the Royal Nonesuch one more time. And I've been struggling along ever since, broke as can be. Where's that ten cents? Hand it over."

I had a good amount of money, so I gave him ten cents, but I asked him to spend it on something to eat and share some with me, because it was all the money I had, and I hadn't eaten anything since yesterday. He didn't say anything. The next minute he turned on me and said:

"Do you think that man would tell on us? We'd make him pay if he did that!"

"How can he blow? Hasn't he run off?"

"No! That old fool sold him and never shared the money with me, and now it's all gone."

"Sold him?" I said, and started to cry; "why, he was my slave, and that was my money. Where is he?—I want my slave."

"Well, you can't get your slave back, that's all—so stop your crying. Look here—do you think you'd dare to tell on us? I'll be damned if I think I'd trust you. Why, if you were to tell on us—"

He stopped, but I had never seen the duke look so menacing before. I continued whimpering and said:

"I don't want to inform on anyone; and I don't have time to inform anyway. I need to get going and find my slave."

He looked somewhat troubled and stood there with his papers fluttering on his arm, thinking and wrinkling his forehead. Finally he said:

"I'll tell you something. We have to stay here for three days. If you promise you won't tell anyone, and won't let the Black man tell anyone, I'll tell you where to find him."

So I made that promise, and he responds:

"A farmer named Silas Ph—" and then he stopped. You see, he had started to tell me the truth, but when he stopped like that and began to think again, I figured he was changing his mind. And that's exactly what he was doing. He didn't trust me; he wanted to make sure I'd be out of the way for the entire three days. So after a moment he said:

"The man who bought him is named Abram Foster—Abram G. Foster—and he lives forty miles back here in the country, on the road to Lafayette."

"All right," I said, "I can walk it in three days. And I'll start this very afternoon."

"No you won't, you'll start right now; and don't waste any time doing it, and don't do any chattering along the way. Just keep your mouth shut and keep moving, and then you won't get into trouble with us, do you hear?"

That was the arrangement I desired, and that was what I was working toward. I wanted to be given the freedom to execute my strategies.

"So get out of here," he says; "and you can tell Mr. Foster whatever you want to. Maybe you can get him to believe that Jim belongs to you—some fools don't require paperwork—at least I've heard there are people like that down here in the South. And when you tell him the poster and the reward are fake, maybe he'll believe you when you explain to him what the plan was for getting them out. Go on now, and tell him anything you want to; but make sure you don't say a word to anyone between here and there."

So I left and headed for the countryside. I didn't look back, but I had a feeling he was watching me. However, I knew I could outlast him at that game. I walked straight into the country for about a mile before I stopped; then I circled back through the woods toward the Phelps place. I figured I'd better start my plan right away without wasting time, because I wanted to keep Jim quiet until those men could get away. I didn't want any trouble with their type. I'd seen enough of them and wanted to be completely rid of them.

Chapter XXXII.

When I arrived there, everything was quiet and had that Sunday feeling, with the heat and bright sunshine; the workers had gone out to the fields; and there were those faint buzzing sounds of bugs and flies in the air that make it feel so lonely, as if everyone has died and disappeared; and when a breeze drifts by and makes the leaves tremble, it makes you feel sad, because it feels like spirits whispering—spirits that have been dead for many, many years—and you always think they're talking about you. Generally speaking, it makes a person wish they were dead too, and finished with it all.

Phelps' place was one of those small, single-family cotton plantations, and they all looked the same. There was a rail fence surrounding a two-acre yard, with a makeshift stile built from logs that had been cut and stood upright like steps, resembling barrels of varying heights, designed for climbing over the fence and for women to stand on when mounting a horse. The large yard contained some patches of sickly grass, but most of it was bare and worn smooth, like an old hat with its surface rubbed away. The main house was a large double log structure for the white family—made of hewn logs with gaps filled in using mud or mortar, and these mud strips had been whitewashed at some point in the past. A round-log kitchen stood nearby, connected to the main house by a wide, open but covered walkway. Behind the kitchen sat a log smokehouse, and on the other side of the smokehouse stood three small log cabins in a row for the enslaved workers. One small hut sat all alone, positioned far back against the rear fence, with some outbuildings located a short distance away on the opposite side. Near the little hut were an ash-hopper and a large kettle for boiling soap. A bench sat beside the kitchen door, holding a bucket of water and a gourd dipper. A hound dog slept there in the sunshine, with more hounds sleeping scattered around the area. About three shade trees grew in a distant corner, and some currant and gooseberry bushes grew in one spot along the fence. Beyond the fence lay a garden and a watermelon patch, followed by the cotton fields, and beyond the fields stretched the woods.

I walked around and climbed over the back fence by the ash bin, and headed toward the kitchen. When I had gone a short distance, I heard the faint hum of a spinning wheel rising and falling again; and then I knew for certain I wished I was dead—for that is the loneliest sound in the whole world.

I continued forward without developing any specific plan, simply trusting that Providence would provide me with the right words when the moment arrived; I had observed that Providence consistently supplied me with the appropriate words whenever I allowed it to work naturally.

When I reached the halfway point, first one dog and then another got up and came after me, and naturally I stopped and turned to face them, staying perfectly still. What a commotion they created! Within fifteen seconds, I found myself at the center of what looked like a wheel—with dog-spokes radiating outward—a circle of fifteen hounds packed tightly around me, their necks stretched upward and noses pointed in my direction, barking and howling; and more were still coming; you could see them leaping over fences and racing around corners from every direction.

A Black woman came rushing out of the kitchen with a rolling pin in her hand, shouting, "Get away, you Tige! you Spot! get away!" and she gave first one and then another of them a smack and sent them howling, and then the rest followed; and the next second half of them came back, wagging their tails around me, and making friends with me. There isn't any harm in a hound, anyway.

And behind the woman comes a little Black girl and two little Black boys wearing nothing but rough linen shirts, and they clung to their mother's dress, and peered out from behind her at me, shy, the way they always do. And here comes the white woman running from the house, about forty-five or fifty years old, bareheaded, and her spinning stick in her hand; and behind her comes her little white children, acting the same way the little Black children were doing. She was smiling so broadly she could hardly stand—and says:

"It's you, at last!—isn't it?"

I blurted out "Yes'm" without thinking.

She grabbed me and hugged me tightly, then gripped both my hands and shook them vigorously. Tears welled up in her eyes and streamed down her face, and she seemed unable to hug and shake me enough, saying over and over, "You don't look as much like your mother as I expected you would, but goodness gracious, I don't care about that—I'm so happy to see you! Oh my, it feels like I could just eat you up! Children, this is your cousin Tom—say hello to him."

But they lowered their heads, put their fingers in their mouths, and hid behind her. So she continued:

"Lize, hurry up and get him a hot breakfast right away—or did you get your breakfast on the boat?"

I told her I had gotten it on the boat. She then headed toward the house, guiding me by the hand, with the children following behind us. Once we arrived, she had me sit in a chair with a woven seat, and she settled herself on a small low stool in front of me, grasping both of my hands, and said:

"Now I can get a good look at you; and my goodness, I've been longing for this moment for so many years, and it's finally here! We've been expecting you for a couple of days or more. What kept you?—did your boat run aground?"

"Yes'm—she—"

"Don't say yes ma'am—say Aunt Sally. Where did she run aground?"

I wasn't sure what to say, since I didn't know whether the boat would be traveling up the river or down. But I rely heavily on instinct, and my instinct told me she would be coming up from down near Orleans. That didn't help me much, though, since I didn't know the names of sandbars in that direction. I realized I'd have to make up a sandbar, or pretend to forget the name of the one we ran aground on—or—Then I came up with an idea and spoke up:

"It wasn't the grounding—that didn't hold us back much. We blew out a cylinder-head."

"Good heavens! Is anyone hurt?"

"No ma'am. Killed a Black man."

"Well, that's fortunate; because sometimes people do get injured. Two years ago last Christmas your uncle Silas was traveling up from New Orleans on the old Lally Rook, and she blew out a cylinder-head and injured a man. And I believe he died later. He was a Baptist. Your uncle Silas knew a family in Baton Rouge that knew his people very well. Yes, I remember now, he did die. Gangrene set in, and they had to amputate his limb. But it didn't save him. Yes, it was gangrene—that was it. He turned blue all over, and died hoping for a glorious resurrection. They say he was a terrible sight to see. Your uncle's been going to the town every day to pick you up. And he's gone again, not more than an hour ago; he'll be back any minute now. You must have met him on the road, didn't you?—elderly man, with a—"

"No, I didn't see anyone, Aunt Sally. The boat docked right at daybreak, and I left my luggage on the wharf-boat and went exploring around town and out into the countryside for a while, to pass the time and avoid arriving too early; so I came down the back way."

"Who did you give the baggage to?"

"Nobody."

"Why, child, it'll be stolen!"

"I don't think it will be where I hid it," I said.

"How did you manage to get your breakfast so early on the boat?"

It was like thin ice, but I said:

"The captain saw me standing around and told me I'd better have something to eat before I went ashore, so he took me to the officers' quarters for lunch and gave me all I wanted."

I was becoming so anxious that I couldn't listen properly. My thoughts were constantly focused on the children; I wanted to pull them aside and question them a bit to figure out who I was supposed to be. But I couldn't find an opportunity, as Mrs. Phelps kept talking and going on and on. Soon she made cold chills run down my spine, because she said:

"But here we are going on like this, and you haven't told me a single word about my sister or any of the others. Now I'll stop talking for a bit, and you can start; just tell me everything—tell me all about every one of them; and how they are, and what they're doing, and what they told you to tell me; and every last thing you can think of."

Well, I could see I was completely stuck—really stuck this time. Providence had been looking out for me up to this point, but now I was firmly trapped with no way out. I realized it was pointless to try to keep going—I had to give up. So I told myself, here's another situation where I have to risk telling the truth. I opened my mouth to start speaking; but she grabbed me and quickly pushed me behind the bed, and said:

"Here he comes! Duck your head down lower—there, that's perfect; no one can see you now. Don't let him know you're here. I'm going to play a trick on him. Kids, don't say a word."

I could see I was in a difficult situation now. But there was no point in worrying; there was nothing to do except stay calm and try to be ready to get out of the way when trouble hit.

I caught just a brief glimpse of the old man when he walked in; then the bed blocked my view. Mrs. Phelps rushed toward him and said:

"Has he come?"

"No," says her husband.

"Good gracious!" she says, "what in the world could have happened to him?"

"I can't imagine," the old gentleman says, "and I have to say it makes me terribly uneasy."

"Worried!" she says; "I'm about to lose my mind! He must have come; and you missed him on the road. I know that's what happened—something tells me so."

"Why, Sally, I couldn't have missed him on the road—you know that."

"But oh, dear, dear, what will Sis say! He must have come! You must have missed him. He—"

"Oh, don't upset me any more than I'm already upset. I don't know what in the world to make of it. I'm at my wit's end, and I don't mind admitting that I'm completely scared. But there's no hope that he's arrived; he couldn't have come without me seeing him. Sally, it's terrible—just terrible—something's happened to the boat, for sure!"

"Hey, Silas! Look over there—up the road! Isn't that someone coming?"

He jumped to the window at the head of the bed, and that gave Mrs. Phelps the opportunity she was waiting for. She quickly bent down at the foot of the bed and pulled me out, and when he turned back from the window, there she stood, beaming and smiling brightly, with me standing quite meekly and nervously beside her. The old gentleman stared and said:

"Why, who's that?"

"Who do you think it is?"

"I have no idea. Who is it?"

"It's Tom Sawyer!"

Good heavens, I nearly collapsed right through the floor! But there wasn't any time to exchange knives; the old man grabbed me by the hand and shook it, and kept on shaking; and all the while the woman danced around and laughed and cried; and then they both fired off questions about Sid, and Mary, and the rest of the family.

But if they were joyful, it was nothing compared to what I felt; it was like being born again, I was so glad to discover who I was. Well, they stuck to me for two hours; and finally, when my jaw was so tired it could barely move anymore, I had told them more about my family—I mean the Sawyer family—than had ever happened to any six Sawyer families. And I explained all about how we blew out a cylinder-head at the mouth of White River, and it took us three days to fix it. Which was perfectly fine, and worked excellently; because they had no way of knowing whether it would actually take three days to fix it. If I had called it a bolt-head it would have worked just as well.

Now I was feeling quite comfortable on one side, and quite uncomfortable on the other. Pretending to be Tom Sawyer was easy and comfortable, and it remained easy and comfortable until eventually I heard a steamboat chugging along down the river. Then I said to myself, what if Tom Sawyer comes down on that boat? And what if he walks in here any minute, and calls out my name before I can give him a signal to stay quiet? Well, I couldn't let that happen; it wouldn't work at all. I had to go up the road and intercept him. So I told the family I thought I would go up to the town and bring down my luggage. The old gentleman wanted to come along with me, but I said no, I could handle the horse myself, and I would rather he didn't go to any trouble for me.

Chapter XXXIII.

So I headed toward town in the wagon, and when I was halfway there, I saw another wagon approaching. Sure enough, it was Tom Sawyer, so I stopped and waited for him to reach me. I called out "Hold on!" and he pulled up alongside me. His mouth fell open like a trunk and stayed that way, and he swallowed two or three times like someone with a dry throat before he finally spoke:

"I haven't ever done you any harm. You know that. So then, what do you want to come back and haunt me for?"

I said:

"I haven't come back—I haven't been gone."

When he heard my voice, it helped him feel a bit better, but he still wasn't completely satisfied. He said:

"Don't try to trick me, because I wouldn't do that to you. I'm being completely honest now—you're not a ghost, are you?"

"I swear, I'm not," I said.

"Well—I—I—well, that should settle it, of course; but I can't seem to understand it at all. Look here, weren't you ever murdered at all?"

"No. I was never murdered at all—I played a trick on them. Come over here and touch me if you don't believe me."

So he did it; and it satisfied him; and he was so glad to see me again he didn't know what to do. And he wanted to know all about it right away, because it was a grand adventure, and mysterious, and so it really excited him. But I said, leave it alone for now; and told his driver to wait, and we drove off a little way, and I told him the kind of trouble I was in, and what did he think we should do? He said, give him a minute, and don't disturb him. So he thought and thought, and pretty soon he says:

"It's all right; I've got it figured out. Take my trunk in your wagon and pretend it's yours. You turn back and take your time, going slow so you arrive at the house when you're supposed to. I'll head toward town for a bit and make a fresh start from there, arriving about fifteen to thirty minutes after you do. When I show up, don't act like you know me at first."

I said:

"All right; but wait a minute. There's one more thing—something that nobody knows but me. And that is, there's a Black man here that I'm trying to help escape from slavery, and his name is Jim—old Miss Watson's Jim."

He says:

"What! Why, Jim is—"

He stopped and began to study. I said:

"I know what you're going to say. You'll tell me it's dirty, despicable business; but what if it is? I'm despicable; and I'm going to steal him, and I want you to keep quiet and not tell anyone. Will you?"

His eyes lit up, and he said:

"I'll help you steal him!"

Well, I let go of everything then, like I'd been shot. It was the most shocking thing I'd ever heard—and I have to say Tom Sawyer dropped considerably in my opinion. But I couldn't believe it. Tom Sawyer helping enslaved people escape!

"Oh, darn!" I said; "you're joking."

"I'm not joking, either."

"Well, then," I said, "joking or not joking, if you hear anything said about a runaway slave, don't forget to remember that you don't know anything about him, and I don't know anything about him."

Then we took the trunk and loaded it into my wagon, and he went his way while I went mine. But naturally I forgot all about driving slowly because I was so happy and lost in thought; so I arrived home much too quickly for such a long journey. The old gentleman was standing at the door, and he said:

"Why, this is wonderful! Who would have thought that mare had it in her to do it? I wish we had timed her. And she hasn't sweated a hair—not a hair. It's wonderful. Why, I wouldn't take a hundred dollars for that horse now—I wouldn't, honest; and yet I would have sold her for fifteen before, and thought that was all she was worth."

That's all he said. He was the most innocent, best old soul I ever saw. But it wasn't surprising; because he wasn't only just a farmer, he was a preacher, too, and had a little one-horse log church down back of the plantation, which he built himself at his own expense, for a church and schoolhouse, and never charged anything for his preaching, and it was worth it, too. There were plenty of other farmer-preachers like that, and they did the same way, down South.

In about half an hour, Tom's wagon pulled up to the front gate, and Aunt Sally spotted it through the window since it was only about fifty yards away, and she says:

"Look, someone's coming! I wonder who it could be? I think it's a stranger. Jimmy" (that's one of the children) "go tell Lize to set another plate for dinner."

Everyone rushed toward the front door because, naturally, a stranger doesn't visit every year, so when one does arrive, it creates more excitement than yellow fever. Tom had already climbed over the fence and was heading toward the house; the wagon was racing up the road toward the village, and we were all crowded together at the front door. Tom wore his best clothes and had an audience—which was always perfect for Tom Sawyer. Under these circumstances, it was no trouble for him to display just the right amount of flair. He wasn't the type of boy to meekly walk up that yard like a sheep; instead, he approached calmly and with importance, like a ram. When he reached us, he lifted his hat with such grace and delicacy, as if it were the lid of a box containing sleeping butterflies that he didn't want to disturb, and said:

"Mr. Archibald Nichols, I presume?"

"No, my boy," the old gentleman says, "I'm sorry to tell you that your driver has deceived you; Nichols's place is about three miles further down the road. Come in, come in."

Tom glanced back over his shoulder and said, "Too late—he's out of sight."

"Yes, he's gone, my son, and you need to come inside and have dinner with us; then we'll get the horses ready and take you down to Nichols's."

"Oh, I can't put you through so much trouble; I wouldn't dream of it. I'll walk—I don't mind how far it is."

"But we won't let you walk—it wouldn't be Southern hospitality to do it. Come right in."

"Oh, please do," says Aunt Sally; "it's not any trouble for us at all, not one bit. You absolutely must stay. It's a long, dusty three miles, and we can't let you walk that distance. Besides, I've already told them to set another place at the table when I saw you coming, so you can't disappoint us now. Come right in and make yourself at home."

Tom thanked them warmly and graciously, allowing himself to be convinced to come inside. Once he entered, he introduced himself as a stranger from Hicksville, Ohio, saying his name was William Thompson, and he made another bow.

Well, he kept going on and on, making up stories about Hicksville and everyone in it that he could think of, and I was getting a little nervous, wondering how this was going to help me get out of my trouble. Finally, while still talking, he leaned over and kissed Aunt Sally right on the mouth, then settled back comfortably in his chair and was about to continue talking. But she jumped up and wiped it off with the back of her hand, and said:

"You audacious puppy!"

He looked somewhat hurt and said:

"I'm surprised at you, ma'am."

"You're surprised—Why, what do you think I am? I have a good mind to take and—Say, what do you mean by kissing me?"

He appeared somewhat humble and said:

"I didn't mean anything, ma'am. I didn't mean any harm. I—I—thought you'd like it."

"Why, you complete fool!" She grabbed the spinning stick, and it seemed like she was barely restraining herself from striking him with it. "What on earth made you think I would like it?"

"Well, I don't know. It's just that they—they—told me you would."

"They told you I would. Whoever told you that is another lunatic. I never heard anything like it. Who are they?"

"Why, everybody. They all said so, ma'am."

It was all she could manage to keep herself under control; her eyes flashed with anger, and her fingers twitched as if she wanted to claw at him; and she said:

"Who exactly is 'everybody'? Give me their names, or there'll be one less fool around here."

He stood up looking upset, fumbled around for his hat, and said:

"I'm sorry, and I wasn't expecting it. They told me to. They all told me to. They all said, kiss her; and said she'd like it. They all said it—every one of them. But I'm sorry, ma'am, and I won't do it anymore—I won't, honest."

"You won't, will you? Well, I should think you won't!"

"No ma'am, I'm being honest about it; I won't ever do it again—until you ask me to."

"Until I ask you! Well, I've never seen anything like it in all my life! I bet you'll be the oldest fool in creation before I ever ask you—or anyone like you."

"Well," he said, "it really surprises me. I just can't understand it. They told me you would, and I believed you would. But—" He stopped and looked around slowly, as if he hoped to find a friendly face somewhere, and his eyes settled on the old gentleman's, and he said, "Didn't you think she would want me to kiss her, sir?"

"Well, no; I—I—actually, no, I don't think I did."

Then he looks around at me in the same way and says:

"Tom, didn't you think Aunt Sally would open her arms wide and say, 'Sid Sawyer—'"

"My goodness!" she exclaims, interrupting and lunging toward him, "you shameless little troublemaker, to trick someone like that—" and she was about to embrace him, but he pushed her away, and says:

"No, not until you ask me first."

So she didn't waste any time and asked him right away. She hugged him and kissed him repeatedly, then handed him over to the old man, who took what remained. After they had calmed down a bit, she said:

"Well, my goodness, I've never seen such a surprise. We weren't expecting you at all, just Tom. My sister never wrote to tell me that anyone else was coming besides him."

"It's because it wasn't intended for any of us to come except Tom," he says; "but I begged and begged, and at the last minute she let me come, too; so, coming down the river, Tom and I thought it would be an excellent surprise for him to come here to the house first, and for me to follow along later and drop in, and pretend to be a stranger. But it was a mistake, Aunt Sally. This isn't a safe place for a stranger to come."

"No—not impudent kids, Sid. You should have gotten your face slapped; I haven't been so upset in I don't know how long. But I don't care, I don't mind the conditions—I'd be willing to endure a thousand such pranks to have you here. Well, to think of that act! I won't deny it, I was completely stunned with amazement when you gave me that kiss."

We ate dinner outside in that wide open walkway between the house and the kitchen, and there was enough food on that table to feed seven families—and it was all hot, too; not like that soggy, tough meat that sits in a cupboard in some damp basement all night and tastes like a chunk of old cold flesh in the morning. Uncle Silas said a pretty long prayer over the meal, but it was worth it; and it didn't cool the food down one bit, unlike the way I've seen those kinds of interruptions do many times before. There was quite a lot of conversation all afternoon, and Tom and I stayed alert the whole time; but it was no use, they didn't happen to mention anything about any runaway slave, and we were afraid to try to steer the conversation in that direction. But at supper that evening, one of the little boys said:

"Dad, can't Tom and Sid and I go to the show?"

"No," says the old man, "I don't think there's going to be any show; and you couldn't go even if there was, because the runaway slave told Burton and me all about that disgraceful performance, and Burton said he would tell the people; so I figure they've driven those shameless con artists out of town by now."

So there it was! But I couldn't help it. Tom and I were supposed to sleep in the same room and bed, so since we were tired, we said good-night and went up to bed right after supper. Then we climbed out of the window and down the lightning rod, and headed for the town. I didn't believe anyone was going to warn the king and the duke, so if I didn't hurry up and give them a warning, they would definitely get into trouble.

On the road, Tom told me everything about how people thought I had been murdered, and how my father disappeared pretty soon after and never came back, and what a commotion there was when Jim ran away. I told Tom all about our Royal Nonesuch scoundrels, and as much of the raft journey as I had time for. As we entered the town and walked up through the center of it—it was about half past eight then—here comes a wild rush of people carrying torches, making terrible whooping and yelling sounds, and banging tin pans and blowing horns. We jumped to one side to let them pass by, and as they went past I saw they had the king and the duke straddling a rail—that is, I knew it was the king and the duke, though they were completely covered in tar and feathers, and didn't look like anything in the world that was human—they just looked like a couple of enormous soldier plumes. Well, it made me sick to see it, and I felt sorry for those poor pitiful rascals. It seemed like I could never feel any anger toward them ever again in the world. It was a terrible thing to see. Human beings can be awfully cruel to one another.

We realized we were too late—there was nothing we could do to help. We asked some people who were hanging around about what happened, and they told us that everyone went to the show acting completely innocent; they stayed quiet and kept hidden until the poor old king was right in the middle of his performance on the stage; then someone gave a signal, and the entire audience stood up and went after them.

So we slowly made our way back home, and I wasn't feeling as confident as I had been before, but rather irritable, humble, and somehow guilty—even though I hadn't done anything wrong. But that's always how it goes; it doesn't matter whether you do right or wrong, a person's conscience doesn't have any sense, and just attacks them regardless. If I had a yellow dog that didn't know any more than a person's conscience does, I would poison it. It takes up more space than all the rest of a person's insides, and yet it's no good at all. Tom Sawyer says the same thing.

Chapter XXXIV.

We stopped talking and started thinking. After a while, Tom said:

"Look here, Huck, what fools we are to not think of it before! I bet I know where Jim is."

"No! Where?"

"In that hut down by the ash-hopper. Why, look here. When we were at dinner, didn't you see a Black man go in there with some food?"

"Yes."

"What did you think the food was for?"

"For a dog."

"So would I. Well, it wasn't for a dog."

"Why?"

"Because part of it was watermelon."

"So that's how it was—I noticed it. Well, it really is amazing that I never thought about a dog not eating watermelon. It shows how a person can see and not see at the same time."

"Well, the man unlocked the padlock when he went in, and he locked it again when he came out. He brought uncle a key about the time we got up from table—same key, I bet. Watermelon shows man, lock shows prisoner; and it isn't likely there are two prisoners on such a little plantation, and where the people are all so kind and good. Jim's the prisoner. All right—I'm glad we found it out detective fashion; I wouldn't give anything for any other way. Now you work your mind, and study out a plan to steal Jim, and I will study out one, too; and we'll take the one we like the best."

What an incredible mind for someone so young! If I had Tom Sawyer's intelligence, I wouldn't trade it to become a duke, or the captain of a steamboat, or a circus clown, or anything else I could imagine. I started working on a plan, but only to keep myself busy; I knew perfectly well where the real plan would come from. Soon enough, Tom says:

"Ready?"

"Yes," I said.

"All right—bring it out."

"My plan is this," I said. "We can easily find out if Jim is in there. Then I'll get my canoe tomorrow night and bring my raft over from the island. Then on the first dark night that comes, we'll steal the key from the old man's pants after he goes to bed, and take off down the river on the raft with Jim, hiding during the day and traveling at night, the way Jim and I used to do before. Wouldn't that plan work?"

"Work? Why, certainly it would work, like rats fighting. But it's too ridiculously simple; there isn't anything to it. What's the good of a plan that isn't any more trouble than that? It's as mild as goose milk. Why, Huck, it wouldn't make any more talk than breaking into a soap factory."

I never said anything, because I wasn't expecting anything different; but I knew very well that whenever he got his plan ready it wouldn't have any of those objections to it.

And it didn't. He explained his plan to me, and I could see right away that it was fifteen times better than mine in terms of style, and it would make Jim just as much of a free man as my plan would, and it might even get us all killed on top of that. So I was pleased with it and said we should go ahead with his idea. I don't need to explain what it was here, because I knew it wouldn't stay the same way it was. I knew he would keep modifying it in every possible way as we moved forward, and adding new complications whenever he had the opportunity. And that's exactly what he did.

Well, one thing was absolutely certain, and that was that Tom Sawyer was serious, and was actually going to help free that enslaved man. That was the thing that was too much for me. Here was a boy who was respectable and well brought up; and had a reputation to lose; and family back home who had good reputations; and he was intelligent and not foolish; and knowledgeable and not ignorant; and not cruel, but kind; and yet here he was, without any more pride, or sense of right and wrong, or conscience, than to lower himself to this business, and bring shame on himself, and shame on his family, in front of everyone. I couldn't understand it in any way at all. It was shocking, and I knew I ought to just speak up and tell him so; and be his true friend, and let him abandon this plan right then and there and save himself. And I did start to tell him; but he silenced me, and said:

"Don't you think I know what I'm doing? Don't I usually know what I'm doing?"

"Yes."

"Didn't I say I was going to help steal the slave?"

"Yes."

"Well, then."

That's all he said, and that's all I said. It wasn't any use to say more; because when he said he'd do something, he always did it. But I couldn't figure out how he was willing to go into this thing; so I just let it go, and never worried about it anymore. If he was determined to have it that way, I couldn't help it.

When we arrived home, the house was completely dark and quiet, so we continued down to the hut by the ash-hopper to examine it. We walked through the yard to see how the hounds would react. They recognized us and didn't make any more noise than country dogs always make when something passes by during the night. When we reached the cabin, we examined the front and both sides, and on the side I wasn't familiar with—the north side—we discovered a square window opening, positioned fairly high up, with just one thick board nailed across it. I said:

"Here's the ticket. This hole's big enough for Jim to get through if we wrench off the board."

Tom says:

"It's as simple as tic-tac-toe, three in a row, and as easy as skipping school. I should hope we can find a way that's a little more complicated than that, Huck Finn."

"Well, then," I said, "how would it work to saw him out, the way I did before I was murdered that time?"

"That's more like it," he says. "It's really mysterious, and troublesome, and good," he says; "but I bet we can find a way that's twice as long. There's no hurry; let's keep on looking around."

Between the hut and the fence on the back side was a lean-to that connected to the hut at the roof line and was built from wooden planks. It stretched the same length as the hut but was narrow—only about six feet wide. The door was located at the south end and secured with a padlock. Tom went over to the soap kettle and looked around until he found the iron tool they used to lift the lid; he took it and pried out one of the metal fasteners. The chain dropped down, and we opened the door and went inside, then closed it behind us and lit a match. We could see that the shed was simply built against a cabin without any actual connection to it, and the shed had no floor or anything inside except some old rusty worn-out hoes and spades and picks along with a broken plow. The match burned out, so we left and pushed the metal fastener back into place, leaving the door locked just as securely as before. Tom was delighted. He said:

"Now we're all right. We'll dig him out. It'll take about a week!"

Then we headed toward the house, and I went through the back door—you just have to pull a leather latch-string since they don't lock their doors—but that wasn't romantic enough for Tom Sawyer; nothing would satisfy him except climbing up the lightning rod. However, after he climbed halfway up about three times and failed each time, falling every time, and the last time nearly cracking his skull open, he figured he had to give up; but after he rested he decided he would give it one more try for luck, and this time he succeeded.

In the morning we were up at daybreak, and down to the slave quarters to pet the dogs and make friends with the enslaved person who fed Jim—if it was Jim who was being fed. The enslaved people were just finishing breakfast and heading out to the fields; and Jim's caretaker was filling up a tin pan with bread and meat and other food; and while the others were leaving, the key arrived from the house.

This Black man had a good-natured, simple face, and his hair was tied up in little bunches with thread. That was to keep witches away. He said the witches were bothering him terribly these nights, and making him see all kinds of strange things, and hear all kinds of strange words and noises, and he didn't believe he had ever been bewitched for so long before in his life. He got so worked up, and got to going on so much about his troubles, he forgot all about what he had been going to do. So Tom says:

"What's the food for? Going to feed the dogs?"

The man's face gradually broke into a smile, like ripples spreading when you throw a stone into a mud puddle, and he said:

"Yes, Master Sid, a dog. Strange dog, too. Do you want to go and look at him?"

"Yes."

I nudged Tom and whispered:

"You're leaving right here at daybreak? That wasn't the plan."

"No, it wasn't; but it's the plan now."

So, damn him, we went along, but I really didn't like it. When we got inside we could barely see anything because it was so dark; but Jim was definitely there, and he could see us; and he calls out:

"Why, Huck! And good Lord! Isn't that Mr. Tom?"

I knew exactly how it would turn out; I had expected it all along. I didn't know what to do; and even if I had known, I couldn't have done anything about it, because that man burst in and said:

"Why, for goodness' sake! Does he know you gentlemen?"

We could see quite clearly now. Tom looked at the Black man steadily with a kind of wondering expression and said:

"Who knows us?"

"Why, this runaway slave."

"I don't think he does; but what made you think of that?"

"What brought him there? Didn't he just this minute call out like he knew you?"

Tom says, sounding confused:

"Well, that's really strange. Who called out? When did he call out? What did he say?" And he turns to me, completely calm, and says, "Did you hear anybody call out?"

Of course there wasn't anything to be said except one thing; so I said:

"No; I haven't heard anyone say anything."

Then he turns to Jim and looks him over as if he had never seen him before, and says:

"Did you sing out?"

"No, sir," says Jim; "I haven't said anything, sir."

"Not a word?"

"No, sir, I haven't said a word."

"Have you ever seen us before?"

"No, sir; not that I know of."

So Tom turns to the Black man, who was looking wild and distressed, and says, kind of sternly:

"What do you think is wrong with you, anyway? What made you think someone called out?"

"Oh, it's those darn witches, sir, and I wish I was dead, I really do. They're always at it, sir, and they nearly kill me, they scare me so much. Please don't tell nobody about it, sir, or old Master Silas will scold me, because he says there aren't any witches. I just wish he was here right now—then what would he say! I just bet he couldn't find any way to get around it this time. But it's always just like that; people who are set in their ways stay set in their ways; they won't look into nothing and find it out for themselves, and when you find it out and tell them about it, they don't believe you."

Tom gave him a dime and said we wouldn't tell anyone; he told him to buy some more thread to tie up his wool with, and then he looked at Jim and said:

"I wonder if Uncle Silas is going to hang this Black man. If I were to catch a Black man who was ungrateful enough to run away, I wouldn't give him up, I'd hang him." And while the Black man stepped to the door to look at the dime and bite it to see if it was good, he whispers to Jim and says:

"Never let anyone know that you're acquainted with us. And if you hear digging sounds at night, that's us working to set you free."

Jim only had time to grab us by the hand and squeeze it; then the enslaved man came back, and we said we'd come again some time if he wanted us to; and he said he would, especially if it was dark, because the witches went for him mostly in the dark, and it was good to have folks around then.

Chapter XXXV.

It would be almost an hour until breakfast, so we left and headed down into the woods, because Tom said we needed to have some light to see how to dig, and a lantern creates too much light and might get us into trouble; what we needed was a bunch of those rotting pieces of wood that are called fox-fire, which just produce a soft kind of glow when you place them in a dark area. We gathered an armful and hid it in the weeds, then sat down to rest, and Tom said, sounding somewhat dissatisfied:

"Darn it, this whole situation is as simple and clumsy as it could possibly be. And that makes it incredibly hard to come up with a challenging plan. There's no guard to drug—there really should be a guard. There isn't even a dog to slip a sleeping potion to. And Jim is chained by one leg with a ten-foot chain to his bed frame: all you have to do is lift up the bed and slide the chain off. And Uncle Silas trusts everyone; he gives the key to that empty-headed slave and doesn't send anyone to watch him. Jim could have escaped through that window opening by now, except it wouldn't do any good to try traveling with a ten-foot chain attached to his leg. Why, blast it, Huck, it's the most foolish setup I've ever seen. You have to create all the obstacles yourself. Well, we can't change it; we have to work with what we've got. At least there's one thing—there's more glory in freeing him through plenty of challenges and risks, when none of those were provided by the people whose job it was to provide them, and you had to think them all up yourself. Just look at that lantern situation. When you get down to the plain truth, we simply have to pretend that a lantern is dangerous. Why, we could use a whole torch parade if we wanted to, I think. Now that I'm thinking about it, we need to find something to make a saw from as soon as we get the chance."

"What do we want of a saw?"

"What do we need it for? Don't we have to saw off the leg of Jim's bed to get the chain loose?"

"Why, you just said someone could lift up the bed and slip the chain off."

"Well, if that isn't just like you, Huck Finn. You can come up with the most childish ways of approaching something. Why, haven't you ever read any books at all?—Baron Trenck, or Casanova, or Benvenuto Cellini, or Henry IV, or any of those heroes? Who ever heard of freeing a prisoner in such an old-fashioned way as that? No; the way all the best authorities do it is to saw the bed leg in two, and leave it just like that, and swallow the sawdust, so it can't be found, and put some dirt and grease around the sawed area so the sharpest guard can't see any sign of it being sawed, and thinks the bed leg is perfectly solid. Then, the night you're ready, give the leg a kick, down it goes; slip off your chain, and there you are. Nothing to do but attach your rope ladder to the castle walls, climb down it, break your leg in the moat—because a rope ladder is nineteen feet too short, you know—and there are your horses and your loyal servants, and they scoop you up and throw you across a saddle, and away you go to your native Languedoc, or Navarre, or wherever it is. It's magnificent, Huck. I wish there was a moat around this cabin. If we have time, the night of the escape, we'll dig one."

I said:

"Why do we need a moat when we're planning to sneak him out from underneath the cabin?"

But he never heard me. He had forgotten me and everything else. He had his chin resting in his hand, lost in thought. Soon he sighed and shook his head, then sighed again and said:

"No, it wouldn't work—there isn't enough necessity for it."

268

"For what?" I asked.

"Why, to saw Jim's leg off," he says.

"Good heavens!" I said. "Why, there's no need for that at all. And what would you want to saw his leg off for anyway?"

"Well, some of the best authorities have done it. They couldn't get the chain off, so they just cut their hand off and escaped. And a leg would be even better. But we have to let that go. There isn't enough necessity in this case; and, besides, Jim's a Black man, and wouldn't understand the reasons for it, and how it's the custom in Europe; so we'll let it go. But there's one thing—he can have a rope ladder; we can tear up our sheets and make him a rope ladder easily enough. And we can send it to him in a pie; it's mostly done that way. And I've eaten worse pies."

"Why, Tom Sawyer, how you talk," I said; "Jim doesn't have any use for a rope ladder."

"He needs it. The way you're talking, you should think before you speak; you don't know anything about it. He has to have a rope ladder; they all do."

"What on earth can he do with it?"

"Do with it? He can hide it in his bed, can't he? That's what they all do; and he has to, too. Huck, you never seem to want to do anything that's normal; you want to be starting something new all the time. Suppose he doesn't do anything with it? Isn't it there in his bed, as a clue, after he's gone? And don't you think they'll want clues? Of course they will. And you wouldn't leave them any? That would be a fine mess, wouldn't it! I never heard of such a thing."

"Well," I said, "if it's in the regulations, and he has to have it, all right, let him have it; because I don't want to go against any regulations; but there's one thing, Tom Sawyer—if we go tearing up our sheets to make Jim a rope ladder, we're going to get into trouble with Aunt Sally, just as sure as you're born. Now, the way I see it, a hickory-bark ladder doesn't cost anything, and doesn't waste anything, and is just as good to load up a pie with, and hide in a straw mattress, as any rag ladder you can make; and as for Jim, he hasn't had any experience, and so he doesn't care what kind of a—"

"Oh, come on, Huck Finn, if I was as clueless as you I'd keep my mouth shut—that's what I'd do. Who ever heard of a state prisoner escaping with a hickory-bark ladder? Why, it's completely ridiculous."

"Well, all right, Tom, do it your own way; but if you'll take my advice, you'll let me take a sheet from the clothesline."

He said that would work. And that sparked another idea, and he says:

"Borrow a shirt, too."

"What do we need a shirt for, Tom?"

"Want it so Jim can keep a journal in it."

"Keep a journal, my foot—Jim can't even write."

"What if he can't write—he can still make marks on the shirt, can't he, if we fashion him a pen from an old pewter spoon or a piece of an old iron barrel hoop?"

"Listen, Tom, we can pluck a feather from a goose and create a better one ourselves; and we can do it faster, too."

"Prisoners don't have geese wandering around the castle tower to pluck feathers from, you fool. They always craft their writing instruments from the hardest, most durable, most difficult piece of old brass candlestick or similar material they can find; and it takes them weeks upon weeks and months upon months to shape it properly, because they have to do it by scraping it against the wall. They wouldn't use a goose feather even if they had one available. It's not the proper way."

"Well, then, what are we going to make his ink from?"

"Many people make it using iron rust and tears, but that's the ordinary kind that women use. The best experts use their own blood. Jim can do that, and when he wants to send any small, everyday mysterious message to let the world know where he's being held prisoner, he can write it on the bottom of a tin plate with a fork and throw it out the window. The Iron Mask always did that, and it's a really good method too."

"Jim doesn't have any tin plates. They feed him from a pan."

"That's nothing; we can get him some."

"Nobody can read his plates."

"That doesn't have anything to do with it, Huck Finn. All he has to do is write on the plate and throw it out. You don't have to be able to read it. Why, half the time you can't read anything a prisoner writes on a tin plate, or anywhere else."

"Well, then, what's the point in wasting the plates?"

"Why, damn it all, those aren't the prisoner's plates."

"But those are someone's plates, aren't they?"

"Well, suppose it is? What does the prisoner care whose—"

He stopped talking right there because we heard the breakfast horn blowing. So we headed back to the house.

During the morning I took a sheet and a white shirt from the clothesline; I found an old sack and put them in it, and we went down and collected the fox-fire, putting that in as well. I called it borrowing, because that's what my father always called it; but Tom said it wasn't borrowing, it was stealing. He said we were playing the role of prisoners; and prisoners don't care how they get something as long as they get it, and nobody blames them for it, either. It's not a crime for a prisoner to steal what he needs to escape with, Tom said; it's his right; and so, as long as we were playing prisoners, we had a perfect right to steal anything on this property that we had the slightest use for to help ourselves escape from prison. He said if we weren't prisoners it would be completely different, and only a mean, low-down person would steal when he wasn't a prisoner. So we decided we would steal everything we could get our hands on. And yet he made a huge fuss, one day after that, when I stole a watermelon from the slave quarters and ate it; and he made me go and give the slaves a dime without telling them what it was for. Tom said that what he meant was, we could steal anything we needed. Well, I said, I needed the watermelon. But he said I didn't need it to escape from prison with; that's where the difference was. He said if I had wanted it to hide a knife in, and smuggle it to Jim to kill the guard with, it would have been all right. So I let it go at that, though I couldn't see any advantage in playing a prisoner if I had to sit down and think through a lot of fancy distinctions like that every time I saw a chance to grab a watermelon.

Well, as I was explaining, we waited that morning until everyone had settled into their daily routines, and no one was visible anywhere around the yard; then Tom carried the sack into the shed while I positioned myself at a distance to keep watch. After a while he came out, and we went and sat down on the woodpile to talk. He says:

"Everything's fine now except for the tools; and that's easily fixed."

"Tools?" I asked.

"Yes."

"Tools for what?"

"Why, to dig with. We're not going to gnaw him out, are we?"

"Aren't those old broken picks and tools in there good enough to dig a person out with?" I said.

He turns toward me with a look so full of pity it could make anyone cry, and says:

"Huck Finn, have you ever heard of a prisoner having picks and shovels, and all the modern conveniences in his cell to dig himself out with? Now I want to ask you—if you have any sense at all—what kind of chance would that give him to be a hero? Why, they might as well just hand him the key and be done with it. Picks and shovels—why, they wouldn't give those to a king."

"Well, then," I said, "if we don't want the picks and shovels, what do we want?"

"A couple of case-knives."

"To dig out the foundations from underneath that cabin?"

"Yes."

"Damn it, that's stupid, Tom."

"It doesn't matter how foolish it is, it's the right way—and it's the regular way. And there isn't any other way that I've ever heard of, and I've read all the books that give any information about these things. They always dig out with a case-knife—and not through dirt, mind you; generally it's through solid rock. And it takes them weeks and weeks and weeks, and forever and ever. Why, look at one of those prisoners in the bottom dungeon of the Château d'If, in the harbor of Marseilles, who dug himself out that way; how long was he at it, do you think?"

"I don't know."

"Well, guess."

"I don't know. A month and a half."

"Thirty-seven years—and he escaped in China. That's exactly the type of person he is. I wish the foundation of this fortress was made of solid rock."

"Jim doesn't know anyone in China."

"What does that have to do with anything? That other guy didn't either. But you're always getting sidetracked. Why can't you focus on the main point?"

"Alright—I don't care where he emerges, as long as he gets out; and I don't think Jim cares either. But there's one thing for sure—Jim's too old to be dug out with a case knife. He won't survive it."

"Yes, he'll survive that long too. You don't think it's going to take thirty-seven years to dig through a dirt foundation, do you?"

"How long will it take, Tom?"

"Well, we can't risk taking as long as we should, because it might not take very long for Uncle Silas to hear from down there by New Orleans. He'll find out Jim isn't from there. Then his next move will be to advertise for Jim, or something like that. So we can't risk taking as long digging him out as we should. By rights I think we should take a couple of years; but we can't. With things being so uncertain, what I suggest is this: that we really dig right in, as quickly as we can; and after that, we can pretend, to ourselves, that we worked at it for thirty-seven years. Then we can grab him and rush him away the first time there's an alarm. Yes, I think that'll be the best way."

"Now, that makes sense," I said. "Pretending doesn't cost anything; pretending isn't any trouble; and if it serves a purpose, I don't mind pretending we were at it for a hundred and fifty years. It wouldn't be a strain on me at all, once I got the hang of it. So I'll head along now and steal a couple of case knives."

"Give us three," he says; "we need one to make a saw from."

"Tom, if it's not against the rules and improper to suggest it," I said, "there's an old rusty saw blade over there stuck under the wooden siding behind the smokehouse."

He looked somewhat tired and dejected, and said:

"There's no point in trying to teach you anything, Huck. Go ahead and steal the knives—three of them." So I did it.

Chapter XXXVI.

As soon as we figured everyone was asleep that night, we climbed down the lightning rod and locked ourselves in the lean-to, then pulled out our pile of fox-fire and got to work. We cleared everything out of the way, about four or five feet along the middle of the bottom log. Tom said he was right behind Jim's bed now, and we'd dig underneath it, and when we finished nobody in the cabin would ever know there was a hole there, because Jim's bedspread hung down almost to the ground, and you'd have to lift it up and look under to see the hole. So we dug and dug with the case knives until nearly midnight; and then we were exhausted, and our hands were blistered, and yet you couldn't tell we'd accomplished anything at all. Finally I said:

"This isn't a thirty-seven year job; this is a thirty-eight year job, Tom Sawyer."

He never said anything. But he sighed, and pretty soon he stopped digging, and then for quite a while I knew that he was thinking. Then he said:

"It's no use, Huck, it's not going to work. If we were prisoners it would, because then we'd have as many years as we wanted, and no hurry; and we wouldn't get but a few minutes to dig, every day, while they were changing watches, and so our hands wouldn't get blistered, and we could keep it up right along, year in and year out, and do it right, and the way it ought to be done. But we can't fool around; we've got to rush; we don't have any time to spare. If we were to put in another night this way we'd have to knock off for a week to let our hands get well—couldn't touch a case-knife with them sooner."

"Well, then, what are we going to do, Tom?"

"I'll tell you. It isn't right, and it isn't moral, and I wouldn't want it to get out; but there's only one way: we have to dig him out with the picks, and pretend we're using case-knives."

"Now you're talking!" I said. "Your thinking gets clearer and clearer all the time, Tom Sawyer," I said. "Picks are the right tool, moral or not moral; and as for me, I don't care at all about the morality of it, anyway. When I set out to free a slave, or take a watermelon, or get a Sunday-school book, I'm not particular about how it gets done as long as it gets done. What I want is to free that slave; or what I want is that watermelon; or what I want is that Sunday-school book; and if a pick is the most practical tool available, that's what I'm going to use to dig out that slave or get that watermelon or that Sunday-school book; and I don't care one bit what the authorities think about it either."

"Well," he says, "there's an excuse for picks and pretending in a situation like this; if there wasn't, I wouldn't approve of it, and I wouldn't stand by and watch the rules get broken—because right is right, and wrong is wrong, and a person has no business doing wrong when he isn't ignorant and knows better. It might work for you to dig Jim out with a pick, without any pretending, because you don't know any better; but it wouldn't work for me, because I do know better. Give me a case-knife."

He had his own with him, but I gave him mine. He threw it down and said:

"Give me a case-knife."

I wasn't sure what to do—but then an idea came to me. I searched through the old tools, found a pickaxe and handed it to him, and he took it and started working without saying a word.

He was always exactly that meticulous. Completely principled.

So I grabbed a shovel, and we took turns picking and digging, making dirt fly everywhere. We kept at it for about half an hour, which was as long as we could manage to stay on our feet, but we had made quite a decent hole to show for our efforts. When I went upstairs, I looked out the window and saw Tom doing everything he could with the lightning rod, but he couldn't manage it because his hands were so sore. Finally he said:

"It's no use, it can't be done. What do you think I should do? Can't you think of any way?"

"Yes," I said, "but I think it's not the proper way. Come up the stairs, and pretend it's a lightning rod."

So he did it.

The next day, Tom took a pewter spoon and a brass candlestick from the house to make some pens for Jim, along with six tallow candles. I waited around the slave quarters looking for an opportunity and managed to take three tin plates. Tom said it wasn't enough, but I told him that nobody would ever notice the plates that Jim threw out because they would land in the dog-fennel and jimson weeds beneath the window opening—then we could bring them back and he could use them again. This satisfied Tom. Then he said:

"Now, what we need to figure out is how to get these things to Jim."

"Take them in through the hole," I said, "when we get it finished."

He just looked scornful and said something about how nobody had ever heard of such a ridiculous idea, and then he went back to thinking. After a while, he said he had figured out two or three ways to do it, but there wasn't any need to decide on any of them yet. He said we had to inform Jim first.

That night we climbed down the lightning rod a little after ten o'clock, bringing one of the candles with us, and listened beneath the window opening, where we could hear Jim snoring; so we tossed it inside, and it didn't wake him up. Then we got to work with the pick and shovel, and in about two and a half hours we had finished the job. We crawled in under Jim's bed and into the cabin, and felt around until we found the candle and lit it, and stood over Jim for a while, and saw that he looked strong and healthy, and then we woke him up gently and gradually. He was so happy to see us he nearly cried; and called us honey, and all the affectionate names he could think of; and wanted us to find a cold chisel right away to cut the chain off his leg with, and escape without wasting any time. But Tom showed him how irregular that would be, and sat down and explained all our plans to him, and how we could change them at a moment's notice if there was any alarm; and told him not to be afraid at all, because we would make sure he got away safely. So Jim said that was fine, and we sat there and talked about old times for a while, and then Tom asked many questions, and when Jim told him that Uncle Silas came in every day or two to pray with him, and Aunt Sally came in to check if he was comfortable and had plenty to eat, and both of them were as kind as they could possibly be, Tom says:

"Now I know how to fix it. We'll send you some things by them."

I said, "Don't do anything like that; it's one of the most foolish ideas I've ever heard," but he didn't pay any attention to me and kept going. That was his way once he had made up his mind about his plans.

So he explained to Jim how they would need to secretly deliver the rope-ladder pie and other large items through Nat, the enslaved man who brought him food, and Jim needed to stay alert and not act surprised, and make sure Nat didn't see him opening these things; and they would hide small items in his uncle's coat pockets for Jim to take out secretly; and they would attach things to his aunt's apron strings or place them in her apron pocket whenever they had the opportunity; and he explained what these items would be and their purpose. He also told him how to write a journal on his shirt using his own blood, along with all the other details. He explained everything to Jim. Jim couldn't understand the reasoning behind most of it, but he figured they were white people and knew better than he did; so he accepted it and promised he would follow Tom's instructions exactly.

Jim had plenty of corncob pipes and tobacco, so we had a really good, friendly time together. Then we crawled out through the hole and headed home to bed, with hands that looked like they had been chewed up. Tom was in high spirits. He said it was the best fun he had ever had in his life, and the most intellectual. He said that if he could only figure out a way to do it, we would keep it up for the rest of our lives and leave Jim to our children to get out. He believed Jim would come to like it better and better the more he got used to it. He said that in that way it could be stretched out to as much as eighty years, and would be the best time on record. And he said it would make us all famous for having a hand in it.

In the morning we went out to the woodpile and chopped up the brass candlestick into manageable pieces, and Tom put them and the pewter spoon in his pocket. Then we went to the slave quarters, and while I distracted Nat, Tom pushed a piece of candlestick into the middle of a cornbread that was in Jim's plate, and we went along with Nat to see how it would work, and it worked perfectly; when Jim bit into it it nearly broke all his teeth; and there had never been anything that could have worked better. Tom said so himself. Jim never let on that it was anything more than just a piece of rock or something like that which always gets into bread, you know; but after that he never bit into anything without first poking his fork into it in three or four places.

And while we were standing there in the dim light, a couple of hounds came bursting in from under Jim's bed; they kept pouring in until there were eleven of them, and there was barely room in there to breathe. Good heavens, we forgot to secure that lean-to door! The black man Nat just shouted "Witches" once, and collapsed onto the floor among the dogs, and began groaning like he was dying. Tom yanked the door open and threw out a piece of Jim's meat, and the dogs went after it, and in two seconds he was out himself and back again and shut the door, and I knew he had secured the other door too. Then he went to work on the black man, coaxing him and comforting him, and asking him if he had been imagining he saw something again. He sat up, and blinked his eyes around, and said:

"Master Sid, you'll say I'm a fool, but if I didn't believe I saw nearly a million dogs, or devils, or something, I wish I may die right here in these tracks. I did, most surely. Master Sid, I felt them—I felt them, sir; they were all over me. Darn it, I just wish I could get my hands on one of those witches just once—only just once—that's all I'd ask. But mostly I wish they'd leave me alone, I do."

Tom says:

"Well, I'll tell you what I think. What brings them here right at this runaway slave's breakfast time? It's because they're hungry; that's the reason. You should make them a witch pie; that's what you need to do."

"But my goodness, Master Sid, how am I going to make him a witch pie? I don't know how to make it. I haven't ever heard of such a thing before."

"Well, then, I'll have to make it myself."

"Will you do it, honey? Will you? I'll worship the ground under your foot, I will!"

"Alright, I'll do it, since it's you asking, and you've been good to us and helped us with the runaway slave. But you have to be extremely careful. When we come by, turn your back; and then whatever we've placed in the pan, don't let on that you see it at all. And don't look when Jim empties the pan—something might happen, I don't know what. And most importantly, don't touch the witch-things."

"Handle him, Master Sid? What are you talking about? I wouldn't lay the weight of my finger on him, not for ten hundred thousand billion dollars, I wouldn't."

Chapter XXXVII.

That was all settled. So then we left and went to the junk pile in the back yard, where they kept the old boots, and rags, and broken bottle pieces, and worn-out tin items, and all kinds of trash, and searched around until we found an old tin washpan, and plugged up the holes as best we could, to bake the pie in, and carried it down to the cellar and filled it with stolen flour and headed off for breakfast, and discovered a couple of roofing nails that Tom said would come in handy for a prisoner to scratch his name and troubles on the dungeon walls with, and slipped one of them into Aunt Sally's apron pocket which was hanging on a chair, and the other one we tucked into the band of Uncle Silas's hat, which was sitting on the dresser, because we had heard the children mention that their father and mother were going to the runaway slave's house this morning, and then we went to breakfast, and Tom slipped the pewter spoon into Uncle Silas's coat pocket, and Aunt Sally hadn't arrived yet, so we had to wait a little while.

And when she arrived, she was heated, flushed, and irritated, and could barely wait for the blessing; then she began pouring out coffee with one hand while rapping the nearest child's head with her thimble with the other, and said:

"I've searched everywhere, high and low, and it's completely baffling what happened to your other shirt."

My heart dropped down into my chest among my lungs and other organs, and a hard piece of cornbread crust started down my throat right after it and collided with a cough on the way down, and got shot across the table, and hit one of the children in the eye and made him curl up like a fishing worm, and caused him to let out a cry as loud as a war whoop, and Tom turned kind of blue around the face, and it all added up to quite a chaotic situation for about a quarter of a minute or so, and I would have given up everything for half its worth if there had been someone willing to take it. But after that we were all fine again—it was the sudden shock of it that caught us so off guard. Uncle Silas says:

"It's extremely strange and curious, I can't understand it. I know perfectly well I took it off, because—"

"Because you only have one on. Just listen to the man! I know you took it off, and I know it by a better way than your scattered memory, too, because it was on the clothesline yesterday—I saw it there myself. But it's gone, that's the bottom line, and you'll just have to change to a red flannel one until I can get time to make a new one. And it'll be the third I've made in two years. It just keeps a person constantly busy to keep you in shirts; and whatever you manage to do with them all is more than I can figure out. A person would think you would learn to take some sort of care of them at your age."

"I understand that, Sally, and I really do try my best. But it shouldn't be entirely my responsibility, because, you know, I don't see them or have anything to do with them except when they're on me; and I don't think I've ever lost a single one of them off of me."

"Well, it's not your fault if you haven't, Silas; you would have done it if you could, I suppose. And the shirt isn't all that's missing, either. There's a spoon gone; and that's not all. There were ten, and now there are only nine. The calf got the shirt, I think, but the calf never took the spoon, that's for sure."

"Why, what else is gone, Sally?"

"Six candles are missing—that's what happened. The rats could have taken the candles, and I believe they did; I'm surprised they don't make off with the entire house, considering how you're always planning to plug up their holes but never actually do it; and if they weren't foolish they'd make their beds in your hair, Silas— you'd never even notice; but you can't blame the spoon on the rats, and I know that for certain."

"Well, Sally, I'm at fault, and I admit it; I've been negligent; but I won't let tomorrow pass without sealing up those holes."

"Oh, I wouldn't rush; next year will work just fine. Matilda Angelina Araminta Phelps!"

The thimble strikes sharply, and the child quickly pulls her hands out of the sugar bowl without any hesitation. Just then the Black woman steps into the hallway and says:

"Ma'am, there's a sheet missing."

"A sheet gone! Well, for the land's sake!"

"I'll fill up those holes today," says Uncle Silas, looking sorrowful.

"Oh, shut up! Do you think the rats took the sheet? Where did it go, Lize?"

"I honestly have no idea, Miss Sally. She was on the clothesline yesterday, but she's gone now: she's not there anymore."

"I think the world is coming to an end. I've never seen anything like it in all my life. A shirt, and a sheet, and a spoon, and six can—"

"Ma'am," said a young light-skinned woman, "there's a brass candlestick missing."

"Get out of here, you hussy, or I'll take a skillet to you!"

Well, she was absolutely furious. I started looking for an opportunity; I figured I would slip out and head for the woods until things calmed down. She kept raging on and on, carrying out her tirade all by herself, while everyone else stayed very meek and quiet; and finally Uncle Silas, looking somewhat foolish, pulls that spoon out of his pocket. She stopped, with her mouth hanging open and her hands raised; and as for me, I wished I was in Jerusalem or anywhere else. But not for long, because she says:

"It's exactly what I thought. So you had it in your pocket the whole time, and you probably have the other things in there as well. How did it end up there?"

"I really don't know, Sally," he says, somewhat apologetically, "or you know I would tell you. I was studying my text in Acts Seventeen before breakfast, and I think I must have put it in there without noticing, meaning to put my Testament in instead, and it must be so, because my Testament isn't there; but I'll go and check; and if the Testament is where I left it, I'll know I didn't put it in, and that will show that I set the Testament down and picked up the spoon, and—"

"Oh, for heaven's sake! Give me a break! Get out of here now, all of you; and don't come near me again until I've gotten my peace of mind back."

I would have heard her even if she had only whispered it to herself, much less spoken it aloud; and I would have gotten up and obeyed her even if I had been dead. As we were passing through the sitting room, the old man picked up his hat, and the shingle nail fell out onto the floor, and he simply picked it up and placed it on the mantelpiece, without saying anything, and went out. Tom saw him do it, and remembered about the spoon, and said:

"Well, there's no point in sending things through him anymore—he's not reliable." Then he says: "But he did us a favor with the spoon, anyway, without knowing it, so we'll go and do him a favor without him knowing it—plug up his rat holes."

There were quite a few of them down in the cellar, and it took us a full hour, but we completed the job thoroughly and properly. Then we heard footsteps on the stairs, so we blew out our light and hid ourselves; and here comes the old man, carrying a candle in one hand and a bundle of items in the other, looking as distracted as ever. He wandered around aimlessly, going from one rat hole to another, until he had visited them all. Then he stood there for about five minutes, picking melted wax drippings off his candle and thinking. Then he turned away slowly and absent-mindedly toward the stairs, saying:

"Well, I honestly can't remember when I did it. I could show her now that I wasn't to blame because of the rats. But never mind—let it go. I don't think it would do any good."

And so he continued mumbling as he went upstairs, and then we left. He was a really nice old man. And he always is.

Tom was quite troubled about how to get a spoon, but he insisted we had to have one, so he thought it over. After he figured it out, he explained his plan to me. We went and lingered near the spoon basket until we saw Aunt Sally approaching, then Tom started counting the spoons and setting them aside, while I slipped one up my sleeve, and Tom said:

"Why, Aunt Sally, there are only nine spoons here."

She says:

"Go on and play, and don't bother me. I know better—I counted them myself."

"Well, I've counted them twice, Aunty, and I can only come up with nine."

She appeared completely out of patience, but naturally she came to count—anyone would have.

"I swear there are only nine!" she said. "What in the world—darn these things, I'll count them again."

So I slipped back the one I had, and when she finished counting, she said:

"Forget about that annoying junk, there's ten now!" and she looked both irritated and flustered. But Tom says:

"Why, Aunty, I don't think there's ten."

"You idiot, didn't you see me count them?"

"I know, but—"

"Well, I'll count them again."

So I snatched one, and they came out to nine, just like the other time. Well, she was furious—trembling all over, she was so angry. But she counted and counted until she got so confused she'd start to count a spoon in the basket sometimes; and so, three times they came out right, and three times they came out wrong. Then she grabbed the basket and slammed it across the house and knocked the cat sideways; and she said get out and let her have some peace, and if we came bothering around her again between that time and dinner she'd whip us. So we had the extra spoon, and dropped it in her apron pocket while she was giving us our marching orders, and Jim got it safely, along with her shingle nail, before noon. We were very satisfied with this scheme, and Tom said it was worth twice the trouble it took, because he said now she could never count those spoons the same way twice again to save her life; and wouldn't believe she'd counted them right if she did; and said that after she'd nearly counted her head off for the next three days he figured she'd give up and threaten to kill anybody who wanted her to ever count them again.

So we put the sheet back on the line that night, and stole one out of her closet; and kept on putting it back and stealing it again for a couple of days until she didn't know how many sheets she had anymore, and she didn't care, and wasn't going to torment herself about it anymore, and wouldn't count them again to save her life; she would rather die first.

So we were all set now with the shirt, the sheet, the spoon, and the candles, thanks to the calf and the rats and our deliberately confused counting; and as for the candlestick, it didn't matter much since that issue would blow over eventually.

But that pie was quite a challenge; we had endless trouble making it. We prepared it deep in the woods and cooked it there; we finally finished it, and it turned out very well, too; but it didn't happen in just one day; we had to go through three wash-pans worth of flour before we were done, and we got burned pretty badly all over in various spots, and our eyes were stung by the smoke; because, you see, we only wanted a crust, and we couldn't support it properly, and it kept collapsing. But naturally we figured out the right method eventually—which was to bake the ladder inside the pie as well. So then we worked with Jim on the second night, and ripped up the sheet into small strips and twisted them together, and well before dawn we had a beautiful rope that could have hanged someone. We pretended it took nine months to make it.

And in the morning we carried it down to the woods, but it wouldn't fit into the pie. Since it was made from a complete sheet, there was enough rope for forty pies if we had wanted them, with plenty remaining for soup, sausage, or whatever else you might choose. We could have had an entire dinner.

But we didn't need it. All we needed was just enough for the pie, so we threw the rest away. We didn't cook any of the pies in the wash-pan—we were afraid the solder would melt; but Uncle Silas had a fine brass warming-pan that he thought highly of, because it belonged to one of his ancestors with a long wooden handle that came over from England with William the Conqueror in the Mayflower or one of those early ships and was hidden away up in the attic with a lot of other old pots and things that were valuable, not because they were useful, since they weren't, but because they were relics, you know, and we sneaked it out, privately, and took it down there, but it failed on the first pies, because we didn't know how, but it worked perfectly on the last one. We took it and lined it with dough, and set it in the coals, and loaded it up with rag rope, and put on a dough roof, and shut down the lid, and put hot embers on top, and stood off five feet, with the long handle, cool and comfortable, and in fifteen minutes it turned out a pie that was a satisfaction to look at. But the person who ate it would want to bring along a couple of barrels of toothpicks, because if that rope ladder wouldn't give him serious trouble I don't know what I'm talking about, and give him enough stomach-ache to last him until next time, too.

Nat wasn't watching when we placed the witch pie in Jim's pan, and we put the three tin plates at the bottom of the pan underneath the food. Jim received everything without any problems, and as soon as he was alone, he broke open the pie and concealed the rope ladder inside his straw mattress. He then scratched some marks on a tin plate and threw it out through the window opening.

Chapter XXXVIII.

Making pens for them was an extremely difficult job, and so was working with the saw; Jim believed the inscription would be the most challenging task of all. That's the one the prisoner has to scratch onto the wall. But he had to do it; Tom said it was absolutely necessary; there had never been a case of a state prisoner not scratching his inscription to leave behind, along with his coat of arms.

"Look at Lady Jane Grey," he says; "look at Guildford Dudley; look at old Northumberland! Why, Huck, suppose it is considerable trouble?—what are you going to do?—how are you going to get around it? Jim's got to do his inscription and coat of arms. They all do."

Jim says:

"Why, Master Tom, I don't have any coat of arms; I don't have anything but this old shirt, and you know I have to keep the journal on that."

"Oh, you don't understand, Jim; a coat of arms is very different."

"Well," I said, "Jim's right, anyway, when he says he doesn't have a coat of arms, because he doesn't."

"I suppose I knew that," Tom says, "but you can be sure he'll have one before he leaves this place—because he's going to leave properly, and there won't be any flaws in his record."

While Jim and I worked on filing our pens using pieces of broken brick—Jim making his from brass and me making mine from the spoon—Tom began working on designing the coat of arms. After a while, he said he had come up with so many good ideas that he could hardly decide which one to choose, but there was one he thought he would settle on. He said:

"On the coat of arms we'll have a golden diagonal stripe in the lower right section, a purple X-shaped cross in the middle, with a lying dog as the main symbol, and under his paw a chain with battlements, representing slavery, with a green chevron at the top with decorative edges, and three curved lines on a blue background, with the center point standing upright on a zigzag indented pattern; crest, a runaway slave, black, with his bundle over his shoulder on a diagonal stripe indicating illegitimate birth; and a couple of red figures for supporters, which is you and me; motto, Maggiore fretta, minore atto. Got it out of a book—means the more haste, the less speed."

"Wow," I said, "but what does the rest of it mean?"

"We don't have time to worry about that," he says; "we need to get to work immediately."

"Well, anyway," I said, "what are some of these terms? What's a fess?"

"A fess—a fess is—you don't need to know what a fess is. I'll show him how to make it when he gets to it."

"Come on, Tom," I said, "I think you could tell a person. What's a bar sinister?"

"Oh, I don't know. But he has to have it. All the nobility does."

That was simply how he operated. If he didn't feel like explaining something to you, he just wouldn't do it. You could press him for answers for an entire week, and it wouldn't make any difference.

He had taken care of all the coat of arms business, so now he began working to complete the remaining part of that task, which involved creating a sorrowful inscription—he said Jim needed to have one, just like everyone else had done. He came up with many options and wrote them down on paper, then read them aloud:

Here a captive heart broke free.

Here a poor prisoner, abandoned by the world and his friends, wore away his sorrowful life.

Here a lonely heart broke, and a weary spirit found its rest, following thirty-seven years of solitary imprisonment.

Here, without a home or friends, after thirty-seven years of harsh imprisonment, died a noble foreigner who was the illegitimate son of Louis XIV.

Tom's voice shook as he read them aloud, and he nearly broke down completely. When he finished reading, he couldn't decide which inscription Jim should carve into the wall since they were all excellent; but finally he decided to let Jim carve all of them. Jim said it would take him a year to scratch so much writing onto the logs with a nail, and besides, he didn't know how to form letters; but Tom said he would outline them for him, and then Jim would only need to trace over the lines. Then shortly after, he said:

"Now that I think about it, the logs won't work; they don't have log walls in a dungeon: we need to carve the inscriptions into a rock. We'll get a rock."

Jim said the rock was worse than the logs; he said it would take him such a terribly long time to dig them into a rock that he would never get out. But Tom said he would let me help him do it. Then he took a look to see how Jim and I were getting along with the pens. It was extremely tedious, hard work and slow, and didn't give my hands any chance to heal from the sores, and we didn't seem to make any progress at all; so Tom says:

"I know how to fix it. We need to get a rock for the coat of arms and sad inscriptions, and we can accomplish two things with that same rock. There's a flashy big grindstone down at the mill, and we'll steal it, and carve the things on it, and sharpen the pens and the saw on it, too."

It wasn't a bad idea at all, and it wasn't a bad grindstone either, but we figured we'd give it a try. It wasn't quite midnight yet, so we headed out to the mill, leaving Jim behind to work. We stole the grindstone and started rolling it home, but it turned out to be an incredibly difficult job. Sometimes, no matter what we did, we couldn't stop it from tipping over, and it nearly crushed us every single time. Tom said it was going to get one of us for sure before we finished. We managed to get it halfway there, and then we were completely exhausted and soaked with sweat. We could see it was no use—we had to go get Jim. So he lifted up his bed and slipped the chain off the bed leg, wrapped it around his neck several times, and we crawled out through our hole and went down there. Jim and I got behind that grindstone and moved it along easily, while Tom supervised. He could supervise better than any boy I'd ever seen. He knew how to do everything.

Our hole was fairly large, but it wasn't big enough to get the grindstone through; however, Jim took the pick and quickly made it large enough. Then Tom marked out those things on it with the nail, and set Jim to work on them, using the nail as a chisel and an iron bolt from the junk in the lean-to as a hammer, and told him to work until the rest of his candle burned out, and then he could go to bed, and hide the grindstone under his straw mattress and sleep on it. Then we helped him fasten his chain back on the bed leg, and were ready for bed ourselves. But Tom thought of something, and said:

"Do you have any spiders in here, Jim?"

"No, sir, thank goodness I haven't, Master Tom."

"All right, we'll get you some."

"But bless you, honey, I don't want any. I'm afraid of them. I'd just as soon have rattlesnakes around."

Tom paused for a moment or two to think, then said:

"It's a good idea. And I think it's been done. It must have been done; it makes sense. Yes, it's an excellent idea. Where could you keep it?"

"Keep what, Mars Tom?"

"Why, a rattlesnake."

"Good gracious alive, Master Tom! Why, if there was a rattlesnake to come in here I'd take and bust right out through that log wall, I would, with my head."

"Come on, Jim, you wouldn't be scared of it once you got used to it. You could train it."

"Tame it!"

"Yes—it's easy enough. Every animal appreciates kindness and affection, and they would never consider harming someone who shows them care. Any book will confirm this. Just give it a try—that's all I'm asking; simply attempt it for two or three days. Why, you can make him so attached to you in a short time that he'll adore you; and sleep beside you; and won't leave your side for even a moment; and will allow you to drape him around your neck and place his head in your mouth."

"Please, Master Tom—don't talk like that! I can't stand it! He'd let me put his head in my mouth—as a favor, isn't that right? I bet he'd wait a very long time before I ask him. And more than that, I don't want him to sleep with me."

"Jim, don't be so foolish. A prisoner has to have some kind of simple pet, and if a rattlesnake has never been tried before, well, there's more glory to be gained by being the first person to ever try it than any other way you could think of to save your life."

"Why, Mars Tom, I don't want any such glory. Snake takes and bites Jim's chin off, then where is the glory? No, sir, I don't want any such doings."

"Darn it, can't you at least try? I just want you to give it a shot—you don't have to stick with it if it doesn't work out."

"But the trouble is all over if the snake bites me while I'm trying to tame him. Master Tom, I'm willing to tackle most anything that isn't unreasonable, but if you and Huck bring a rattlesnake in here for me to tame, I'm going to leave, that's for sure."

"Well, then, forget it, forget it, if you're going to be so stubborn about it. We can get you some garter snakes, and you can tie some buttons on their tails, and pretend they're rattlesnakes, and I suppose that'll have to be enough."

"I can stand them, Master Tom, but I'll be blamed if I couldn't get along without them, I tell you that. I never knew before that it was so much bother and trouble to be a prisoner."

"Well, it always is when it's done right. Do you have any rats around here?"

"No, sir, I haven't seen any."

"Well, we'll get you some rats."

"Why, Mars Tom, I don't want any rats. They're the most troublesome creatures to disturb a person, and rustle around over him, and bite his feet, when he's trying to sleep, I ever saw. No, sir, give me garter snakes, if I've got to have them, but don't give me any rats; I haven't got any use for them, scarcely."

"But Jim, you have to have them—everyone does. So don't make any more fuss about it. Prisoners are never without rats. There's no case of it ever happening. And they train them, and pet them, and teach them tricks, and the rats become as friendly as flies. But you have to play music for them. Do you have anything to play music on?"

"I don't have anything except a coarse comb and a piece of paper, and a jaw harp; but I suppose they wouldn't put any value in a jaw harp."

"Yes they would. They don't care what kind of music it is. A jew's harp is plenty good enough for a rat. All animals like music—in a prison they absolutely love it. Especially painful music; and you can't get any other kind out of a jew's harp. It always interests them; they come out to see what's wrong with you. Yes, you're all right; you're set up very well. You want to sit on your bed at night before you go to sleep, and early in the mornings, and play your jew's harp; play 'The Last Link is Broken'—that's the thing that'll catch a rat quicker than anything else; and when you've played for about two minutes you'll see all the rats, and the snakes, and spiders, and things begin to feel worried about you, and come. And they'll just swarm all over you, and have a wonderful good time."

"Yes, they will, I reckon, Master Tom, but what kind of time is Jim having? Blessed if I can see the point. But I'll do it if I have to. I reckon I better keep the animals satisfied, and not have any trouble in the house."

Tom took a moment to think it over and see if there wasn't anything else; and soon he said:

"Oh, there's one thing I forgot. Do you think you could grow a flower here?"

"I don't know, but maybe I could, Master Tom; but it's pretty dark in here, and I don't have any use for a flower anyway, and it would be a lot of trouble."

"Well, you should try it anyway. Some other prisoners have done it."

"One of those big cattail-looking mullein stalks would grow in here, Master Tom, I reckon, but it wouldn't be worth half the trouble it would cause."

"Don't you believe it. We'll get you a small one and you can plant it in that corner over there, and grow it. And don't call it mullein, call it Pitchiola—that's what it's properly called when it's in a prison. And you need to water it with your tears."

"Why, I have plenty of spring water, Master Tom."

"You don't want spring water; you want to water it with your tears. It's the way they always do."

"Why, Master Tom, I bet I can grow one of those mullein stalks twice as fast with spring water while another man is just starting one with tears."

"That's not the point. You have to do it with tears."

"She'll die in my hands, Master Tom, she surely will, because I hardly ever cry."

So Tom was completely puzzled. But he thought it through, and then said Jim would have to make do the best he could with an onion. He promised he would sneak over to the slave quarters and secretly drop one in Jim's coffee pot in the morning. Jim said he would "just as soon have tobacco in his coffee," and complained so much about it, and about all the work and trouble of growing the mullein, and playing music to attract the rats, and caring for and encouraging the snakes and spiders and other creatures, on top of all the other work he had to do with pens, and inscriptions, and journals, and other things, which made being a prisoner more troublesome and worrisome and demanding than anything he had ever attempted, that Tom nearly lost all patience with him; and said he was simply loaded down with more spectacular opportunities than any prisoner ever had in the world to make a reputation for himself, and yet he didn't have enough sense to value them, and they were practically wasted on him. So Jim felt sorry, and said he wouldn't act that way anymore, and then Tom and I headed off to bed.

Chapter XXXIX.

In the morning we went up to the village and bought a wire rat trap and brought it back down, then opened up the best rat hole, and in about an hour we had caught fifteen of the finest rats you ever saw. We took the trap and put it in a safe place under Aunt Sally's bed. But while we were gone looking for spiders, little Thomas Franklin Benjamin Jefferson Alexander Phelps found it there and opened the door to see if the rats would come out, and they did. Aunt Sally came in, and when we got back she was standing on top of the bed raising holy hell, and the rats were doing everything they could to keep her entertained. So she took a hickory switch and gave us both a good beating, and it took us nearly two hours to catch another fifteen or sixteen rats, curse that meddling kid, and they weren't nearly as good as the first batch either, because our first catch had been the best of the bunch. I never saw a finer group of rats than what we caught in that first haul.

We collected an excellent assortment of sorted spiders, bugs, frogs, caterpillars, and various other creatures; and we nearly managed to get a hornet's nest, but we didn't succeed. The family was at home. We didn't give up right away, but stayed with them as long as we could; because we figured we'd tire them out or they'd have to tire us out, and they did it. Then we got some liniment and rubbed it on the stung places, and we were pretty much all right again, but couldn't sit down comfortably. And so we went after the snakes, and grabbed a couple of dozen garter snakes and house snakes, and put them in a bag, and placed it in our room, and by that time it was supper-time, and it had been a really good honest day's work: and hungry?—oh, no, I don't think so! And there wasn't a single snake up there when we went back— we didn't tie the sack properly, and they worked their way out somehow, and left. But it didn't matter much, because they were still on the property somewhere. So we figured we could catch some of them again. No, there wasn't any real shortage of snakes around the house for quite a while. You'd see them dropping from the rafters and other places every now and then; and they usually landed on your plate, or down the back of your neck, and most of the time where you didn't want them. Well, they were beautiful and striped, and there wasn't any harm in a million of them; but that never made any difference to Aunt Sally; she hated snakes, whatever the type might be, and she couldn't tolerate them no matter how you tried to fix it; and every time one of them dropped down on her, it didn't matter what she was doing, she would just put that work down and run away. I never saw such a woman. And you could hear her scream all the way to Jericho. You couldn't get her to pick up one of them with tongs. And if she rolled over and found one in bed she would scramble out and let out a howl that you would think the house was on fire. She disturbed the old man so much that he said he could almost wish there had never been any snakes created. Why, after every last snake had been gone completely out of the house for as much as a week Aunt Sally wasn't over it yet; she wasn't nearly over it; when she was sitting thinking about something you could touch her on the back of her neck with a feather and she would jump right out of her stockings. It was very strange. But Tom said all women were just like that. He said they were made that way for some reason or other.

We received a beating every time one of our snakes crossed her path, and she made it clear these beatings were nothing compared to what she would do if we ever filled the place with them again. I didn't mind the beatings because they weren't that bad, but I was bothered by the trouble we had getting another batch. However, we managed to gather them up along with all the other things, and you never saw a cabin as lively as Jim's was when they would all come swarming out for music and go after him. Jim didn't like the spiders, and the spiders didn't like Jim, so they would wait for him and make things very uncomfortable for him. He said that between the rats and the snakes and the grindstone, there was barely any room for him in bed, and when there was space, a person couldn't sleep because it was so active, and it was always active, he said, because they never all slept at the same time but took turns, so when the snakes were asleep the rats were active, and when the rats went to sleep the snakes came on duty, so he always had one group underneath him getting in his way, and the other group putting on a show above him, and if he got up to find a new spot the spiders would take their shot at him as he moved across. He said if he ever got out this time he would never be a prisoner again, not for any amount of money.

Well, by the end of three weeks everything was in pretty good shape. The shirt was smuggled in early, hidden in a pie, and every time a rat bit Jim he would get up and write a little in his journal while the ink was fresh; the pens were made, the inscriptions and so on were all carved on the grindstone; the bed-leg was sawed in two, and we had eaten up the sawdust, and it gave us a most amazing stomach-ache. We figured we were all going to die, but didn't. It was the most indigestible sawdust I ever saw; and Tom said the same.

But as I was saying, we had finally finished all the work, and we were all pretty exhausted, especially Jim. The old man had written a couple of times to the plantation below New Orleans asking them to come get their runaway slave, but he hadn't received any response because no such plantation existed. So he decided he would place an advertisement for Jim in the St. Louis and New Orleans newspapers. When he mentioned the St. Louis papers, it sent chills down my spine, and I realized we had no time to waste. So Tom said it was now time for the anonymous letters.

"What are those?" I asked.

"Warnings to the people that something is happening. Sometimes it's done one way, sometimes another. But there's always someone spying around who alerts the governor of the castle. When Louis XVI was going to escape from the Tuileries, a servant girl did it. It's a very good method, and so are the anonymous letters. We'll use both of them. And it's common for the prisoner's mother to switch clothes with him, and she stays inside while he slips out wearing her clothes. We'll do that too."

"But listen here, Tom, why do we want to warn anyone that something's going on? Let them figure it out for themselves—it's their problem."

"Yes, I know; but you can't rely on them. It's how they've behaved from the very beginning—left us to handle everything. They're so trusting and simple-minded they don't pay attention to anything at all. So if we don't alert them there won't be anyone or anything to interfere with us, and so after all our hard work and effort this escape will fall completely flat; won't amount to anything—won't be anything to it."

"Well, as for me, Tom, that's how I'd prefer it."

"Darn!" he said, looking disgusted. So I said:

"But I'm not going to make any complaint. Whatever way suits you suits me. What are you going to do about the servant girl?"

"You'll take her place. You sneak in during the middle of the night and steal that yellow girl's dress."

"Why, Tom, that'll cause trouble in the morning; because, of course, she probably doesn't have any but that one."

"I know; but you only need it for fifteen minutes, to deliver the anonymous letter and slip it under the front door."

"All right, then, I'll do it; but I could carry it just as easily in my own clothes."

"You wouldn't look like a servant-girl then, would you?"

"No, but there won't be anyone to see what I look like, anyway."

"That has nothing to do with it. What we need to do is simply perform our duty, and not worry about whether anyone sees us do it or not. Don't you have any principles at all?"

"All right, I'm not saying anything; I'm the servant girl. Who is Jim's mother?"

"I'm his mother. I'll grab a dress from Aunt Sally."

"Well, then, you'll have to stay in the cabin when Jim and I leave."

"Not much. I'll stuff Jim's clothes full of straw and lay it on his bed to represent his mother in disguise, and Jim will take the woman's gown off of me and wear it, and we'll all escape together. When a prisoner of style escapes it's called an evasion. It's always called so when a king escapes, for instance. And the same with a king's son; it doesn't make any difference whether he's a legitimate one or an illegitimate one."

So Tom wrote the anonymous letter, and I stole the yellow servant girl's dress that night, put it on, and slipped it under the front door, just as Tom had instructed me to do. It said:

Beware. Trouble is brewing. Keep a sharp lookout. UNKNOWN FRIEND.

The next night we put up a picture that Tom had drawn in blood, showing a skull and crossbones on the front door; and the following night we placed another one of a coffin on the back door. I had never seen a family in such a panic. They couldn't have been more terrified if the place had been full of ghosts waiting for them behind everything and under the beds and floating through the air. If a door slammed, Aunt Sally would jump and say "ouch!" If anything dropped, she would jump and say "ouch!" If you happened to touch her when she wasn't paying attention, she did the same thing; she couldn't face any direction and feel comfortable, because she believed there was something behind her every time—so she was always spinning around suddenly, and saying "ouch," and before she had turned two-thirds of the way around she would whirl back again, and say it again; and she was afraid to go to bed, but she didn't dare stay up. So the plan was working very well, Tom said; he said he had never seen anything work more perfectly. He said it proved it was done right.

So he said, now for the big moment! The very next morning at the first light of dawn, we prepared another letter and wondered what we should do with it, because we had heard them say at supper that they were going to have a guard watching both doors all night. Tom climbed down the lightning rod to look around, and the guard at the back door was asleep, so he stuck the letter in the back of his neck and returned. This letter said:

Don't betray me, I wish to be your friend. There is a desperate gang of cutthroats from over in the Indian Territory going to steal your runaway slave tonight, and they have been trying to scare you so that you will stay in the house and not bother them. I am one of the gang, but have got religion and wish to quit it and lead an honest life again, and will betray the hellish design. They will sneak down from northward, along the fence, at midnight exactly, with a false key, and go in the slave's cabin to get him. I am to be off a piece and blow a tin horn if I see any danger; but instead of that I

300

will bleat like a sheep as soon as they get in and not blow at all; then while they are getting his chains loose, you slip there and lock them in, and can kill them at your leisure. Don't do anything but just the way I am telling you, if you do they will suspect something and raise a ruckus. I do not wish any reward but to know I have done the right thing.

UNKNOWN FRIEND

Chapter XL.

We were feeling pretty good after breakfast, and I took my canoe and went across the river fishing, bringing along some lunch, and had a great time, and checked on the raft and found it was fine, and got home late for supper, and discovered them in such a panic and worry they didn't know what they were doing, and made us go straight to bed the moment we finished supper, and wouldn't tell us what the problem was, and never mentioned a word about the new letter, but they didn't need to, because we knew as much about it as anyone did, and as soon as we were halfway up the stairs and her back was turned we snuck down to the cellar cupboard and packed up a good lunch and brought it up to our room and went to bed, and got up around half past eleven, and Tom put on Aunt Sally's dress that he had stolen and was about to leave with the lunch, but said:

"Where's the butter?"

"I spread out a chunk of it," I said, "on a piece of cornbread."

"Well, you left it laid out, then—it's not here."

"We can manage without it," I said.

"We can manage with that too," he says. "Just slip down to the cellar and get it. Then climb down the lightning rod and come over. I'll go stuff straw into Jim's clothes to make it look like his mother in disguise, and I'll be ready to bleat like a sheep and push off as soon as you arrive."

So he left, and I went down to the cellar. The chunk of butter, as big as a person's fist, was right where I had left it, so I picked up the piece of cornbread with the butter on it, blew out my light, and started climbing the stairs very quietly, making it to the main floor without any trouble, but then Aunt Sally appeared with a candle, and I quickly shoved the food into my hat and put my hat on my head, and the very next moment she spotted me; and she says:

"Have you been down to the basement?"

"Yes'm."

"What have you been doing down there?"

"Noth'n."

"Noth'n!"

"No'm."

"Well, then, what made you go down there at this time of night?"

"I don't know him."

"You don't know? Don't give me that answer. Tom, I want to know what you've been doing down there."

"I haven't been doing a single thing, Aunt Sally, I hope to God if I have."

I figured she would let me go now, and usually she would have; but I suppose there were so many strange things happening that she was worried about every little thing that wasn't perfectly normal; so she said, very firmly:

"You just walk straight into that sitting room and stay there until I come. You've been up to something you have no business doing, and I guarantee I'll find out what it is before I'm finished with you."

So she left as I opened the door and walked into the living room. My goodness, there was quite a crowd there! Fifteen farmers, and every single one of them carried a gun. I felt extremely sick and slipped into a chair to sit down. They were sitting around, some of them talking quietly in low voices, and all of them restless and uncomfortable, though trying to appear as if they weren't. But I knew they were nervous because they kept taking off their hats and putting them back on, scratching their heads, shifting in their seats, and fidgeting with their buttons. I wasn't comfortable either, but I kept my hat on just the same.

I really wished Aunt Sally would show up and finish dealing with me, give me a beating if she wanted to, and let me leave so I could tell Tom how we had gone too far with this plan, and what a huge mess we had gotten ourselves into, so we could stop messing around immediately, and escape with Jim before these scoundrels lost their patience and came after us.

Finally she arrived and started questioning me, but I couldn't give her straight answers since I didn't know which way was up. These men were so agitated that some wanted to leave immediately and ambush those desperadoes, insisting there were only a few minutes left until midnight, while others tried to convince them to wait for the sheep signal. Meanwhile, Aunt Sally kept firing questions at me, and I was trembling all over, ready to collapse right where I stood from fear. The room was getting hotter and hotter, and the butter began melting and dripping down my neck and behind my ears. Soon, when one of them declared, "I'm in favor of going to the cabin right now and catching them when they arrive," I nearly fainted. A stream of butter trickled down my forehead, and when Aunt Sally noticed it, she turned white as a sheet and exclaimed:

"For heaven's sake, what is wrong with this child? He's definitely got brain fever, and his brains are leaking out!"

And everyone rushes over to look, and she pulls off my hat, and out falls the bread and whatever butter was still there, and she grabs me, and hugs me, and says:

"Oh, what a scare you gave me! And how glad and grateful I am that it's not any worse; because luck is against us, and it never rains but it pours, and when I saw that mess I thought we'd lost you, because I knew by the color and everything it looked just like your brains would if—Dear, dear, why didn't you tell me that was what you'd been down there for? I wouldn't have cared. Now get yourself off to bed, and don't let me see any more of you until morning!"

I was upstairs in a second, and down the lightning rod in another, racing through the darkness toward the lean-to. I could barely get my words out because I was so anxious, but I told Tom as quickly as I could that we had to run for it right now, without wasting a single minute—the house over there was full of armed men!

His eyes simply burned with intensity, and he said:

"No way! Really? Isn't that amazing! Listen, Huck, if I had to do it all over again, I bet I could get two hundred! If we could just wait until—"

"Hurry! Hurry!" I said. "Where's Jim?"

"Right next to you; if you stretch out your arm you can touch him. He's dressed, and everything's ready. Now we'll slip out and give the sheep-signal."

But then we heard the sound of men's footsteps approaching the door, and we heard them start to fiddle with the padlock, and we heard a man say:

"I told you we'd arrive too early; they haven't shown up yet—the door is locked. Here's what we'll do: I'll lock some of you inside the cabin, and you wait for them in the darkness and kill them when they arrive; the rest of you spread out a bit and listen to see if you can hear them approaching."

So they came in, but they couldn't see us in the darkness, and most of them stepped on us while we were scrambling to get under the bed. But we managed to get under there safely, and crawled out through the hole, moving quickly but quietly—Jim went first, then me, and Tom came last, which was exactly how Tom had planned it. Now we were in the lean-to, and we could hear footsteps nearby outside. So we crept to the door, and Tom stopped us there and pressed his eye to the crack, but he couldn't make out anything because it was so dark; he whispered that he would listen for the footsteps to move farther away, and when he nudged us, Jim should slip out first, and Tom would go last. So he put his ear to the crack and listened, and listened, and listened, while the footsteps kept scraping around out there the whole time; and finally he nudged us, and we slid out, crouching down without breathing and making no sound at all, and we moved stealthily toward the fence in single file, and we reached it safely, with Jim and me climbing over it; but Tom's pants got caught on a splinter at the top of the fence, and then he heard the footsteps approaching, so he had to pull himself free, which broke the splinter and made a noise; and just as he dropped down and we started moving, someone called out:

"Who's there? Answer, or I'll shoot!"

But we didn't respond; we just turned on our heels and pushed forward. Then there was a sudden rush, and a bang, bang, bang! and the bullets absolutely whizzed all around us! We heard them call out:

"There they are! They've broken for the river! After them, boys, and turn the dogs loose!"

So here they came, charging forward at full speed. We could hear them approaching because they wore boots and were shouting, but we weren't wearing boots and kept quiet. We were on the path leading to the mill, and when they got fairly close to us, we ducked into the bushes and let them pass by, then fell in behind them. They had kept all the dogs locked up so the animals wouldn't frighten away the robbers, but by now someone had released them, and here they came, making enough noise for a million dogs. However, they were our dogs, so we stood still until they caught up with us. When they saw it was nobody but us and that we offered no excitement for them, they simply greeted us and rushed straight ahead toward the shouting and commotion. Then we picked up speed again and raced along behind them until we were almost at the mill. At that point, we cut up through the bushes to where I had tied my canoe, jumped in, and paddled for our lives toward the middle of the river, making no more noise than absolutely necessary. Then we headed out, relaxed and comfortable, toward the island where my raft was moored. We could hear them yelling and barking at each other all along the riverbank until we had traveled so far away that the sounds grew faint and finally disappeared completely. When we stepped onto the raft, I said:

"Now, old Jim, you're a free man again, and I bet you won't ever be a slave no more."

"And it was a mighty good job too, Huck. It was planned beautifully, and it was done beautifully; and there isn't anybody who can come up with a plan that's more mixed-up and splendid than what that one was."

We were all as happy as we could possibly be, but Tom was the happiest of all because he had a bullet lodged in his calf.

When Jim and I heard that, we didn't feel as confident as we had before. It was hurting him quite a bit, and he was bleeding; so we laid him in the shelter and tore up one of the duke's shirts to bandage him, but he said:

"Give me those rags; I can handle it myself. Don't stop now; don't mess around here, with the escape going so well; grab the oars, and let's get moving! Boys, we pulled this off perfectly—we really did. I wish we could have been the ones to handle Louis XVI; there wouldn't have been any 'Son of Saint Louis, ascend to heaven!' written in his biography; no sir, we would have gotten him across the border—that's what we would have done with him—and pulled it off as smooth as silk, too. Grab the oars—grab the oars!"

But Jim and I were talking things over—and thinking. And after we'd thought for a minute, I said:

"Say it, Jim."

So he says:

"Well, then, this is how it looks to me, Huck. If it was him that was being set free, and one of the boys was to get shot, would he say, 'Go on and save me, never mind about a doctor to save this one?' Is that like Mr. Tom Sawyer? Would he say that? You bet he wouldn't! Well, then, is Jim going to say it? No, sir—I don't budge a step out of this place without a doctor; not if it's forty years!"

I knew he was good inside, and I figured he'd say what he did say—so it was all right now, and I told Tom I was going for a doctor. He made quite a fuss about it, but Jim and I stuck to our decision and wouldn't budge; so he wanted to crawl out and set the raft loose himself; but we wouldn't let him. Then he gave us a piece of his mind, but it didn't do any good.

So when he sees me getting the canoe ready, he says:

"Well, then, if you're determined to go, I'll tell you what to do when you reach the village. Close the door and blindfold the doctor securely, make him promise to keep absolutely silent, and place a bag full of gold coins in his hand. Then lead him through all the back streets and everywhere else in the darkness, and afterward bring him here by canoe, taking a winding route through the islands. Search him and take away his chalk, and don't return it to him until you've brought him back to the village, or he'll mark this raft so he can locate it again. That's how everyone does it."

So I promised I would, and I left, and Jim was supposed to hide in the woods when he saw the doctor coming until the doctor was gone again.

Chapter XLI.

The doctor was an elderly man; a very pleasant, gentle-looking elderly man when I woke him up. I explained to him that my brother and I had been hunting on Spanish Island yesterday afternoon, and we had camped on a section of a raft we discovered, and around midnight he must have kicked his gun while dreaming, because it discharged and wounded him in the leg, and we needed him to go over there and treat it without mentioning anything about it, or letting anyone know, because we planned to return home this evening and surprise our family.

"Who are your people?" he says.

"The Phelpses, down there."

"Oh," he says. And after a minute, he says:

"How did you say he got shot?"

"He had a dream," I said, "and it shot him."

"Strange dream," he says.

So he lit his lantern and grabbed his saddlebags, and we set off. But when he saw the canoe, he wasn't happy with how it looked—he said it was big enough for one person, but didn't seem very safe for two. I said:

"Oh, you don't need to be afraid, sir, she carried the three of us easily enough."

"What three?"

"Well, Sid and I, and—and—and the guns; that's what I mean."

"Oh," he says.

But he placed his foot on the edge of the boat and rocked it back and forth, shaking his head as he said he thought he'd search for a larger one. However, all the boats were locked up and chained, so he took my canoe and told me to wait until he returned, or I could search around some more, or perhaps I should go back home and prepare them for the surprise if I wanted to. But I said I didn't want to, so I explained to him exactly how to find the raft, and then he left.

I came up with an idea pretty quickly. I thought to myself, what if he can't fix that leg right away? What if it takes him three or four days? What are we going to do then—just hang around there until he spills the secret? No way; I know what I'll do. I'll wait, and when he comes back, if he says he needs to go anywhere else, I'll get down there too, even if I have to swim; and we'll grab him and tie him up, and keep him with us, and head out down the river; and when Tom's finished with him we'll pay him what it's worth, or everything we have, and then let him go ashore.

So I crawled into a pile of lumber to get some sleep, and when I woke up next, the sun was high overhead! I rushed out and headed to the doctor's house, but they told me he had left during the night and hadn't returned yet. Well, I thought to myself, that looks really bad for Tom, and I need to get to the island immediately. So I took off, turned the corner, and almost crashed headfirst into Uncle Silas's belly! He says:

"Why, Tom! Where have you been all this time, you rascal?"

"I haven't been anywhere," I said, "just hunting for the runaway slave—me and Sid."

"Why, where on earth did you go?" he says. "Your aunt has been extremely worried."

"She doesn't need to," I said, "because we were fine. We followed the men and the dogs, but they outran us, and we lost them; but we thought we heard them on the water, so we got a canoe and went after them and crossed over, but couldn't find anything; so we searched along the shore until we got tired and worn out; and we tied up the canoe and went to sleep, and didn't wake up until about an hour ago; then we paddled over here to hear the news, and Sid's at the post office to see what he can find out, and I'm heading out to get something to eat for us, and then we're going home."

So then we went to the post office to get Sid, but just as I suspected, he wasn't there. The old man picked up a letter from the office, and we waited a while longer, but Sid didn't show up. Finally, the old man said to come along and let Sid walk home or take a canoe when he finished fooling around—we would ride instead. I couldn't convince him to let me stay and wait for Sid. He said there was no point in it, and I had to come along so Aunt Sally could see we were all right.

When we arrived home, Aunt Sally was so happy to see me that she both laughed and cried at the same time, hugged me tightly, and gave me one of those gentle scoldings of hers that didn't really mean anything, and said she would treat Sid the same way when he arrived.

And the place was completely packed with farmers and their wives for dinner, and you never heard such constant chatter. Old Mrs. Hotchkiss was the worst of all; her tongue never stopped moving. She says:

"Well, Sister Phelps, I've searched that cabin thoroughly, and I believe the man was crazy. I said to Sister Damrell—didn't I, Sister Damrell?—I said, he's crazy, I said—those were my exact words. You all heard me: he's crazy, I said; everything shows it, I said. Look at that grindstone, I said; do you want to tell me that any creature who's in his right mind is going to scrawl all those crazy things onto a grindstone, I said? Here such and such a person broke his heart; and here so and so struggled along for thirty-seven years, and all that—natural son of Louis somebody, and such everlasting nonsense. He's completely crazy, I said; it's what I said in the first place, it's what I said in the middle, and it's what I said last and all the time—the man's crazy—crazy as Nebuchadnezzar, I said."

"And look at that ladder made out of rags, Sister Hotchkiss," says old Mrs. Damrell; "what in the name of goodness could he ever want with—"

"Those exact words I was saying just this minute to Sister Utterback, and she'll tell you so herself. She said, look at that rope ladder, she said; and I said, yes, look at it, I said—what could he have wanted with it, I said. She said, Sister Hotchkiss, she said—"

"But how in the world did they ever get that grindstone in there, anyway? And who dug that hole? And who—"

"Those were my exact words, Brother Penrod! I was saying—pass that dish of molasses, would you?—I was saying to Sister Dunlap, just this minute, how did they get that grindstone in there, I said. Without help, mind you—without help! That's where it is. Don't tell me, I said; there was help, I said; and there was plenty of help, too, I said; there's been a dozen helping that slave, and I bet I'd punish every last slave on this place until I'd find out who did it, I said; and furthermore, I said—"

"A dozen, you say!—forty men couldn't have accomplished everything that's been done. Look at those case-knife saws and tools, how painstakingly they've been crafted; look at that bed-leg sawed off with them, a week's work for six men; look at that figure made out of straw on the bed; and look at—"

"You're absolutely right about that, Brother Hightower! That's exactly what I was telling Brother Phelps himself. He said, 'What do you think about it, Sister Hotchkiss?' he said. 'Think about what, Brother Phelps?' I said. 'Think about that bed leg being sawed off like that,' he said. 'Think about it,' I said. 'I guarantee it didn't saw itself off,' I said—'somebody sawed it,' I said. 'That's my opinion, take it or leave it. It might not be worth much,' I said, 'but for what it's worth, it's my opinion,' I said, 'and if anybody can come up with a better one,' I said, 'let them do it,' I said. 'That's all.' I told Sister Dunlap, I said—"

"Good heavens, there must have been a houseful of slaves in there every night for four weeks to accomplish all that work, Sister Phelps. Look at that shirt—every last inch of it covered over with secret African writing done with blood! There must have been a whole bunch of them at it constantly, all the time, almost. Why, I'd give two dollars to have it read to me; and as for the slaves that wrote it, I believe I'd take and whip them until—"

"People to help him, Brother Marples! Well, I think you'd agree if you'd been in this house for a while. Why, they've stolen everything they could get their hands on—and we were watching all the time, mind you. They stole that shirt right off the line! And as for that sheet they made the rope ladder out of, there's no telling how many times they stole that; and flour, and candles, and candlesticks, and spoons, and the old warming-pan, and nearly a thousand things that I can't remember now, and my new cotton dress; and me and Silas and my Sid and Tom keeping constant watch day and night, as I was telling you, and not one of us could catch hide nor hair nor sight nor sound of them; and here at the last minute, wouldn't you know it, they slip right in under our noses and fool us, and not only fool us but the Indian Territory robbers too, and actually get away with that slave safe and sound, and that with sixteen men and twenty-two dogs right on their heels at that very moment! I tell you, it beats anything I ever heard of. Why, spirits couldn't have done better and been any smarter. And I think they must have been spirits—because, you know our dogs, and there aren't any better; well, those dogs never even got on their track once! You explain that to me if you can!—any of you!"

"Well, it does beat—"

"Good heavens, I never—"

"I swear, I wouldn't have—"

"House-thieves as well as—"

"Good gracious, I would have been afraid to live in such a—"

"Afraid to live! Why, I was so scared I could hardly go to bed, or get up, or lie down, or sit down, Sister Ridgeway. Why, they would steal the very—why, goodness gracious, you can imagine what kind of panic I was in by the time midnight came last night. I hope to heaven I wasn't afraid they would steal some of the family! I was just at that point where I didn't have any reasoning abilities left. It looks foolish enough now, in the daylight; but I said to myself, there are my two poor boys asleep, way upstairs in that lonely room, and I swear to goodness I was so anxious that I crept up there and locked them in! I did. And anybody would have. Because, you know, when you get frightened like that, and it keeps going on, and getting worse and worse all the time, and your mind starts getting confused, and you start doing all sorts of crazy things, and eventually you think to yourself, suppose I was a boy, and was way up there, and the door isn't locked, and you—" She stopped, looking kind of puzzled, and then she turned her head around slowly, and when her eyes fell on me—I got up and took a walk.

I said to myself that I could better explain how we ended up not being in that room this morning if I stepped aside and thought it through a bit. So that's what I did. But I didn't dare go far, or she would have sent for me. When it was late in the day and all the people had left, I came in and told her that the noise and shooting had woken up me and "Sid," and since the door was locked and we wanted to see what was happening, we climbed down the lightning rod, and we both got hurt a little, and we never wanted to try that again. Then I went on and told her everything I had told Uncle Silas earlier; and she said she would forgive us, and maybe it was all right anyway, and about what you might expect from boys, since all boys were a pretty reckless bunch as far as she could tell; and so, as long as no harm had come of it, she figured she'd better spend her time being grateful that we were alive and well and she still had us, instead of worrying about what was past and done. So then she kissed me and patted me on the head and fell into a kind of thoughtful mood; and pretty soon she jumped up and said:

"Good heavens, it's almost nighttime, and Sid still hasn't come home! What has happened to that boy?"

I see my opportunity, so I jump up and say:

"I'll run straight into town and get him," I said.

"No you won't," she says. "You'll stay right where you are; one person getting lost at a time is enough. If he isn't here for supper, your uncle will go."

Well, he wasn't there for supper, so right after supper uncle went.

He came back around ten o'clock feeling somewhat worried; he hadn't come across any sign of Tom. Aunt Sally was quite anxious, but Uncle Silas told her there was no reason to worry—boys will be boys, he said, and you'll see this one show up in the morning safe and sound. So she had to accept that. But she said she would stay up for him for a while anyway, and keep a light on so he could see it.

When I went upstairs to bed, she came with me carrying her candle, tucked me in, and took such good care of me that I felt terrible and couldn't bear to look at her. She sat down on the bed and talked with me for a long time, telling me what a wonderful boy Sid was, and she seemed like she never wanted to stop talking about him. She kept asking me every so often if I thought he might have gotten lost, or hurt, or maybe drowned, and could be lying somewhere right now suffering or dead, with her not there to help him, and tears would fall silently down her face. I kept telling her that Sid was fine and would be home in the morning for sure. She would squeeze my hand or kiss me and ask me to say it again, and to keep saying it, because it made her feel better and she was so worried. When she was about to leave, she looked straight into my eyes so steadily and gently, and said:

"The door won't be locked, Tom, and there's the window and the rod; but you'll be good, won't you? And you won't go? For my sake."

Laws knows I desperately wanted to go check on Tom, and I had every intention of going; but after that happened, I wouldn't have gone, not even if you offered me entire kingdoms.

But she was on my mind and Tom was on my mind, so I slept very restlessly. And twice I went down the rod during the night, and slipped around to the front, and saw her sitting there by her candle in the window with her eyes looking toward the road and tears in them; and I wished I could do something for her, but I couldn't, except to promise that I would never do anything to hurt her again. And the third time I woke up at dawn, and slid down, and she was still there, and her candle was almost burned out, and her old gray head was resting on her hand, and she was asleep.

Chapter XLII.

The old man went uptown again before breakfast, but he couldn't find any trace of Tom. Both of them sat at the table thinking without saying anything, looking sad, while their coffee grew cold and they didn't eat anything. After a while, the old man said:

"Did I give you the letter?"

"What letter?"

"The one I picked up yesterday from the post office."

"No, you didn't give me any letter."

"Well, I must have forgotten it."

So he searched through his pockets, and then went off somewhere he had left it, and brought it back, and gave it to her. She says:

"Why, it's from St. Petersburg—it's from Sis."

I thought another walk would help me feel better, but I couldn't move. However, before she could tear it open, she dropped it and ran—because she saw something. And so did I. It was Tom Sawyer lying on a mattress, along with that old doctor, and Jim wearing her calico dress with his hands tied behind his back, surrounded by a crowd of people. I quickly hid the letter behind the first thing I could find and rushed forward. She threw herself at Tom, crying, and said:

"Oh, he's dead, he's dead, I know he's dead!"

And Tom turned his head slightly and mumbled something that showed he wasn't thinking clearly; then she threw up her hands and said:

"He's alive, thank God! And that's enough!" and she quickly kissed him and rushed toward the house to prepare the bed, shouting instructions in every direction to the servants and everyone else as fast as she could speak, with every step she took.

I followed the men to see what they were going to do with Jim, while the old doctor and Uncle Silas went after Tom into the house. The men were very angry, and some of them wanted to hang Jim as an example to all the other enslaved people in the area, so they wouldn't try to run away like Jim had done, causing so much trouble and keeping a whole family terrified for days and nights. But the others said not to do it, that it wouldn't work at all; he wasn't their enslaved person, and his owner would show up and make them pay for him for sure. So that calmed them down a little, because the people who are always most eager to hang an enslaved person who hasn't behaved properly are always the very ones who aren't most willing to pay for him once they've gotten their satisfaction from him.

They cursed Jim quite a bit, though, and gave him a slap or two on the side of his head from time to time, but Jim never said anything, and he never let on that he knew me, and they took him to the same cabin, and put his own clothes on him, and chained him up again, and not to a bed leg this time, but to a big metal fastener driven into the bottom log, and chained his hands, too, and both legs, and said he wasn't going to have anything but bread and water to eat from now on until his owner came, or he was sold at auction if the owner didn't come within a certain amount of time, and they filled up our hole, and said a couple of farmers with guns had to stand guard around the cabin every night, and a bulldog tied to the door during the daytime; and about this time they were finished with the job and were winding down with a kind of general farewell cursing, and then the old doctor comes and takes a look, and says:

"Don't be any rougher on him than you have to be, because he's not a bad man. When I got to where I found the boy, I could see I couldn't cut the bullet out without some help, and he wasn't in any condition for me to leave him to go and get help; and he got a little worse and a little worse, and after a long time he became delirious, and wouldn't let me come near him anymore, and said if I marked his raft he'd kill me, and all sorts of wild nonsense like that, and I could see I couldn't do anything at all with him; so I said, I have to get help somehow; and the minute I said it, out crawls this man from somewhere and says he'll help, and he did it, too, and did it very well. Of course I figured he must be a runaway slave, and there I was! and there I had to stay right there all the rest of the day and all night. It was quite a predicament, I tell you! I had a couple of patients with chills, and of course I would have liked to go up to town and see them, but I didn't dare, because the man might get away, and then I'd be to blame; and yet no boat came close enough for me to call out to. So there I had to stay completely until daylight this morning; and I never saw a man who was a better nurse or more faithful, and yet he was risking his freedom to do it, and was completely exhausted, too, and I could see plainly enough he'd been worked very hard lately. I respected the man for that; I tell you, gentlemen, a person like that is worth a thousand dollars—and kind treatment, too. I had everything I needed, and the boy was doing as well there as he would have done at home—better, maybe, because it was so quiet; but there I was, with both of them on my hands, and there I had to stay until about dawn this morning; then some men in a boat came by, and as good luck would have it the man was sitting by the makeshift bed with his head resting on his knees, sound asleep; so I motioned them in quietly, and they slipped up on him and grabbed him and tied him before he knew what was happening, and we never had any trouble. And the boy being in a kind of restless sleep, too, we muffled the oars and tied up the raft, and towed it over very carefully and quietly, and the man never made the slightest disturbance or said a word from the start. He's not a bad person, gentlemen; that's what I think about him."

Someone says:

"Well, it sounds very good, doctor, I have to say I'm grateful."

Then the others softened up a little, too, and I was really thankful to that old doctor for doing Jim that good turn; and I was glad it matched my judgment of him, too; because I thought he had a good heart in him and was a good man the first time I saw him. Then they all agreed that Jim had acted very well, and deserved to have some recognition for it, and a reward. So every one of them promised, right out and sincerely, that they wouldn't curse him anymore.

Then they came out and locked him up. I hoped they would say he could have one or two of the chains removed, because they were extremely heavy, or that he could have meat and vegetables with his bread and water; but they didn't think of it, and I figured it wasn't best for me to interfere, but I decided I'd get the doctor's story to Aunt Sally somehow or other as soon as I'd gotten through the difficult situation that was lying just ahead of me— explanations, I mean, of how I forgot to mention about Sid being shot when I was telling how he and I spent that awful night paddling around hunting the runaway slave.

But I had plenty of time. Aunt Sally stayed in the sick-room all day and all night, and every time I saw Uncle Silas wandering around I avoided him.

The next morning I learned that Tom was doing much better, and they told me Aunt Sally had gone to take a nap. So I quietly made my way to the sick-room, thinking that if I found him awake we could come up with a story for the family that would be believable. But he was sleeping, and sleeping very peacefully too; he looked pale, not flushed and feverish the way he had been when he arrived. So I sat down and waited for him to wake up. After about half an hour Aunt Sally came quietly into the room, and there I was, caught off guard again! She gestured for me to stay quiet, and sat down beside me, and began to whisper, saying we could all be happy now, because all the signs were excellent, and he had been sleeping like that for a very long time, and looking better and more peaceful all the while, and most likely he would wake up in his right mind.

So we sat there watching, and after a while he stirred a little, opened his eyes quite naturally, took a look around, and said:

"Hello! Wait, I'm at home! How is that possible? Where's the raft?"

"It's all right," I said.

"And Jim?"

"The same," I said, but I couldn't say it very boldly. But he never noticed, and said:

"Good! Splendid! Now we're all right and safe! Did you tell Aunty?"

I was about to say yes, but she interrupted and asked, "About what, Sid?"

"Why, about the way the whole thing was done."

"What whole thing?"

"Why, the whole thing. There's only one; how we set the runaway slave free—me and Tom."

"Good heavens! Set the run— What is this child talking about! Oh my, oh my, he's out of his head again!"

"No, I'm not out of my mind; I know exactly what I'm talking about. We did set him free—Tom and I. We planned to do it, and we accomplished it. And we did it with style, too." He had gotten

319

started, and she never interrupted him, just sat there staring and staring, letting him continue on, and I could see there was no point in me jumping in. "Why, Aunt Sally, it took us an enormous amount of work—weeks of it—hours and hours, every night, while you were all sleeping. And we had to steal candles, and the sheet, and the shirt, and your dress, and spoons, and tin plates, and case-knives, and the warming-pan, and the grindstone, and flour, and just countless other things, and you can't imagine how much work it was to make the saws, and pens, and inscriptions, and one thing after another, and you can't imagine half the excitement it provided. And we had to create pictures of coffins and such things, and anonymous letters from the robbers, and climb up and down the lightning-rod, and dig the hole into the cabin, and make the rope ladder and send it in baked inside a pie, and send in spoons and other tools hidden in your apron pocket—"

"Good heavens!"

"—and fill the cabin with rats and snakes and other creatures to keep Jim company; and then you kept Tom here so long with the butter in his hat that you nearly ruined the whole plan, because the men arrived before we got out of the cabin, and we had to hurry, and they heard us and started shooting at us, and I got hit, and we ducked off the path and let them pass by, and when the dogs came they weren't interested in us, but went toward the loudest noise, and we reached our canoe, and headed for the raft, and we were all safe, and Jim was a free man, and we did it all by ourselves, and wasn't it wonderful, Aunt Sally!"

"Well, I've never heard anything like this in my entire life! So it was you two little troublemakers who've been causing all this chaos, turning everyone's minds upside down and scaring us all nearly to death. I have half a mind right now to give you the punishment you deserve this very instant. Just think—here I've been, night after night, worrying sick—you just get better first, you young rascal, and I swear I'll give both of you the beating of your lives!"

But Tom was so proud and excited that he just couldn't contain himself, and his tongue kept running—with her interrupting and getting furious the whole time, and both of them talking at once, like a gathering of cats; and she says:

"Well, you better enjoy yourself while you can, because I'm warning you—if I catch you interfering with him again—"

"Interfering with who?" Tom asks, his smile disappearing as he looks surprised.

"With who? Why, the runaway slave, of course. Who'd you think?"

Tom looks at me with a very serious expression and says:

"Tom, didn't you just tell me he was all right? Hasn't he escaped?"

"Him?" says Aunt Sally; "the runaway slave? Indeed he hasn't. They've got him back, safe and sound, and he's in that cabin again, on bread and water, and weighed down with chains, until he's claimed or sold!"

Tom shot straight up in bed, his eyes blazing and his nostrils flaring open and closed like fish gills, and shouted out to me:

"They have no right to lock him up! Push!—and don't waste a minute. Set him free! He's not a slave; he's as free as any creature that walks this earth!"

"What does the child mean?"

"I mean every word I'm saying, Aunt Sally, and if nobody else goes, I'll go myself. I've known him my entire life, and so has Tom over there. Old Miss Watson died two months ago, and she felt ashamed that she had ever planned to sell him down the river, and she said as much; she freed him in her will."

"Then why on earth did you want to set him free, since he was already free?"

"Well, that's quite a question, I have to say; just like women! Why, I wanted the adventure of it; and I would have waded neck-deep in blood to—goodness alive, AUNT POLLY!"

If she wasn't standing right there, just inside the door, looking as sweet and satisfied as an angel who had eaten her fill of pie, I swear I've never seen anything like it!

Aunt Sally rushed toward her and nearly squeezed the life out of her with hugs, crying all over her, while I discovered a perfect hiding spot under the bed since things were becoming quite uncomfortable for us, it seemed to me. I peered out, and after a short time Tom's Aunt Polly freed herself and stood there staring at Tom through her glasses—practically boring holes right through him, you understand. Then she said:

"Yes, you'd better turn your head away—I would if I were you, Tom."

"Oh my goodness!" says Aunt Sally; "has he changed so much? Why, that isn't Tom, it's Sid; Tom's—Tom's—why, where is Tom? He was here just a minute ago."

"You mean where's Huck Finn—that's what you're asking! I figure I haven't raised a rascal like my Tom all these years without being able to recognize him when I see him. That would be quite something. Come out from under that bed, Huck Finn."

So I did it. But I wasn't feeling bold about it.

Aunt Sally was one of the most confused-looking people I had ever seen—except for one person, and that was Uncle Silas, when he came in and they told him everything. It kind of made him feel overwhelmed, you could say, and he didn't understand anything at all for the rest of the day, and preached a prayer meeting sermon that night that gave him quite a reputation, because even the oldest man in the world couldn't have understood it. So Tom's Aunt Polly told everyone who I was and what my situation was; and I had to explain how I was in such a difficult position that when Mrs. Phelps mistook me for Tom Sawyer—she interrupted and said, "Oh, go ahead and call me Aunt Sally, I'm used to it now, and there's no need to change"—that when Aunt Sally mistook me for Tom Sawyer I had to go along with it—there wasn't any other choice, and I knew he wouldn't mind, because it would be perfect for him, being a mystery, and he'd turn it into an adventure and be completely satisfied. And that's exactly what happened, and he pretended to be Sid, and made things as easy as he could for me.

And his Aunt Polly confirmed that Tom was correct about old Miss Watson freeing Jim in her will; and so, as it turned out, Tom Sawyer had gone through all that trouble and effort to free a man who was already free! I had never been able to understand before, until that very moment and that conversation, how someone with his upbringing could help another person free an enslaved man.

Well, Aunt Polly said that when Aunt Sally wrote to her that Tom and Sid had arrived safely, she told herself:

"Look at that! I should have seen this coming, letting him take off like that without anyone keeping an eye on him. So now I have to go and trek all the way down the river, eleven hundred miles, and figure out what that guy is up to this time, since I couldn't seem to get any answers out of you about it."

"Why, I never heard anything from you," says Aunt Sally.

"Well, that's strange! I actually wrote to you twice asking what you meant by saying Sid was here."

"Well, I never got them, Sis."

Aunt Polly turned around slowly and sternly, and said:

"You, Tom!"

"Well—what?" he says, somewhat irritably.

"Don't you 'what' me, you impudent thing—hand over those letters."

"What letters?"

"Those letters. I swear, if I have to get my hands on you I'll"

"They're in the trunk. There, now. And they're exactly the same as they were when I took them from the office. I haven't looked through them, I haven't touched them. But I knew they would cause trouble, and I thought if you weren't in any hurry, I would—"

"Well, you definitely need a good scolding, there's no doubt about that. And I wrote another letter to tell you I was coming; and I suppose he—"

"No, it came yesterday; I haven't read it yet, but it's all right, I've got that one."

I wanted to offer to bet two dollars that she hadn't, but I figured it was probably safer not to. So I didn't say anything.

Chapter The Last

The first time I caught Tom alone I asked him what his plan was for the escape—what he intended to do if the escape worked perfectly and he managed to free a man who was already free? He told me that what he had planned from the very beginning was this: if we successfully got Jim out safely, we would take him down the river on the raft and have adventures all the way to the mouth of the river, then tell him he was actually free, and bring him back home on a steamboat in grand style, pay him for his lost time, send word ahead and gather all the enslaved people from the area, and have them escort him into town with a torchlight procession and a brass band, making him a hero, and us too. But I figured things worked out just fine the way they did.

We freed Jim from his chains right away, and when Aunt Polly, Uncle Silas, and Aunt Sally discovered how well he had helped the doctor care for Tom, they showered him with attention and treated him wonderfully, giving him all the food he wanted, a great time, and no work to do. We brought him up to the sick room where we had an exciting conversation, and Tom gave Jim forty dollars for being our prisoner so patiently and doing such a good job of it, and Jim was absolutely thrilled and burst out saying:

"There, now, Huck, what did I tell you?—what did I tell you up there on Jackson Island? I told you I got a hairy breast, and what's the sign of it; and I told you I been rich once, and going to be rich again; and it's come true; and here she is! There, now! don't talk to me—signs is signs, mind I tell you; and I knew just as well that I was going to be rich again as I's standing here this minute!"

And then Tom kept talking and talking, and he says, let's all three of us slip out of here one of these nights and get some equipment, and go on exciting adventures among the Indians, over in the Territory, for a couple of weeks or so; and I said, all right, that sounds good to me, but I don't have any money to buy the equipment, and I think I couldn't get any from home, because it's likely that father has been back by now, and taken it all away from Judge Thatcher and spent it on drinking.

"No, he hasn't," Tom says; "it's all there still—six thousand dollars and more; and your father hasn't ever been back since. He hadn't when I left, anyway."

Jim speaks in a somewhat serious tone:

"He's not coming back anymore, Huck."

I said:

"Why, Jim?"

"Never mind why, Huck—but he isn't coming back anymore."

But I kept pressing him; so finally he says:

"Don't you remember the house that was floating down the river, and there was a man in there, covered up, and I went in and uncovered him and didn't let you come in? Well, then, you can get your money when you want it, because that was him."

Tom is completely well now and wears his bullet around his neck on a watch chain, constantly checking the time, so there's nothing more to write about, and I'm really glad about that, because if I had known what trouble it was to write a book I wouldn't have attempted it, and I'm not going to do it again. But

I think I need to head out for the Territory before the others, because Aunt Sally is going to adopt me and civilize me, and I can't stand it. I've been through that before.

THE END.

YOURS TRULY,

HUCK FINN.

Thank You For Reading

You've Just Read a Piece of the Greatest Library Ever Rebuilt

Thank you for reading.

This book is one of thousands we're restoring, reimagining, and translating as part of the **Modern Library of Alexandria** — a global movement to preserve and share humanity's most important ideas.

What was once lost to fire and time is now rising again — not just as memory, but as living, breathing knowledge, freely accessible to all.

What You Can Do Next:

- **Keep Reading.**

  Discover more legendary works — in beautiful print, audiobook, or digital form — at LibraryofAlexandria.com.

- **Build Your Own Library.**

  Every title is available as a paperback, hardcover, or collectible boxset — at true printing cost. Craft a personal library worthy of display.

- **Spread the Light.**

  Share this book. Tell others about the movement. Help us translate every timeless work into every language, so no reader is ever left behind.

By finishing this book, you've already taken part in something extraordinary.

Join us at LibraryofAlexandria.com

Together, we're rebuilding the greatest library the world has ever known.

With appreciation,

The Modern Library of Alexandria Team

Visit:
www.libraryofalexandria.com
Or scan the code below: